What Others Are Saying

This fascinating book helped me to understand some of the many joys and sorrows of missions work. I especially enjoyed learning about the Bible translation process.

—Rosie Zakes, homeschooler, Minnesota

Your heart will be stirred by Edna's recounting the journey that she and her husband, Paul, took to reach the remote Tunebo people of Colombia, South America. Enduring all, they lived among this group of people with one goal in mind— to translate the Word of God into the Tunebo language that they may know of Jesus's saving grace. This book will cause you to consider your own commitment to the cause of Christ.

—Dave Gibson, pastor of missions and evangelism, Grace Church, Eden Prairie, Minnesota

The story of the work of Paul and Edna Headland with the Tunebo tribe in Colombia is a testimony, in the words of Eugene Peterson, to "a long obedience in the same direction." It is, indeed, a life-long obedience.

Most missionary accounts narrate such obedience, of course, but the obedience usually results in conversions, founding of churches, perhaps even expansion of the mission within and beyond its first recipients. The Headlands labored for nearly thirty years among the Tunebo without seeing such rewards. Called to translate the Scriptures into the language of a people who were adverse to virtually everything outside their tribe—literacy, paper, medicine, even allowing "outsiders" to learn their language—the Headlands were indomitable in their efforts to understand, affirm, honor, and serve "the least of these." They entitle their story, *His Grace Is Sufficient*, and this is truly a story of the sufficiency of the grace of Jesus Christ.

—James R. Edwards, Bruner-Welch Professor of Theology, Whitworth University, Spokane, Washington

My husband and I came into Wycliffe as a new generation of recruits ready to build on the solid foundation that colleagues like Paul and Edna Headland established in earlier decades. The lessons they lived and modeled, as portrayed in *His Grace Is Sufficient: Bible Translation with the Tunebo of Colombia,* are the building blocks that have given this current generation the momentum to meet the challenge of completing the remaining Bible translations around the world. Their endurance, reliance on prayer, creativity, eternity-mindfulness, and absolute confidence in God's sovereignty continue to set the framework from which we work today.

—Dallas Creson, wife of Bob Creson, President CEO,
Wycliffe Bible Translators, USA

I have been blessed by reading the draft of this book—a book that can change your life commitment to do your part in reaching a lost world. As pastor of the Headland's sending and supporting church I had the extraordinary privilege of becoming acquainted with Paul and Edna and their extremely difficult, sometimes dangerous, and often discouraging work. My wife, Dee, and I were also blessed to be able to go where they served with this unreached group in the Andes Mountains of Eastern Colombian.

I highly recommend this book be read by those passionate about reaching people for Christ, who hear God's call on their lives and need assurance that God can sustain them. In this book, you will see how the grace of God and the assurance of His call helped the Headlands to stay with this ministry through often troubling times.

—Dr. Robert Ricker, former president of Baptist General Conference and former pastor of Grace Church of Edina,
Minnesota

Some books I savor in bite-sized chunks each day. *His Grace Is Sufficient* I gobbled up the whole bag full; I read it in two sittings. If you want to be transported to a world you can never visit and an era you can't return to, this is the book. Full disclosure: I'm a friend and colleague of the author and her husband; I was eager to learn details of a story of which I only knew snatches.

Edna Headland relates the story of their family's ministry from the 1960s to 1980s of literacy and medical work and Bible translation among a people living in a remote region near the Colombia-Venezuela border. The detailed and personal record is invaluable. American linguist-missionaries live alongside marginalized indigenous people for over twenty years, learning, sharing, struggling, influencing, and experiencing deprivation, rejection, danger, grief, confusion, as well as ecstasy, deep friendship, rescue, success, and joy.

God's grace, which is sufficient, is the powerful theme of the book from beginning to end. The Headlands were an incarnational ministry, before the term became popular. At times, their assurance of God's call and grace was enough for them to carry on. Sometimes they had to be carried by caring friends and colleagues. Their account of trust in God is sure to enrich yours.

—Donald Hekman, former president of Wycliffe Bible Translators, Canada

Throughout history, many peoples and civilizations have seen themselves as central characters on the world stage. The Tunebo people of Colombia have gone a step further and convinced (or deceived) themselves that their ceremonial dances actually hold the world together!

How does one reach such a people with the Good News? This book recounts the story of a young couple who devoted twenty-six years of their lives to such an effort! Their approach—Bible translation. Their strategy—a lifetime of living with, befriending, loving, and ministering to a small group of people who were by turns suspicious yet generous, hostile yet friendly, indifferent yet hardworking. Read these pages and be challenged by the commitment, endurance, and faith of Paul and Edna as they sought—and still seek—to see the Tunebo people won for His Kingdom!

—Steve Walter, PhD, Applied
Anthropology Department,
Graduate Institute of Applied Linguistics

If you have ever attempted to imagine the calling, the equipping, the sacrifice, and the daily struggles and victories in the life of a missionary, you can do more than imagine it as you follow the lives of Paul and Edna Headland and their Bible translation work among the Tunebo people.

His Grace Is Sufficient reveals the depth and breadth of God's care for the Headlands; whether by meeting simple needs, by providing for them when traumatic issues arose, or by amazing them with incredible God-ordained victories, God was there. During physical challenges, Satanic attacks, militant conflicts, and political inquiries, and even when simply misunderstood, Paul and Edna discovered that God's grace is always, always sufficient.

What an amazing story—not only of God's grace, but also His sovereignty—in calling two individuals to become one in marriage and in mission for the glorious purpose of translating and taking His Word to the Tunebo people of Colombia, South America. *His Grace Is Sufficient* will encourage all who have a heart for God and His work, who long for the fulfillment of Acts 1:8 in taking the Gospel to the "ends of the earth."

On a personal note, it has been my privilege to serve as Paul and Edna Headland's pastor for the past twenty-four years. During that time, I have listened with joy to reports of the ongoing fruit of their work, but as I read *His Grace Is Sufficient*, I gained a much deeper appreciation of the price paid by Paul and Edna as they stayed the course and accomplished the work assigned them by the Father.

—Dr. Mike Simmons, senior pastor,
Hillcrest Baptist Church, Dallas, Texas,
trustee, International Mission Board

His Grace
——— *is* ———
Sufficient

II Cor 12:9

Edna Headland

His Grace
—is—
Sufficient

Bible Translation with the Tunebo of Colombia

FOREWORD BY DR. LUIS PALAU

EDNA HEADLAND

His Grace Is Sufficient
Copyright © 2017 by Edna Headland. All rights reserved.

Dedicatory Prayer for the Tunebo

SIRU, TETÚ, AJÁT Bah quin conro. Behmá wacjá Jesucristo, uw siwin acu chinjacro. Uwat Bah chihtá cácayta acu conro. Bah chihtá rahcuayta acu conro. Jesucristo ajc cuitar conro.

God, Father, I cry to you. Your son, Jesus Christ, died to save the Tunebo people. I pray for the people to accept your message. I pray for them to obey your message. I cry (to you) in the name of Jesus Christ.

Contents

FOREWORD

I LOVE MISSIONARIES and missionary stories! My own father would be in hell if missionaries had not come to Argentina, South America, where we lived, and brought us the Good News of Jesus Christ and the Bible, the Word of God.

As I held the manuscript of Edna Headland's book about their experience as missionary-translators with the Tunebo people of Colombia, South America, I said to my wife, "I feel I was there." That is as it should be. I was transported to the village where Edna and her husband Paul invested their time and treasure, all they knew and valued, to deposit the very words of God, the Bible, into the language of these indigenous people.

The drama that was involved in the preparation, travel, orientation, and struggle to make this happen is laid out before us with a high degree of honesty and transparency. It was hard! But in each situation, the Lord's grace proved to be sufficient to sustain them.

You'll read that Edna and Paul gave twenty-six years to the translation of the Scriptures into the Tunebo language. But it's not a simple project. You'll come to appreciate all that is involved in preparation, language learning, cultural adjustments, isolation, and loneliness. You will also be made more aware of what it means to be outside of Christ, without hope, as you get a glimpse of the culture and customs of the Tunebos.

I greatly admire Edna and Paul for their concept and practice of servanthood and honor them for being the living sacrifices they were, living years with one tribal group, the Tunebos. As I read, I kept thinking of the apostle Paul's words, "And so, dear brothers and sisters, I plead with you to give your bodies to God because of all he has done for you. Let them be a living and holy sacrifice—the kind he will find acceptable. When you think of what Christ has done for you, is this too much to ask?" (Rom. 12:1, NLT).

This book will remind you that for some, this sacrifice is real and all-encompassing. It will show you the adjustments the Headlands made, the surrendering of their "rights," the obedience of faith in action as the apostle Paul teaches us in 1 Corinthians 9, their profound devotion to the Savior and their love for this group of people who are lost without Christ.

This couple died to their own ambitions and easy living so that others might live as Paul teaches us in 2 Corinthians 5. Missionaries are often unrecognized by the Christian community and diminished and ridiculed by secular anthropologists. Yet the Master said, "Well done, thou good and faithful servant: thou hast been faithful over a few things, I will make thee ruler over many things: enter thou into the joy of thy lord" (Matt. 25:23, KJV).

All of us who serve in the cause of the spread of the gospel struggle to find words to honor, thank, and bless the support systems that sustain us in our mission. Paul and Edna have a strong band of friends, family, and churches that have stood by them, praying, encouraging, and supporting them financially through the years. This book will bless all those who had some part in sending the Headlands to Colombia.

Someone has said, "We cannot propagate the gospel at less cost than it took to procure it," and "We as Christians do not make sacrifices. We are sacrifices." The narrative reminds us of the lostness of those who have never heard the gospel and the high cost of obedience.

My wife Pat and I were part of the 1960–1961 graduate class at Multnomah School of the Bible with Edna before she met Paul. As we moved out into ministry, we were assigned by our respective sending agencies to Colombia, South America. We kept up with and sought to encourage each other, especially during the four years that we lived there. While Paul and Edna were led to one group in the mountains, Pat and I were led to evangelize in the large cities. At the time, the evangelical community in Colombia was very small. Today is another story! The number of Christ followers in Colombia has grown. The Colombian church is sending missionaries out to finish the task of reaching those who have not clearly heard the Good News.

Your faith and your commitment to intercessory prayer will be strengthened as you read of answers to prayer. The experiences of the Headlands remind us that, especially in sectors where Satan has long-held strongholds, there is a need for serious warfare against the powers of darkness. We don't always understand what's going on, but we know we need to stand by those like the Headlands on the forefront.

Edna expresses so clearly their sadness and even frustration as assaults against their work came over and over. The enemy had so many costumes: the animistic taboos of the people, the influx of leftist militants, the physical terrain, and even the climate.

Why didn't the Tunebos respond to the gospel? It's not over yet. Another indigenous group in Latin America had a Christian witness among them for over a hundred years without one known convert! One day it all changed, and today this group has an organized church that is totally self-governing and self-propagating.

Someday, on that great day of resurrection, we shall all kneel at the feet of the One who made heaven possible, from every kindred, tribe, and nation. That includes the Tunebos!

Dr. Luis Palau
International Evangelist, Author
Founder of Luis Palau Association

PREFACE

THE YOUNG MAN we had hired to accompany me and carry my water, my raincoat, and our two-way radio, had run on ahead when I stopped a few minutes to visit. I kept thinking, *Surely I will find him waiting for me at the next bend in the trail.* But I finally realized that wasn't going to happen. He had deserted me. I could still feel the sting of his brother's taunting remark, "You have already eaten, and you didn't give me anything. You're selfish!" He and I both knew he couldn't have eaten my food if I had given it to him. I had learned that the hard way. The Tunebo taboos forbade anyone from taking cooked food from outsiders. He may have been teasing, but I couldn't shrug it off. It particularly hurt that day as I struggled up the steep, slippery trail feeling half sick. I pushed on well past the usual resting place, trying to catch my companion before I finally sat down, giving way to tears. I poured out my complaints to the Lord. He reminded me that He had struggled up a hill carrying His own cross. He had been mocked and ridiculed. He had done it for me. Wow! That gave me an instant attitude check. It was a reminder that His grace is sufficient. If He had done that for me, He would give me strength for this hike. He would give me a forgiving heart.

The apostle Paul experienced much greater hardships in his missionary journeys than I could imagine. He enumerated them as follows:

> Are they servants of Christ? [I am out of my mind to talk like this.] I am more. I have worked much harder, been in prison more frequently, been flogged more severely,

and been exposed to death again and again. Five times I received from the Jews the forty lashes minus one. Three times I was beaten with rods, once I was pelted with stones, three times I was shipwrecked, I spent a night and a day in the open sea, I have been constantly on the move. I have been in danger from rivers, in danger from bandits, in danger from my fellow Jews, in danger from Gentiles; in danger in the city, in danger in the country, in danger at sea; and in danger from false believers. I have labored and toiled and have often gone without sleep; I have known hunger and thirst and have often gone without food; I have been cold and naked. Besides everything else, I face daily the pressure of my concern for all the churches. Who is weak, and I do not feel weak? Who is led into sin, and I do not inwardly burn?

If I must boast, I will boast of the things that show my weakness. The God and Father of the Lord Jesus, who is to be praised forever, knows that I am not lying. (2 Cor. 11:23–31, NIV)

In the next chapter, Paul goes on to tell how God assured him, "My grace is sufficient for you. For my strength is made perfect in weakness" (2 Cor. 12:9, NKJV).

To better understand Paul's stresses and put them in our context, I compared them to some of my own experiences:

I have walked steep, slippery mountain trails, slept on planks with just a flea-ridden blanket, eaten questionable food, and lain in strange beds shaking with fever. Five times, I have had my house broken into and my things stolen. I spent three days on the airstrip in the rain only to miss my daughter's eighth-grade graduation, missed family Christmases, weddings, birthdays, found no plane to be able to go to my mother's funeral, made two trips to the States for the sudden deaths of both my sisters and left my children in the States for school. I have seen thirty-five friends and acquaintances in a village of five hundred people die in a malaria epidemic and gone through two coworkers kidnappings and one's murder, had language helpers who we taught to read and who showed an interest in the gospel disappear from the village because they couldn't stand the pressure. Communist guerillas took over the area where we worked. Besides everything else, I faced daily my concern for the lost condition of the Tunebos.

As with the apostle Paul, Jesus has also shown me, "My grace is sufficient for you, Edna. For my strength is made perfect in your weakness."

He sustained me with His all-sufficient grace by miracles just when I needed them, answers to prayer, and specific messages from His word. My hope is that this story will encourage you, the reader, that His grace can carry you through the difficult circumstances in life.

The story shows how the *Tunebo New Testament* has been translated at high cost. The same is true of other New Testaments in other languages of Colombia and around the world. As with the Tunebos, in many of these places, there is still no church. The Word of God and other materials are available in Uwa/Tunebo and many languages for the next generation of missionaries to use to evangelize, disciple, and teach people to obey. My heart's desire is that this book might help young people see the need to use the New Testaments that have been translated to reach people in their heart languages. I pray that our work and that of other translators will not be in vain so that one day there will be a vibrant church among the Tunebos and other groups, singing God's praises and learning from His word each in their own language.

I also pray that the book will motivate God's people to pray that Satan's bondage on the Tunebos and other groups like them would be broken so that they might receive freedom in Christ. I hope that reading the book will motivate those who send out young workers to pray for God's grace to sustain them.

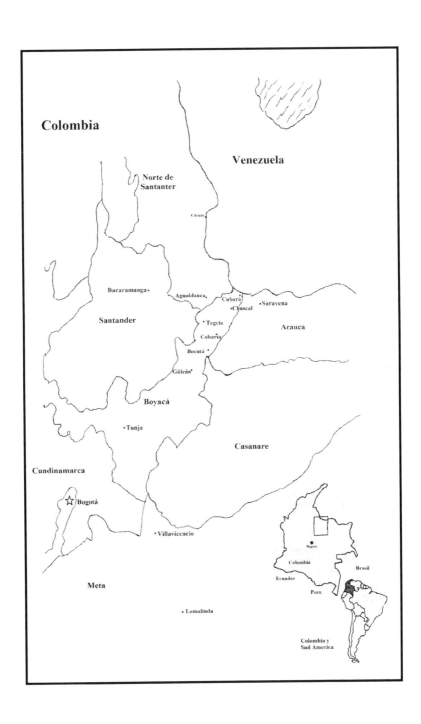

Colombia

Venezuela

Norte de
Santanter

Cúcuta

Bucaramanga•

Aguablanca•   •Cubará
                    •Chuscal   •Saravena
Santander   •Tegría   Arauca
                Cobaría
            Bocutá •
        Güicán•

        Boyacá

    •Tunja

                        Casanare

Cundinamarca

☆ Bogotá

                •Villavicencio

    Meta

            •Lomalinda

Colombia
Ecuador   Bogotá
Peru   Brasil

Colombia y
Sud America

1

LOST CONTACT

Where are they?

"*Cobaría, Cobaría. Bogotá.*"

Silence.

"*Bogotá* calling *Cobaría.*"

No response.

"I haven't heard from Paul and Edna since the day after they moved higher in the rugged Andes Mountains near the Tunebo settlement of Cobaría," the radio operator reported to Clarence Church, the director, after a few days of no contact.

As each day passed without contact, Clarence became more concerned. "What could have happened to the Headlands?" He knew the Tunebos were suspicious of outsiders. Neighbors had been unfriendly. The nearest mail contact was still three walking days from the village.

Arrangements were made with Jungle Aviation and Radio Service (JAARS) to send seasoned pilot Ralph Borthwick on a reconnaissance flight. Cargo included a duplicate radio outfit, so any part of the radio equipment that was not working could be replaced, and a duffle bag of supplies, in case an overland trip from the nearest airstrip proved necessary. Also included to be airdropped was a white bed sheet with signaling instructions for ground-to-air communication for every conceivable situation.

Nearing the village, Borthwick again tried radio contact. Still no response, but when he overflew Cobaría and saw us outside with our own signaling sheet as instructed, he knew we were still able to receive messages. We could hear him on our Zenith Trans-Oceanic Radio.

A most interesting two-way conversation took place as the plane kept circling.

"If transmitter not functioning, place sheet on ground."

No move. Apparently that was not the trouble.

"If battery lost its charge, lay sheet on ground, one person sit on it."

Paul laid the sheet out and sat on it.

"I read that battery not functioning. If that is only problem, wave sheet."

We promptly responded by following his instructions and vigorously waved the sheet.

"If you are well and everything is all right, two people sit on the sheet."

I rebelled. I was not willing to sit on the sheet to acknowledge that everything was all right. I was desperately lonely, everything seemed out of control, and now my beloved husband was ordering me to join him in sitting on the sheet. He ordered, "Sit down. If you don't, they will have to walk two days to get here to see what's wrong." Tears in my eyes, I acquiesced and sat on the sheet.

"I'll leave a fresh battery in Cubará, and a friend will bring it to you next week. Stand clear. I'll make two passes and drop a bundle each time."

Down came a five-week accumulation of mail and another bundle of fresh vegetables, each with long red location-identifying streamers flying. A friendly farewell dip of the wing, then to Cubará, the small frontier town at the foot of the mountains near the Colombia-Venezuela border, to leave the battery as promised.

George M. Cowan, president of Wycliffe, writing in a letter dated September 1964, summed up the JAARS flight this way. "Routine? No, not when it is your son, daughter, personal friend, or church member they are serving! Not when it is long-forgotten Bible-less tribes they are reaching."

The Makings of a Missionary

What was the background of this young couple that motivated them to go to the remote Tunebo village of Cobaría?

Paul

Paul was born April 17, 1938, in Los Angeles, California where his parents had grown up. At the beginning of World War II, the family moved to Long Beach, where his father worked for Douglas Aircraft. When the war ended, they moved back to Los Angeles, where they lived with his maternal grandmother, who was suffering from advanced cancer.

A year later, his grandmother died, and they moved into the house where Paul spent the rest of his growing up years. In each of the moves, even though neither parent attended church, Paul's dad made sure he and his brother Tom got to Sunday school every week. Each summer, the two boys spent a few weeks with their great-aunt Ida, who daily read to them from the Bible.

One Sunday at Angeles Mesa Presbyterian Church, Paul signed the card in the pew. He checked the box that indicated he wanted a call from the pastor. Not realizing Paul was only twelve, the senior pastor of the church, Bill Stoddard, came to visit. That was the beginning of the church's influence in the lives of the Headlands. Joe Stephens, the youth pastor, was single and became a frequent guest at the Headland's dinner table. The conversations over meals focused on the Lord and the Bible. Paul's parents eventually started attending regularly with the boys and opened their hearts to the Lord.

Joe suggested Paul, then thirteen, would profit from going to Bible camp. Although Paul had learned a lot in Sunday school, it was at Tahquitz Pines Christian Camp that he realized his need for cleansing from sin and accepted Christ. Soon after that, he felt God calling him into the ministry.

Paul had a number of experiences that helped him develop his communication skills and his perspective on ministry and missions. He held leadership roles among the youth in his church. Upon high school graduation, he went to Whitworth College (now Whitworth University), a Christian school in Spokane, Washington. There he participated in student gospel teams who held services in area churches. During his junior and senior years, he served on weekends as pastor in two small rural churches.

In his sophomore year, during a chapel talk by a missionary, he realized that the Lord might be calling him to missionary service overseas. Previously at Angeles Mesa Presbyterian Church, he had heard the presentation of a Wycliffe missionary and had said to himself, *If I ever go into missions, it will be with the Wycliffe Bible Translators.* Now that seed thought began to germinate and influence his choice of college courses.

While their sons were in college, Paul's parents attended a missions meeting where Dick Hillis was speaking. He encouraged parents to commit their children to go to the mission field. Paul's parents prayerfully went to the altar together and gave their sons to the Lord for His service wherever He led them.

The summer after his sophomore year, when Paul saw Tom, who was home from Mexico City College, Tom said, "Hey, Paul, let me tell you about an exciting mission." He had met Wycliffe members and had been attending meetings where they shared about their work. Paul told Tom he also had felt that the Lord might be leading him into missions and of his interest in Wycliffe. Both were very thrilled with the possibility of working with indigenous people groups.

When Paul was a senior, a Wycliffe missionary spoke in the Whitworth chapel service. After being touched by his message, Paul sought him out to talk with him personally. That was enough. He knew this was God's plan for him. Paul yielded to God's call to missions and His leading to Wycliffe Bible Translators.

The next year, when he graduated from Whitworth, he had only a quarter in his pocket. He sold his old car for $25. With no more money than that, he realized that the Summer Institute of Linguistics (SIL) course all Wycliffe missionary candidates were required to take would have to be postponed. However, there was a jungle training course to be held in the spring. Paul would have the opportunity to earn some money and take that part of the training first. Although it was not the usual order of training, Paul was accepted to participate in the Jungle Camp program in the spring of 1961. He and his brother Tom attended together and were *champa* (jungle hut) partners. Paul's camping experience on Headland family vacations helped him do well.

That summer following Jungle Camp, Paul went to Norman, Oklahoma, for the initial SIL course. His first taste of linguistics left him hungry for more. During the summer, in consultation with Wycliffe's leaders, it was decided that Paul's next phase of training would be seminary. He immediately enrolled at Fuller Seminary in Pasadena, California, where he took the courses needed to prepare for Bible translation.

By the end of the year at Fuller, his funds were once again depleted. It seemed like the second summer of Linguistics training at Norman would have to be postponed. Then he saw a note on the bulletin board, "$200 Scholarship for training for Bible translation." The exact amount needed for the course! He applied, received the scholarship, and was on his way to Oklahoma again.

It was there at the University of Oklahoma that he noticed another missionary trainee, Edna Blake, wiping off tables in the dining room in preparation for the influx of students for the summer course.

Edna

Early on the morning of January 1, 1939, in Parkers Prairie, Minnesota, excitement was in the air. In their upstairs bedrooms, my sister, Joan, and four brothers, Clyde, Dick, John, and Larry, were awakened by the sound of commotion downstairs. They heard my first baby cry followed by footsteps as my dad climbed the stairs to announce my arrival. "You have a new baby sister, Edna Romayne."

By 1942, the mounting costs of raising a growing family of six children became a staggering challenge for my dad. The United States was actively engaged in World War II, making jobs available in industry. My dad took advantage of the promise of higher-paying employment, and we moved to the city of St. Paul, Minnesota.

In the summer of 1944, the desire for home ownership became a fulfillment. My dad made a down payment on a four-room imitation brick house on a full acre of land on the outskirts of Edina, a suburb of Minneapolis, one of the ten wealthiest suburbs in the United States. The price was right. However, ours may have been one of the few houses in the whole city with no indoor plumbing.

I had the advantage of a good education in the Edina school system. At the same time, I felt the disadvantages and at times the humiliation of being a poor kid in a wealthy community.

My mother and dad both worked, but with so many kids, there were always older ones to take care of the younger ones. I had my turn at baby sitting as another brother, Dennis, and a sister, Lois, were born after we moved to Edina. We all learned from the give-and-take of family life. We had lots of fun playing soft ball, kick the can, and other outdoor games in summer and sledding, skating, table games, or roughhousing in winter.

The best thing for me about living in Edina was attending Edina Baptist Church with the family. The pastor, Glenn Anderson, had a deep love for God, and he faithfully presented the truth of the Scriptures. It was through his ministry and my Sunday school teachers that I came to know the Lord and gave my life to Him. Soon after we joined the church, we attended the wedding where Glenn married Eileen. They were role models of a wonderful family throughout my growing up years.

The church always had a strong emphasis on missions. Whenever an altar call for missions was given, I was among the first to go forward to present myself as willing to go. The Lord started to work in my heart when I was still in kindergarten. Pastor Glenn's sister, Ruth, who was on home leave from missionary work in Brazil, taught Vacation Bible School. I was deeply moved by her stories. God continued to touch my heart each time a missionary spoke. In the sixth grade, when I was assigned to write a paper about what I wanted to be when I grew up, I didn't hesitate to write that I wanted to be a missionary in South America. My mother's heart was also touched by the needs of the lost in other countries. She fervently prayed that her children would become missionaries.

In 1956, five missionaries were killed while trying to make contact with an unreached indigenous group on the Curaray River in the jungle in Ecuador, South America. That event was followed by an emphasis on missions and a call for missionaries to replace the five who had died. This served to strengthen my call to missions. About the same time, our youth director went to serve on staff at Wycliffe's jungle training camp in Mexico. When he returned, he invited a Wycliffe member to talk to the young people about the needs of groups who had never had the opportunity to hear of Christ in their own language. That was my introduction to Bible translation and the needs of indigenous groups. God deeply impressed this need on my heart. I had always thought of missions as going to a people who had never heard the gospel, but I was unaware of Bible translation.

Then as I came to that difficult stage in life of deciding what the next step is after high school graduation, I went to Pastor Anderson for counsel. I had two interests: nursing and physical education. I wanted to know which one would be most helpful on the mission field. He wisely advised me to pursue nursing, which

I did at The Swedish Hospital School of Nursing in Minneapolis. I have often said I was never sorry I was a nurse except to wish that I were a doctor.

As I neared the end of nurse's training, I corresponded with a mission I was interested in. I learned that they required all their candidates to have Bible school or seminary training. They recommended Multnomah School of the Bible in Portland, Oregon, because it offered a one-year graduate course in Bible. God graciously sent a nurse, who had attended Multnomah, to work at The Swedish Hospital. She highly recommended that I enroll there. I followed her suggestion, applied, and was accepted. Within two weeks of graduating from The Swedish Hospital School of Nursing, I was back in school again. In those two weeks, I had traveled with my sister-in-law by car to the East Coast for a vacation, taken state board exams in Minnesota, and traveled by train to Portland.

At Multnomah, I met Vurnell Newgard, a nurse from Minneapolis who was a new member of Wycliffe Bible Translators. I also met Clarence Church, another member of Wycliffe, who was studying while on home leave from Guatemala. Conversations with them convinced me that this was the work to which God was calling me. After a wonderful year studying the Bible and making great friends, I boarded the train with Vurnell for Grand Forks, North Dakota, to attend the Summer Institute of Linguistics at the University of North Dakota. At that time, I was thinking, *I can be the nurse partner of a linguist/translator.* But in the course of the summer, I learned to enjoy linguistics. At the end of the summer, I was accepted as an approved candidate of Wycliffe Bible Translators. At that time, I had a scholarship loan from The Swedish Hospital that had paid for my first semester at Multnomah. I couldn't become a member until the loan was paid off. (I had paid for my second semester there and the summer SIL course by working part-time at Providence Hospital in Portland.) In the fall, I worked and paid off the loan to meet the last requirement. When I went to Jungle Camp in December, I was made a member of Wycliffe Bible Translators and the Summer Institute of Linguistics (SIL), the organization Wycliffe members serve with on the field.

Jungle Camp

Vurnell,[1] Elwood Jacobsen, and I left the snow and cold of Minnesota at 4:00 a.m. on December 29, 1961. Destination: Mexico and Jungle Camp. We arrived in Mexico City on January 3 for several days of orientation to SIL's policies and an introduction to the cultural training required by Wycliffe Bible Translators and the Summer Institute of Linguistics for all their new members. We also met our fellow jungle campers while becoming familiar with Mexican culture and history as we visited the pyramids, museums, and other places of interest. The language barrier made us fully aware that we were visitors and guests in a foreign country.

Mexico City was not our final destination; we traveled for two more days deeper into southern Mexico to Tuxtla, where we waited for the weather to clear for the last leg of our journey, a thirty-six minute flight into the jungle. After our short flight, we arrived at Jungle Camp[2] on Sunday, January 14, for three months of training in jungle living while having contact with the Tzeltal Indian culture.

---

[1] Vurnell had married Elwood in the fall.

[2] Jungle Camp was a program designed to equip and orient the missionary candidates of Wycliffe Bible Translators to the practical aspects of primitive living situations. For many years all new Wycliffe missionaries attended this program, however, with the changing world situation and with missionaries coming from many parts of the world substitute programs have been developed. These are closer to the area of service and are contextualized to the needs of the particular area and culture of service.

We had classes in language and culture, missionary orientation, simple medicine for tropical diseases, and Christian living. We were also introduced to the practical aspects of missionary living with classes in mechanics, carpentry, swimming, and canoeing. We all shared in the work of making group meals as we learned to cook the foods available. My favorite time of the day came at four o'clock in the afternoon when we went to visit the Tzeltal Indians in the surrounding villages. I learned a few greetings and other phrases in their language by practicing the methods that were part of the training.

Paul had his own memories of Jungle Camp a year earlier, in April of 1961. I loved to compare notes with him as he told of getting up at 3:30 a.m. to begin a twenty-mile hike on foot or on mule from the main center to a new and unsettled area in the jungles of southern Mexico.

I had the similar experience in another area. For six weeks, we put into practice the things we had previously learned at the main center. We were divided into teams of two or three. My team of three built our own *champa* (hut) and prepared our own meals on wood fires using a mud stove we made ourselves. We gathered as a group to take survival classes that culminated in a survival experience. In my case, it was a simulated plane crash in an unknown jungle location. I survived although I spent the night alone in the jungle and never got a fire started.

After the three months of training, we had one more assignment to complete before leaving the jungle. To reach the airstrip where we would get the plane to leave, we were required to take a day's trip downriver on balsa rafts that we constructed ourselves.

Jungle Camp prepared us for many of the hardships we would later face in our ministry in the Andes Mountains of Colombia. We sometimes laughed, however, when reflecting on the number of times we had to get off the mules in Jungle Camp because our instructors thought the trail was too steep. If we had followed their rules, we would never have gotten on the mules in the rugged Andes.

From Jungle Camp in Mexico, I traveled to Guatemala City and on to the small town of Cubulco. The intent of this visit was to provide more cross-cultural experiences under the supervision of highly respected SIL translators Helen Neuenswander and Mary Shaw. In addition to their translation work, Helen carried on a large medical ministry with the Achi Indians.[3] Helen had a stream of Indians at the door starting at seven o'clock in the morning. I mostly observed but helped a little with the medical work in the clinic.

After Jungle Camp and being in Guatemala, I went for the second course of linguistic training that summer at the University of Oklahoma in Norman. By that time, I realized I was getting close to being assigned to a country of service. I needed someone with whom to work. The Summer Institute of Linguistics does not send people to work individually in an Indian village. They send teams of at least two, either two single women, or two men, or a married couple. I began to get concerned about who my coworker might be. In June, I sent out a prayer letter saying, "I would like you to pray for the will of God concerning an assignment to a field and a partner."

Since childhood God had placed South America on my heart as the place to serve. That summer SIL was seeking workers for Colombia. Cameron Townsend, the founder of Wycliffe Bible Translators and the Summer Institute of Linguistics, had recently signed a contract with the Colombian Ministry of Government for SIL to do linguistic work and translation for the indigenous groups there. It was an amazing opportunity. Colombia had not welcomed American Protestants during the years of La Violencia, 1948–1958, when there was political violence with

---

[3]   Achi is a Mayan language spoken by about fifty thousand people in Guatemala.

fighting between political Conservatives and Liberals as well as persecution of Protestants.[4] I joined a Colombia prayer group and began to seek an assignment there.

Like every young girl, I dreamed of being married, but I committed this area of my life to the Lord. The two single translators I had visited in Guatemala were happy and satisfied in their ministry. They helped me realize that being a single missionary was not a terrible fate. There were at least three single girls for every guy at Norman that summer, so it seemed likely that I would be single. In fact, a young woman student and I had begun talking about working together, although another student, Paul Headland, and I had begun dating at the beginning of the summer.

We were divided into small groups to study and analyze a language. Paul and I were in the same group. Each student also had a work assignment for an hour a day to keep costs down. My work assignment was serving breakfast in the cafeteria line. Paul apparently noticed me in the language group and again while serving breakfast. When I finished serving and sat down to eat with one of the older single missionaries, he came over and invited me to go bowling the first Saturday night. I didn't realize at the time that it was the diversion of senior missionaries to pair off the young ones. They had figured us out as a couple long before we did. We had a few more casual dates. Then Paul stunned me by inviting another girl to accompany him to an evening lecture where all my friends and I saw him walk her right down to the front. Apparently he thought we might be getting too serious and he should see about some of the other girls he had on his "list." She was not yet committed to missions, so he crossed her

---

4   For more information see http://www.academia.edu/4255210/The_unfortunate_irritant_in_US_Colombian_relations_1948-1958,http://www.britannica.com/EBchecked/topic/126016/Colombia/25342/La-Violencia-dictatorship-and-democratic-restoration.

off the "list" and came back to me. A week or two later, we had a particularly good time together visiting a Kiowa Church some distance from Norman, and our relationship grew closer as the summer went on.

The board of directors would soon be meeting. I was up for assignment, and Paul was seeking membership in Wycliffe. I went out on a scorching hot Sunday afternoon and crawled under a bush for shade. There I prayed seeking God's direction. I told the Lord I was willing to be Paul's wife.

A few days later on lunch break, we sat together on the lawn under a tree outside my dorm. During our conversation, Paul seemed intent on coming up with all kinds of ideas of what I could do for the next year so I could avoid going to the field so soon. He suggested that I could study for a master's degree in linguistics or work in nursing to gain more experience. Somehow none of his ideas appealed to me until he finally said, "Will you marry me?" I said, "Yes, I will!"

Paul explained his situation this way in a letter to his folks dated August 14, 1962:

> In principle, I would not have asked her this early in our relationship, but if I had waited until I could afford a ring and until I had spent some time in her home and she in mine, then she would already have received an assignment. She would be preparing to leave for the field before there could be much said.

He went on to say

> We are thinking in terms of either Christmas or next April...Of course, all this will be off if I don't get into Wycliffe.

We had made our engagement conditional on his becoming a member of Wycliffe. The Lord confirmed His working to bring us together when the Wycliffe Board of Directors accepted

Paul as an approved candidate. We both received tentative assignments to Colombia. Five other couples and four singles received their assignments to Colombia at the same time. After receiving our assignment on Saturday, August 18, we announced our engagement. "Paul Headland has staked his claim and now Miss Blake will change her name."

I was able to visit Paul's home in Southern California for a few days right after the summer course. Together we visited my brother Dick in the San Francisco Bay area. From there, I went back to work at The Swedish Hospital in Minnesota, and Paul returned to study at Fuller Seminary. We didn't see each other again until six days before the wedding. In the days before cell phones, e-mail, or Skype, long-distance phone calls were very expensive. We wrote daily letters sent by snail mail. Even with those letters when Paul got off the plane, the thought, *Help, I am marrying a total stranger*, went through my mind.

On December 18, 1962, I walked down the aisle at Edina Baptist Church on my dad's arm to meet Paul at the altar. The church was decorated with Norway pine Christmas trees and the bridesmaids wore red-velvet dresses. I wore my friend Bea Carlson's beautiful wedding dress. I had gone shopping with her when she bought the dress several years earlier. I thought then, *Someday I will wear that dress*. Paul sang, "The Lord's Prayer." The congregation sang "Great Is Thy Faithfulness," a message that has proved true for more than fifty years of marriage.

We left Minneapolis naively heading to my sister and brother-in-law's summer cabin in Northern Minnesota for our honeymoon. The weather was so cold we could not get the car started once we arrived at the cabin. (People actually froze to death in their cars that week.) A local farmer who checked on us helped us get to the store for food. We kept the oil heater going but were still cold so we also burned wood in the fireplace. One night, after we were settled down to sleep, I said to Paul, "I smell smoke." As a new husband, he dutifully went to check, even though he was probably thinking, *What do you expect? We have been burning wood all day.* It was a good thing he went. He discovered a spark had jumped from the fire and was smoldering on a stack of newspapers. God protected us from both freezing and burning. When it was time to go home, the farmer pushed our car with his tractor to get it started.

It never felt so good to get back to my parents' warm house in Edina. After spending Christmas with my family, we moved to Pasadena, California, where Paul was attending Fuller Seminary. I took a job at Alta Vista Hospital in Pasadena as head nurse on a medical-surgical floor, where I was in charge of the other employees in the unit on the day shift. During this same period, we spoke in churches and in homes. We explained our future work in an effort to raise financial support for our Bible translation ministry.

At the end of spring quarter in April, Paul completed the courses he was taking at Fuller Seminary. We packed our wedding gifts and the gear we had purchased into six steel drums and shipped them off to Colombia by ocean freight. Then we traveled across country to Minnesota where we continued to speak and contact friends.

2

A GROUP IN THE MOUNTAINS

No One to Meet Us

ON JULY 15, 1963, we said good-bye to our family and friends in Minnesota and boarded the plane for Bogotá, Colombia, via Miami and Panama. I was so excited to be on my way to the work God had commissioned us to do; I didn't give a thought to how my parents must have felt. They were saying good-bye to their twenty-four-year-old daughter going off to an unknown situation in a foreign country just two years after they had lost their son serving with the Navy in Korea.

On July 16, we arrived safely in Bogotá. When we got out of customs, we looked expectantly for our friends but saw none. We wondered if we were in the wrong place. Being young and naïve, although I was not really expecting the red carpet treatment, I did anticipate at least a small welcoming committee since a number of our friends were already in Colombia. We didn't even have the address of the SIL group house[1] handy. We had to dig in the duffle bag to find it.

---

[1] Wycliffe members serve under the Summer Institute of Linguistics (SIL) on the field. In Spanish, it is called *Instituto Linguistico de Verano* (ILV). The group house is a building where members who were in the city for medical reasons, shopping, or in transit to an assignment could stay.

After finding the paper with the address, Paul surveyed the situation, took things in stride, got our bags together, found the airport exit for street transportation, and using our limited Spanish language skills, flagged down a taxi to take us to the SIL group house.

When we arrived at the address, Paul unloaded our luggage and paid the driver. We rang the doorbell and were greeted by a maid and some children who knew nothing of our expected arrival. The children dashed off to find their mothers. Much to our relief, we saw the familiar face of Kay Church, a dear friend, who warmly greeted us. She told us they planned to meet us at the airport the following day, when they thought we were arriving. All our other friends were in the jungle being allocated to their places of service.

We were soon taken to our temporary quarters, a small apartment on the third floor of the building. Weary after traveling all night, after a quick bite to eat, we crawled into bed for a nap. Before drifting off to sleep, we offered a word of praise and thanks to God for our safe arrival and for the way He worked out the myriad of details leading up to this milestone in our lives.

Spanish Study

On August 15, we began a sixteen-week Spanish course at the University of the Andes. During the course, we lived in a Colombian home with two very proper maiden ladies. They were still wearing black to indicate they were mourning their brother's death. We lived in the room that had been his. The picture window in our room gave us a view of the culture on the street below as we saw among other things children in uniform on their way to school and horse-drawn wagons among the cars.

Each day the maid in the ladies' home served the four of us breakfast and afternoon tea. The time together gave us opportunity to ask mundane questions like where to buy laundry soap as well as more important questions about the culturally appropriate way to receive gifts. As we conversed we gained a greater fluency in Spanish.

Tunebo Chief Seeks Help

While we were studying Spanish, José, the leader of the Tunebo[2] people, made the arduous four-day trail trip over the mountains to a town where he boarded a bus for Bogotá, the capital city of Colombia. Little did we know that our lives would become inextricably joined. José was in search of "the government." He had been told they could help his people.

Years earlier, as an older teen, José had lived in town and had learned to speak Spanish. When he returned home, he learned his parents and many other people dear to him had died. Facing the difficult life there without them, he was tempted to return to the "outside" permanently. But instead, he found a wife and stayed. Through the years, settlers came into the Tunebo traditional lands bringing their diseases with them. Smallpox swept the area. José and others escaped the dreaded disease by isolating themselves in the mountains, but he never forgot the horrible decimation that had come from contact with outsiders.

Over time the Tunebos noticed José's ability to speak Spanish as well as his other leadership qualities and started to look to him for direction. He became the head chief in Cobaría. A leading shaman taught him the traditional rituals and songs for their ceremonial dances, which they believed kept the world from coming to an end. The shaman warned José, "Don't ever stop

---

[2]   The Tunebo are also called *U'wa* or *Uwa*, meaning people. In literature written before the 1970s, they were referred to as Tunebo, which is how we refer to them in the first two-thirds of the book. It is one and the same group.

performing these yearly ceremonies or the world will come to an end."

In 1963, when José arrived in Bogotá to report to "the government," he saw dozens of towering building, hundreds of buses, and streets crowded with people rushing by without so much as glancing at him. He had no idea where to go or whom to talk to on behalf of his people's need for protection of their children and their land. Eventually someone guided him to the Indian Affairs office, and he was granted an appointment with the head of the department. José, in his humble yet dignified way, communicated clearly the situation of his people. Settlers were taking their land. They were killing off their wild game with shotguns, and there was very little left. He also reported that his people were very unhappy that their children were being taken away. He made it clear he wanted the government to do something.

As our Spanish study drew to a close, we sought advice from the Indian Affairs Department of the Ministry of Government, the department SIL had a contract with, asking what group they would recommend. José's request was still in the mind of the head of the department. He strongly urged us to consider the Tunebo. We had asked God at one time for a group in the mountains. We took this as His answer. We requested and were assigned to the Tunebo people. (Being young, naïve, and idealistic, we didn't have a clue what we would face in the years ahead.)

November 22, 1963, the same day that President John Kennedy was shot, we successfully completed the Spanish course. When the announcement came over the radio, the owner of the small store where we were shopping exclaimed loudly, "The President of the United States has been murdered!" The maid in the home where we lived wailed off and on for several days after she heard that President Kennedy was dead. He was popular in the Catholic country of Colombia through the introduction of the Peace Corps, an important program for the underdeveloped people in small towns in rural areas of the country. Many homes displayed flags with a black bow tied in the middle to indicate mourning.

After Spanish study, we had only a little over a month to prepare for our first tribal assignment. During that time, we attended the first SIL Colombia group conference in which we became charter members of the branch. We enjoyed cultural experiences and introductions to a number of important people arranged by "Uncle Cam" Townsend.

In the midst of those experiences and preparation, we celebrated our first Christmas far away from family. We had a quiet breakfast with friends. When they left, we crawled back under the covers and slept the entire day. It was the only time we ever did that. I believe it was from culture shock and missing our families.

Tunebo Survey

Right after Christmas, Paul went out with a survey team to the Tunebo area to find a good location for us to live among the people. The team wanted to find the area where the language spoken was understood by the most people and was the most prestigious in which to translate the Scriptures. Of course, the people needed to be willing to accept us living among them and learning their language. In Paul's first radio contact, he reported they had had a good meeting with the Roman Catholic bishop. It should be noted that in 1953, the Colombian government had renewed a contract with the Vatican, giving all education and governance of Indian Territories over to the Roman Catholic Church. When "Uncle Cam" signed SIL's contract with the Indian Affairs Department of the Ministry of Government of Colombia, he agreed that SIL linguists would live on or near Catholic mission stations wherever that was possible. The bishop in charge of the area gave the all-clear for Paul and the team to continue further up the mountain to survey beyond the mission station. When Paul had been gone over a week with the survey team, I was anxious to hear if they had found a village and house for us to live in.

Plane Lost

I soon had more to be concerned about than a house in the village. On Sunday morning, the JAARS plane was returning our dear friends, Stan and Junia Schauer, to the group they worked with in the Amazon jungle. The pilot, Ralph Borthwick, on loan from the Peru branch of SIL, followed the best map available, but it led him to the wrong river. Nothing on that river was indicated on the maps, and he became completely disoriented as to his location. By afternoon all but twenty minutes of the gas supply was used up. When Ralph saw a clear stretch of beach on the river, he did what any good pilot would do—he landed there.

On Monday morning, another small plane flew up a river intending to refuel the stranded plane, but was unable to locate it on the river where they expected to find it. The next day, Tuesday, a high-flying commercial aircraft happened to spot the JAARS plane on a different river; however, it was Wednesday before they finally got gas to them.

The pilot, translation team, and the plane were all fine. They refueled and flew the Schauers on to their allocation among the Yucuna Indians on the Mirití River. Later we learned of three small commercial plane crashes in Colombia over the weekend with a number of casualties. In our group prayer meeting, we praised the Lord for His protection and care in this incident. In my personal prayers, I thanked the Lord for caring for my friends and asked for His protection as I knew my flight was the next one scheduled.

3

THERE AT LAST

Beginning Our Life's Work

A FEW DAYS later, with fear and trepidation, I crawled into the same small plane beside the same pilot for my first flight to Cubará, Boyacá. We climbed to fourteen thousand feet to get over the rugged, snow-covered mountains. This was Ralph's first trip after being lost in the jungle. I don't know if he was normally that quiet, but he didn't say a word the whole two-hour trip. I was scared to death. I could feel my muscles tense as I looked at the clouds and rugged mountain peaks. I feared we might get lost and hit one of those peaks hidden behind a cloud.

It came as quite a relief to see Paul, Al, and Vic waving their hands in welcome as we approached the airstrip. Paul had mules there ready for the trip to Chuscal, the combined boarding school, cattle ranch, and Catholic mission station.

Based on Junia Schauer's suggestions from her jungle experience, I took what I thought was enough food to last us four or five months. It had been hard to buy food, not knowing exactly how much we would use during our planned stay or what we could buy in the area. As a new bride, I faced the difficulty of planning, shopping, and packing for approximately 450 meals, uncertain of housing accommodations and with no refrigeration.

The pilot, Al, and Vic loaded the plane for their return trip and took off, leaving Paul and me with the mule driver. He packed our supplies onto the mules, and Paul helped me mount one of them. After a brief stop in Cubará, we started our mule train up to Chuscal at about two o'clock in the afternoon.

Someone had told us we would need a cat to keep the mice under control, so we took a kitten. I had to carry the scratching, squirming kitten with me on the mule. It was panting so much I thought he was going to die from the heat. We arrived about dark at Chuscal on the edge of the Tunebo area where we spent our first month studying their language.

The Tunebo Indians were a traditional Chibchan people group who lived on the slopes of the rugged Andes Mountains.[1] They had been pushed back little by little into this rainy rough area as settlers came in and took the better lands. They had a spoken language, but no materials in writing in their language available to them.[2] Most of them were monolingual in Tunebo. They would not be able to be reached through Spanish. We were there to learn to speak and write their language, to develop an alphabet, to analyze the grammar, to translate the New Testament, and to develop materials to teach them to read and write. It was our prayer and deepest desire that through the Scriptures they would come to know the Lord and establish a church to worship Him.

We rented a room in the foreman's house near the Catholic mission boarding school and ranch in Chuscal. The school had been started in this location in December 1958 by the Teresa

---

[1] Different Catholic Missions had some contact with the Tunebo people off and on since the early 1600s. (Márquez, María Elena, 1988, p. 15.)

[2] In 1926–1927, a French priest, Enrique Rochereau, wrote a description of the Tunebo language and grammar as well as a vocabulary list. (La Lengua Tuneba y sus Dialectos, [Ensayo Gramatical] Imprenta de Diócesis—Pamplona 1926; Fasciculo Segundo [Vocabularios] Imprenta de la Diócesis—Pamplona 1927.) These works were written to help the nuns learn the language. They were valuable and of some help to us in the early analysis of the language.

Sisterhood just five years before our arrival.[3] It had previously been located in an area farther away. We learned the children in the school had been brought there from their homes in the Tunebo villages of Cobaría, Tegría, Bocutá, Rinconada and Agua Blanca. Spanish was the language of instruction and the children were strongly discouraged from using their own language. Most of them learned their numbers well but not all of them learned to read. The children stayed there year around. When they grew up most never went back to live with their families but rather settled nearby and took on a Colombian farm lifestyle. Surrounding the mission there were also a number of Spanish speaking Colombian settlers.

During the four weeks in Chuscal, the foreman's wife cooked for us as well as a few farm hands. We ate lots of rice, beans, fried bananas, and fried meats. One of the Tunebos who worked in the mission helped us with language learning. Although we thought some of the suspicion they originally felt toward us diminished as we shared our plans with them, unbeknownst to us our language helper was reporting everything we said and all the phrases we were learning to those in authority. Obviously, they didn't trust "this young couple" who had come to live and work with the Tunebos.

We visited in homes of the acculturated Tunebos who lived about twenty to thirty minutes' walk from where we were staying. We learned the phrase, "What is this?" and used it to learn the words for all the common objects. The people seemed to enjoy our efforts and watched us carefully write each word as we had learned in our phonetics class.

One day, we started out at 6:30 in the morning to accompany Padre Builes, the Catholic priest, to the village of Tablón. He had been working in the area for fifteen years when we arrived. Along the way, he told us of some of the improvements that he had made

---

[3]   María Elena Marquéz, p. 15.

in the area, including building two wooden bridges across rivers, a small school, and a chapel in Cobaría, among other things. He was a dedicated austere man who supported himself and his projects by saying masses for the dead as requested by people in the city. He was very familiar with the rugged overgrown trails on which he frequently hiked to visit sick Tunebos.

After climbing uphill until about 10:00 or 10:30, we had our first sight of Tunebos in their traditional culture. The women we saw wore dark-colored wraparound ponchos made of wool. They placed the square poncho under one arm and over the other shoulder where they fastened it with decorative and utilitarian bone needles. They carried their babies with a strap on their back, tucked inside their wraparound poncho. Most of the people were hunting, so we only met a few. We were fascinated watching a woman coiling clay and carefully forming it into a cooking pot using only a piece of gourd to smooth it. We were shocked to see another woman, lying in a lean-to hut in the midst of a banana patch, apparently left there to die.

When we had been in Chuscal for two or three weeks, we wanted to make contact with the traditional Tunebos who spoke the language. Those who were living near Chuscal, many of whom had grown up in the Roman Catholic mission, spoke Spanish since they had been discouraged from speaking their own language. Our desire was to work with the traditional people so we could learn to speak the language. Paul had been told to contact the two leaders of Cobaría, José, who had gone to Bogotá seeking help, and Alvaro.

A young man who lived near the mission expressed a willingness to make a trip to Cobaría with Paul. In addition to locating and speaking with the Indian leaders, Paul planned to look over a plot of land that some thought might be suitable for an airstrip. Early one morning, Paul and his young guide set out for the highlands. It was the dry season and not raining much, so they made good time. By late afternoon, they arrived at the potential airstrip site.

Paul looked it over and asked himself, *What do I need to see in order to know if it would be suitable? I have never built an airstrip before.* He just didn't have the background to be able to evaluate the possibility of the land for an airstrip. Besides, he was exhausted after climbing mountain trails all day. But his visit to the area alerted some of the homesteaders of his plan to use an airplane to travel in and out of the area—an incredible idea to them.

Soon Paul and his guide arrived at the mission outpost in Cobaría where they spent the night. The next morning they set out for the lowlands again, but this time on the other side of the river. The trails on that side were narrow, not well kept, and hard to find. After a few hours on the trail, they arrived at José's house; unfortunately, he was in another area. Paul had missed his contact. Paul's guide had relatives nearby with whom he made arrangements for hammocks and some food for the night.

Wow, thought Paul. *I get to spend the night right here in a leaf hut among the traditional people. This is what I came to Colombia to do!*

In the morning, Paul met a young father, who spoke a little Spanish. Paul took out his word list. *I'll ask for some of these words I learned from the cook in Chuscal. I wonder if they'll be the same.* He asked the first word. "How do you say *sol*?" he asked, hoping and expecting that the Spanish word for *sun* would be recognized.

The man responded, "*Riha*."

Paul knew that wasn't the word for *sun*, at least the one he learned in Chuscal. "Say it again," Paul said, now using a Tunebo phrase he had learned and used frequently in Chuscal as he worked on learning to pronounce the language and write it down in the correct phonetic alphabet. But the man would not repeat it.

Paul went on to another word. "How do you say *casa*?" he asked, pointing to the hut nearby hoping and expecting that the Spanish word for *house* would be understood.

"*Sihyora*," he responded. Paul looked down at his list. He saw that (at least in Chuscal) the word *sihyora* meant *moon*. The man wouldn't repeat that word either.

Is this what the homesteaders and priest meant when they told us the people would not teach us their language? Is this what happens when they lie? Paul wondered. Then he prayed, "Lord, all the linguistic training in the world couldn't enable me to learn a language under these conditions. You have to intervene for us."

Paul knew he could not confront his new contact. At least not at this stage he couldn't. He would only get into a battle that he couldn't win. He went on. There were three or four chickens right there. He pointed to one, made a sound like a chicken, and asked, "How do you say *gallina*?" he asked, hoping for the Tunebo word for *chicken*.

"*Cárucua*," was the response. It was the word for *tree*.

Paul continued down the one hundred word list for ten or fifteen more words, but he only pretended to write them down. In his heart, he was praying, "Lord, I don't think you brought me to Colombia and out here to face this. I really need you badly. Please change their minds about teaching me the language."

That night, there was a full moon as he lay in his hammock and listened to the crickets, frogs, and other sounds in the tropical mountains where the Tunebos lived. He wondered, *Will I ever learn to speak Tunebo?*

Move to Cobaría

On February 8, 1964, Paul and I relocated from Chuscal to Cobaría to await the arrival of the Indians who would soon be returning from another area where they had spent the summer months (summer in Cobaría is December through February).

Filled with youthful enthusiasm, excitement, and the spirit of adventure, we were eager to move on to the work God had called and prepared us to do. We set out on foot for the two-day trip up the mountains. I was carrying the cat; Paul was carrying a car battery for our two-way radio on a pole stretched between himself and a young Tunebo fellow. We hiked all day and finally stopped for the night at a settler's home. They kindly shared their simple meal and a bed.

We started out early the next morning climbing higher up and down the ridges. Finally we came to an open spot where we could see the whole area. The panoramic view of the numberless mountain ranges was breathtaking. I was awestruck with the beauty of the mountains, streams, waterfalls, and valleys. Paul excitedly pointed out, "Look! Right over there is the mission outpost where we are going." I looked at the mountains and the rivers between where we were and where we were going and burst into tears. I was already exhausted, and the thought of walking all that way was overwhelming.

About twenty minutes later, we arrived at a very humble house of some settlers. The parents had gone on a four days' walk up the mountain for supplies. They left the younger children in the care of Diego[4], their teenage son. He offered us lemonade. We were refreshed, and I somehow was able to climb the next two hours to the mission outpost. We didn't know it at the time, but it was the beginning of a lifelong friendship with Diego.

At long last, we arrived in Cobaría in the Eastern Andes Mountains of Colombia. We made temporary arrangements with the caretaker for a single room at the Catholic mission outpost school, a half-hour walk from the remote Tunebo village. We anticipated moving to a house nearer the Indians when they returned to Cobaría.

We arrived to an empty village because the Tunebos had not returned from their migration to the lowlands. There were no people anywhere. While we were staying down below in Chuscal, we had some regular language assistants. However, there were no Indians available to help us learn the language in Cobaría.

---

[4] Many pseudonyms are used throughout the book to protect our friends.

We later learned that the Tunebos followed a yearly migration cycle that coincided with the growing season of the crops planted at each elevation. They lived in Cobaría from March until June and again from August to November. Every Tunebo family had two or three huts with gardens, located at varying elevations approximately a half-day's walk from each other. From mid-November to early March, and again during June and July, they lived in the lowlands. They planted different crops at each elevation; in Cobaría, it was mainly corn in addition to several varieties of root plants, squash, peppers, red beans, lima beans, and a small green banana. In the lowlands, they grew coca, manioc (a potato-like tuber called *yuca* in Spanish), various other root plants, avocados, corn, and many varieties of bananas. They depended mainly on their crops for food although they also gathered many wild greens, hunted, and set traps in all their locations.

While one crop was growing, they migrated back to a place where the harvest was ready. Their harvests usually produced just enough so that when the food was gone at one location, the crops were ready at another. When a move took place, all the people tied their doors shut, put their packs on their backs, and left. Everyone was gone within a short period of time, leaving the first area deserted. Because of the limitations of how much they could carry and leaving their houses unguarded, the Tunebos preferred not to accumulate material possessions. They said, "No one ever steals from us because we have nothing worth stealing."

The fact that Tunebos didn't have cash crops and the nearest road was so far away also limited their access to manufactured products. Machetes, axes, and a few clothes were the exceptions. Salt was the only consumable item brought in.

Unlike the Tunebos, we couldn't just put a pack on our back and get along with the food in our garden for the next three months. We had no garden. We needed the food we had purchased in town. We had made the mistake of going ahead of the man whom we hired to take our supplies to Cobaría. After we left Chuscal, he decided he couldn't do it. We prayed the rest of the supplies would arrive in Cobaría without problems. Thankfully, someone else realized our dilemma, packed his mules, and brought part of our things. However, because he was afraid to take his mules over the two wooden bridges to get to where we were staying, he left them at Diego's family's house. Later, Paul arranged to get carriers to take our things the last two hours over the trail.

While we waited for the people to return from their migration, Paul had a contact with one man in the village. The man was monolingual in Tunebo, speaking no Spanish. Here's how Paul described the incident in a letter to his parents on February 15, 1964.

> I had seen smoke in a nearby house yesterday and made plans to make a contact today. When I arrived this morning, it was raining. A man was standing outside in nothing but a G-string. As I approached, he sat down under the porch of the leaf house. With hesitation, I proceeded to sit down beside him. I then eagerly tried out my limited, newly acquired language skills by using a typical Tunebo greeting. He almost immediately got up and brought me some dried corn, dried beans, and some dried red peppers to take home for a meal. (Years later, we learned he was terribly frightened and hoped that Paul would leave as soon as he gave him food.) Before too long, I took off my poncho and placed it beside me. The Indian, obviously cold from the rain and lack of clothes went inside without saying a word and sat down by the fire. Curious, I stepped toward the door. He quickly handed me a piece of wood to sit on. As we sat together, I asked him the few questions which I knew in Tunebo. He seemed to like the idea of a non-Indian who could speak his language. He smiled but didn't laugh. He gave me the Tunebo words for a few of the objects in the small room. All too soon he stood up and said, "*Bar biru.*" (I'm going.) He began to straighten things up and put on his clothes. We walked the thirty

or forty yards together until the trail parted. He went on toward the lowlands as I hurried home for breakfast.

At this time, we still did not have all our supplies from Chuscal. Our meals had been rather slim the last two weeks. We were eating rice, beans, and oatmeal every day. When Paul came home with food after his contact, I was elated. My mouth watered as I anticipated the spicy aroma of the pepper-seasoned beans filling the room.

I had been soaking some beans for two days and had already started cooking them. That afternoon I added the whole red pepper—which Paul had gotten from the Indian—to the pot of beans. Within a very short time, I felt a terrible burning on the skin on my face and my eyes watered. I quickly concluded it was the result of touching my face after handling the pepper. In a panic, I ran to the fireplace to taste the beans. One bite and my throat burned.

Even after taking out all the pepper, washing the beans, and cooking them in fresh water, we were only able to eat about two bites. Our meal was ruined; I was distraught. There went the meal that we had our mouths watering for all day. It was challenging to be a young bride trying to learn to cook with unfamiliar foods over a wood fire with the pot balanced on the rocks. The popcorn we called supper did not satisfy the hunger pangs we felt. We went to bed hungry.

While waiting to make more permanent arrangements, we moved from the room in the Catholic mission outpost to a room in the house of a school teacher next door. It was just one big room with mud walls, plank flooring, and a shingle roof. We partitioned off a sleeping area with a tarp we had brought with us. In spite of the fact that we were located about eight degrees north of the equator, at an altitude of five thousand feet, the nights were cool. We were happy to have sleeping bags. At one end of the room, we had a mud stove and a few kitchen supplies.

Cooking with firewood in our homemade mud stove proved to be a challenge with nearly continuous rain during the rainy season. For one week, I struggled every day blowing and fanning, trying to get the fire hot enough to boil our soup. I was using firewood Paul had brought in from the forest. Finally we found two Tunebo boys who knew what kind of wood to get. To me the wood they brought appeared to be just as wet, but it burned a lot better, making it possible to cook faster. We ate a lot of food that was either burned or half-cooked until I learned to control the fire. I had no choice but to use firewood; any other kind of fuel was prohibitive with the high cost of transportation. For fifteen cents, the Indians brought a load of firewood that lasted about a week.

Our rent was $4 per month, but our cash was diminishing quickly, and we didn't have enough to pay the owner. Paul made a deal with him to fix the plank floor in exchange for rent the next two months. After language study all day, Paul enjoyed working an hour with the carpentry tools his dad had given him. Besides fixing the floor, he made two three-legged stools from poles, binding three poles together in the middle with wire and spreading the ends, one end for legs and the other for a board that served as a seat. These stools gave us something to sit on while we analyzed the language and ate.

4

A House with Half a Roof

When your children ask their fathers in time to come, saying,
"What are these stones?" then you shall let your children
know, saying, "Israel crossed over this Jordan on dry land";
for the Lord your God dried up the waters of the Jordan.

—Joshua 4:21b–23a (NKJV)

God's Miraculous Provision
of a House in the Village

DURING THE LONG month of waiting for the people to return to the village of Cobaría, we hiked up the mountain to the village at different times to see if someone might have returned. On one of those trips, it started to rain. We sought shelter in an abandoned Tunebo house that had no doors. It was about ten feet by ten feet. The cap and much of the leaf roof was missing. The remaining leaves were blackened from years of cooking inside with no chimney.

While we huddled there together out of the rain, we prayed, "Lord, please give us a good reception among the people, and please give us a house in the village. Even if it has to be this tiny leaf hut with only half a roof and totally blackened from smoke, give us a house in the village. Lord, we also need someone to teach us the language."

We had been told, "The Tunebos will never teach you their language. They will never let you live among them." Only a work of God could open the door!

A few weeks later, the people returned. Paul contacted José, the main chief. He was one of the very few people in Cobaría who could understand some Spanish. While in town as a teenager, José had lived with a deeply spiritual Catholic leader, José Ignacio Afanador, whose name he took. Before leaving to go back home, the leader had told young José, "Don't forget to think about God." Maybe the advice of Bishop Afanador was still in José's mind as Paul told him about our vision to translate God's Word into Tunebo. Paul explained that to be able to translate, we would have to live among them and learn their language. Inwardly quaking but outwardly bold, he said, "We need a house. Is there a house in the village we can live in?"

Paul watched as José's eyes scanned the village, stopping at what seemed to be each house. Then he thought for a while and finally said, "We'll see."

A few days later, about twenty Tunebo men gathered outside the house where we were staying. While the others waited, one of the men who knew Spanish came into the house and asked us pointed questions. "Who sent you here? How long will you stay? What are you going to do? Will you help us? Are you going to take our land?" Each time we answered a question, he went back outside and reported to the others what we had said. Then, for what seemed to us forever, they discussed it in their language. Then he came back in with another question and went out again for a long discussion. We couldn't understand a thing.

Suddenly, without warning, all the men except one left. He remained to say good-bye. He also said, "We'll be down to get you tomorrow."

Paul and I were excited, bewildered, and exhausted. "Wow," Paul said. "That interview was more intense than any we had when we applied to Wycliffe!"

I asked Paul, "What did the man mean when he said, 'We'll be down to get you tomorrow?'" Paul wasn't sure but thought it was good.

All the next day, we waited, but they didn't come. The following day, we decided to visit the chief again. When we arrived, he took us to a house. He indicated for us to stay outside while he went inside. Once again, we were grilled with similar questions. The long discussions were repeated while we waited. Finally, the chief said, "Come on, I'll show you a house." We crossed a small stream and arrived at a small house with no doors, smoke blackened walls, and half a roof. The very house where we had prayed that rainy day! It was God's answer to our prayer! It was *a stone of remembrance*[1] for the altar of our faith. Many times in the years to come, when things got difficult, we would look back and remember that God had worked a miracle to allow us to live in the village.

José then asked us, "Is there anything else you need?"

"Yes, we need someone to teach us the language an hour a day. To begin with, it should be someone who knows Spanish."

"Okay, I'll send someone tomorrow at two o'clock."

The next day at two o'clock, we waited. The village seemed deserted since the people were all working in their fields. We were concerned because we had read that at one time it had been punishable by death for Tunebos to teach an outsider the language. Despite that, shortly after the appointed time, José himself appeared to help us learn the language as promised. Because of the long-time prohibition of teaching the Tunebo language to anyone from the outside, as chief, he was the only one at liberty to help us.

---

[1] Then you can tell them, "They remind us that the Jordan River stopped flowing when the Ark of the Lord's Covenant went across." These stones will stand as a memorial among the people of Israel forever (Joshua 4:7, NLT).

He came not only that day but for an hour every day in the months to come. He continued helping us with language and translation for the next seventeen years. God had answered the second part of our prayer. It was no small miracle that the Tunebos allowed us to live in their village and taught us their language!

We were humbled and amazed at the Lord's working. "Oh, the depth of the riches of the wisdom and knowledge of God! How unsearchable his judgments, and his paths beyond tracing out!" (Rom. 11:33, NIV).

It was incredulous to the local priest that the Tunebos had given us a house right among them in the village and were even teaching us the language. He emphatically let both us and the Tunebos know he was not happy. The Tunebos had already fixed the roof and the doors of the tiny house, and we had prepared to move, but now we were confronted with a dilemma. Were we going to move against the priest's will? We consulted with our director, Clarence Church, by radio. It was always reassuring to us when his booming voice came over the radio. I had known him both at Multnomah and at Jungle Camp where he served on staff. He advised us to continue to live in the teacher's house and use the house in the village for an office. We followed his advice with confidence.

5

SETTLING IN TO A NEW LIFE

Gift Exchange

WHILE WE WERE still living in the teacher's house, in the afternoons after school, a few Tunebo children came right into our room (the door was open all day except when we were gone). Although they came in, they didn't sit down and frequently just stood outside by the window and watched us. They taught us the greetings, "*As racaro.*" (I've come.), repeating them over and over. We were to respond with "*¿Bar raqui?*" (You've come?) In turn we taught them the English word *kitty*.

Each day, as we hiked to our little "office" in the village, we stopped to rest at the first house we came to where Sinará lived with his wife. We noted that his house, like the other houses in the village, was made totally from materials gathered from the forest. The roof of leaves was held with vines to a frame of split palm. The rounded roof extended all the way to the ground on three sides. Outside in some of the yards, squash, peppers, edible roots, and beans grew right up to the house. A bow and arrow frequently stood near the door.

Sinará did not invite us in, so we either sat on a leaf on the ground outside the door or exchanged greetings while standing for a few minutes. On our first visits to not only Sinará's but to all the houses, we didn't see any children. We wondered if they were like a group, we had learned about in our studies, who felt so threatened they deliberately stopped having children. It turned out the Tunebos were actually hiding their children for fear we might take them. When we began to see children peeking out from behind their mothers, we took it as an indication of increasing trust.

During planting season, the people had very little to eat. They made trips of a few days or a week to the lowlands to bring up bananas and avocados from their gardens.

One afternoon, when we stopped by Sinará's house, he had just returned from a trip to the lowlands with his family. He gave us two avocados and a manioc root. Then his wife got out an avocado and two *yuca*. Then Sinará turned to his young son and said something we didn't understand. The little boy, not more than five years old, opened a small woven bag and got out an avocado for each of us. He had carried the bag with a head strap with just those two avocados the five-hour walk from the lowlands, and he gave them to us! We were touched!

Something similar happened in each home when we made visits to the village after the Indians had come back from trips to the lowlands. We would return home with a bag of food given to us by the people. An avocado, two small ears of corn or a few bananas from each one added up to so much that we were embarrassed! What did we have to give to them? We soon discovered that they had no matches. (We didn't know at the time they didn't normally use matches). We had a good supply so whenever someone came to our house we gave them a box. Later we realized the best thing we had to give was our medicines; considering the generous spirit of these people, we decided it was best not to charge for them. This would help keep our "accounts" balanced. We learned that their belief was if you accepted a gift, it put you in debt to the donor.

On warm days, we found Sinará and the other Tunebo men wearing just a G-string and a shirt. At other times they wore western shirts, pants, and a ruana (wool poncho) over their shoulders. His wife and the women usually wore a ruana wrapped around them under one arm and over the other shoulder where it was fastened with bone needles like the woman we had seen in Tablon. They wore a long narrow belt woven from red yarn to hold it around their waist.

After a number of months, we were finally allowed into Sinará's home. He quickly grabbed a large leaf from a stack on the bed. He indicated for us to sit on it on one of the two beds of cane poles or split palm. The stack of large leaves served as a pillow. Inside we observed a fireplace consisting of three rocks in the middle of the floor and firewood neatly stacked close by. Clay pots for cooking and storing water sat by the walls or on the fire. Corn was stored on a shelf similar to a loft or attic. There were doors at either end, hung on hinges of rope made of plant fiber.

When we left, Sinará's wife said, "Take your leaves with you."

Sometimes when we left his house, Sinará would follow us down the trail, giving us the names of the plants growing along the way. We gradually began to understand the people and to find our way around the area. Our daily visits gave us the opportunity to build their trust, observe their culture, and learn their traditions.

As we observed this proud, reserved mountain people, we noted how either by choice or fear of changing they maintained their self-sustaining way of life. They managed with things they found in their environment.

The women made clay cooking pots by first digging the clay, grinding all the bits of rock out of it, then making long coils and working them together in the form of a pot, and finally carefully smoothing out all the creases. It was a real work of art. They also made some pots with handles for carrying water. They let them dry out at home for about a month. When the pots were dried to just the right stage, the family took them out to the woods to fire them. They put the pots on a fire and built the fire up all around them.

The men wove hammocks from handspun maguey[2] fiber. They stripped the fiber by pulling it through two sticks, dried it and twisted it into string using just a spindle. Their loom consisted of four sticks in the ground, some sticks to hold the weaving in place, and a shuttle. The men also wove bags in the same way to sell or exchange for salt or machetes. The women wove bags from balsa fiber for their own use.

The major part of their self-sustaining lifestyle was providing all their own food. The men hand-cleared fields for planting. Even though José was busy clearing fields, he was committed to helping us with learning the Tunebo language. We were impressed with José's self-discipline. One day while Paul was getting data from José, there were some younger Indians with us looking at pictures of the Agtas (the group of people Paul's brother worked with in the Philippines). José became curious over their excited exclamations. He joined the boys and looked on with real interest. When he suddenly realized he was supposed to be teaching, he rejoined Paul to continue in his role as language assistant, which he took very seriously.

The first time we used the tape recorder with José, he was fascinated by the machine. He asked, "Can it speak my language?" When he realized it was like a parrot that repeated everything he said, he enthusiastically gave us the words and phrases we needed, played a song on his musical whistle, and sang another song for us. He was mesmerized listening to his own voice.

In the early stages of grappling with the Tunebo language, I was sitting at my typewriter one day, trying to figure out the tenses of Tunebo verbs. I couldn't help but smile as I observed my audience. Three young boys were engrossed in watching me type on my Underwood[3] typewriter. As they discussed among

---

2   Agave, sometimes called century plant.

3   The latest patent on the machine was 1927. Later on one of our friends (a radio technician) came out to visit in the tribe, and he soldered some slugs (changed the key type) using a candle to heat up the solder.

themselves how they thought the typewriter worked, they pointed to various parts of the machine. One of the boys became very curious. He was so intent looking down into the typewriter he nearly got his nose hit with a key.

We were determined to learn to speak the Tunebo language fluently in order to eventually communicate God's Word. To do so, we memorized short dialogues of typical situations learned from José, which we then practiced with the Tunebo people as we visited sitting on leaves on the ground outside their homes.

The Indians were quite impressed when they heard us making an effort to speak to them using words from their language. As a way of learning, we repeated words and phrases they said, often without understanding. Occasionally we noticed everyone laughing after we said something. We weren't sure if they had told us to say something off-color or if it was our poor pronunciation.

An important inroad for us was my training as a nurse. Although we had provided medical help to people from the mission and white settlers before, our first medical case in the Tunebo village was a challenge as well as an opportunity. A Tunebo man came asking for medicine for his sick boy, so we made plans to treat him the following day.

When we arrived, we found the boy in obvious pain and hot with a fever lying on the ground in front of his house. The nurse in me wanted to put him in a bed with clean white sheets, but that was impossible. Based on the information we had, we gave him a medication to reduce the pain and lower his temperature.

No one in the household spoke enough Spanish to get any information on his symptoms beyond what I could observe or to instruct the father on how to give additional dosages of the medicine. Finally, they located a man who understood enough to haltingly translate for us.

That typewriter had an amazing touch to it. We also had a portable Olympia that Paul had bought during his senior year in college.

This incident gave us more incentive to learn to speak the Tunebo language. When we saw the boy again the following day, he was more alert, in less pain, and his temperature was close to normal. I breathed a sigh of relief as I offered a quiet prayer of thanksgiving for God's intervention.

As we visited in the village, we noticed many of the babies and children lying listlessly on their mothers. Eventually their mothers began asking us to treat their babies, who I discovered were suffering from diarrhea. We noticed that when the water level went down, stomach trouble went up. They knew nothing of boiling water to kill germs. There was an added complication because the streams also served as their toilets. They were careful to use water that was upstream from the area designated for toilets, but when there was little water, there was additional danger of contamination and disease.

They also began to call on us to treat injuries and infected sores. One day, a boy got a severe machete cut while working in the field. The wound wouldn't stop bleeding. I was worried, knowing it was getting late and it was almost an hour's climb up the mountain back to our house. Finally after a long time of applying pressure and being unable to control the bleeding, I stitched it closed with an ordinary sewing needle and thread. After applying a good dose of sulfa powder, I carefully bandaged the wound. The parents were very grateful that the bleeding stopped, and I was relieved that he didn't develop an infection. I put sterile suture material and surgical needles at the top of my list of supplies needed.

When the people discovered we had scissors, which worked better than a machete or knife for cutting hair, they reticently came asking for a haircut. One day, someone saw Paul using a grinding wheel for sharpening his machete, and soon a few began to shyly ask if he would sharpen theirs. Each task gave us new areas of vocabulary and opportunities to practice using the language. When people were patient enough with us, we could actually understand and carry on a little superficial conversation. "What would you like?" "I'd like a haircut." "Who is sick?" "My mother (father, sister, brother) has a fever." "Where do you live?"

Although we were developing superficial relations with these reserved people, it wasn't the same as the deep friendships we had left behind. In the remote village of Cobaría where there were no Christians, Easter was like any other day. I was homesick. We spent a lonely morning listening to services on the radio and a tape of a sermon Paul's mother had sent. The music, message, and familiar voices on the tape gave me a little sense of contact with home.

Plans for an Airstrip

The gifts of food from the Tunebos stretched our grubstake, but they were not enough to sustain us. We tried to plant things like lettuce, tomatoes, onions, carrots, and radishes following Uncle Cam's example. But for us it was a total fiasco. Nothing grew. As we planned for the future, we realized we couldn't depend on the settlers near town to bring our supplies; we needed an airstrip.

The day after Easter, Paul went across the canyon to the Tegría area to evaluate a potential site that might serve as an airstrip. It looked feasible, and at that time, it appeared to him it would not need a lot of work. It had been used for pasture land and there were not many trees to remove, but uneven areas needed leveling. Although it was about a two- to three-hour walk from Cobaría, that hurdle was easier than the two- or three-day trip over the trail to the town of Cubará. An airstrip would eliminate the need for using mules to haul our equipment and other supplies from town. We talked to our director on the radio. Based on our description of the location, he thought that it should serve us once we completed the work of leveling the field where needed. We talked to the land owner and found him agreeable to the project. Although it was bad timing from a weather standpoint, we thought we needed to take action while he was open to the idea. Paul hired a group of Tunebos and worked with them cutting the pasture grass, removing some large trees and leveling a few areas.

We had been in the Tunebo area for almost five months. Soon they would be leaving for their lowland activities and the village would be abandoned for two months. We planned to return to Bogotá during that time. We were also looking forward to a vacation on the coast.

6

MIGRATIONS

Who Are We Waiting For?

GETTING TO BOGOTÁ was quite a trip. At the last minute, the Tunebos who were going to carry our packs from Cobaría to Cubará got sick, but the Lord worked in our behalf. We were able to secure a mule from a settler who was going down the mountain as far as Chuscal. We spent the night there. Even though we had complications in the morning securing help with our packs, we still arrived in Cubará around 11:00 am. The following morning, we planned to catch a bus for a long day's trip to a city where we could get a plane to Bogotá.

In Cubará, we ate lunch and got ourselves a very small room with two cots. We had just lain down to take a siesta when we heard a plane circling overhead. Excited, we ran outside to see if it might be landing in this frontier town with no scheduled air service. We watched as it circled to land at the airstrip about two miles out of town. "Where is it going, Paul?" I asked.

His response was short. "I don't know. But anywhere it is going is better than here."

We ran up to a truck passing by, one of the two or three vehicles in town that day. Paul asked if they would take us to the airstrip. The driver agreed; we loaded our duffle bags, and he took us to the airstrip. The plane's final destination after many intermediate stops was Cúcuta, a city with regular plane service to Bogotá. Even though it was a cargo plane, they let us board. While in flight, the pilot radioed the tower in Cúcuta that we were coming. The tower relayed the message to the pilot, who held the Bogotá plane for a few minutes so we could board. The well-dressed passengers waiting in the plane looked disparagingly at "the two young North Americans who looked and smelled the part of the five months they had spent in the village and two days over the trail."

Our friends at the SIL group house welcomed us. We spent the next two days resting and reading three months of accumulated mail. It was great seeing some of our old friends, meeting new ones, and having good Christian fellowship. We reveled in the luxury of hot showers, electric lights, and food we didn't have to cook over a wood fire. The ability to communicate using English was an added pleasure.

From Bogotá, we traveled to Santa Marta, a seaport on the Caribbean coast. Our hotel was directly across from the beach. Each evening, we enjoyed sitting on the hotel balcony watching the sun set over the ocean. The clouds, which usually came for the afternoon, made lovely sunsets. The bay where we swam faced west so the land mass of Panama made the comfortably warm Caribbean water calm. The sunny days went a long way to offset all the cold rainy weather we had experienced in Cobaría for the entire four months we were there.

On returning to Bogotá from vacation, I went to the doctor. He confirmed what we hoped. I was pregnant. Our joy was short-lived, however, as I started spotting that very day and miscarried shortly thereafter.

Development of Lomalinda Center

While in Bogotá, we were updated on plans that had been made during our first conference for the development of a center. The purpose of the center was to provide a place for the translators to work with language assistants away from all the distractions in the Indian villages. It was to be a place to call home when not in the village. A school was planned for the children. A study building for consultant offices and a linguistic library were part of the plan. It would be the hub of operations for the aviation department to fly the translators to the indigenous villages. It was also to provide facilities for the radio department to communicate with the translators in remote locations. Friends of Wycliffe in Santa Ana, California, provided the funds to get it well under way.

In a letter to his parents, Paul wrote,

> Plans are developing for the center in the llanos, the eastern plains of Colombia. There is a lake on the property that can be used for landing float planes.
>
> The Colombia Branch is constructing six temporary buildings so that there will be places to live during the construction of the permanent structures. Titus Nickel, who oversaw the construction of the SIL centers in Peru, Brazil, and the JAARS center in Waxhaw, North Carolina, has arrived to head up the building program. Fortunately, building materials can be procured in Bogotá and transported to the center site one hard day's drive over the road. There are also building material vendors located in a town about a five-hour drive from the planned center. Building costs are reasonable. SIL has a long-term use arrangement on the land, so with the reasonable material costs, our living expenses will be less at the center than in Bogotá.

Tunebo Ceremonial Dances

After a brief time in Bogotá, we returned to Cobaría in early August to be there for their ceremonial dances. We flew three hours to our new airstrip. We were thrilled when the plane landed without incident. However, the pilot told us our airstrip was marginal at best.[1] He wanted us to make changes to smooth out the rough spots before they would come back.[2] We were willing to make the improvements if it meant not having to walk and have our supplies carried two or three days over the trail.

The people were still in the lower village when the plane flew over. A friend told us when he saw the plane, the chief announced, "There's Paul." As if to say, "I told you he'd come back." Many of the Indians did not expect us to return. They couldn't imagine how we could survive there when we didn't even know how to find wood that would burn. The chief sent a delegation from the lower village to greet us. We felt warmly welcomed back by the people. Soon after we got settled at the house, the chief himself came by to see us. We found the Indians were all in good health with more free time than during their planting season. They were home and available to visit more often.

Again José conscientiously followed through on his commitment to help us learn the language. He even sent two young men help us in our language study when he needed to be gone a few days.

As they did every year, on August 8, the Tunebos held the first celebration in a series of eight two-night ceremonies. Part of their strong sense of self-worth was their belief that it was *their* dances that "kept the world going." For sixteen nights, between August and November, large conch shells, sounding like trumpets, were blown at dusk to call the people together. The ceremonies started then and continued until dawn. The Indians marched or danced around a fire inside the ceremonial house five

---

[1]   See Zander, Forrest with Dwight Clough, *His Faithfulness Reaches to the Skies: The Story of a Missionary Pilot*, chapter one, 2015.

[2]   The flight from the SIL center in Lomalinda was a four- to six-hour round trip. It cost $20 per flight hour. To keep our costs down on future trips, we had rice, flour, and other staples brought in when the plane came to pick us up from Cobaría. That way, we didn't have to be as concerned about weight overages when we returned.

abreast, the men in front and the women at the rear. A few shook maracas or rattles made from a gourd with holes drilled in the sides and seeds inside, with a stick through it for a handle. One singer led out singing or chanting many long narratives, naming all the animals and mountain peaks. The others followed several words behind. They sang in an archaic form of Tunebo speech as they danced, sometimes running at a feverish pace. At midnight, when they thought their god was near, they blew the conch shells, and all shouted at the top of their lungs hoping he would hear them. At that time, about ten of them held hands in a chain as they ran and jumped over the fire in the middle. This traditional ceremony was one of the few times there was interaction between Tunebo villages.

We tape recorded the songs to study the traditions, values, and beliefs that influenced their culture and determined their lifestyle. We questioned in our hearts what our presence to observe these ceremonies might mean to the people. We didn't want them to think we believed that one had to yell at the top of his lungs for God to hear. We wanted to communicate with them that God knows even the thoughts of our hearts, but at that point, we didn't know the language well enough.

7

THE DIRECTOR'S VISIT

Peace Corp Visitors

THE DEPARTMENT OF Indian Affairs was concerned about the Tunebo situation. In September 1964, they sent a representative from the office in Bogotá to Cobaría. He recommended the department have some of their workers in Cobaría for a time. (A home economist and an agronomist came but only stayed a few months due to the primitive living conditions.)

After the representative from Indian Affairs left, a Colombian anthropologist and two American Peace Corps volunteers came to the area to observe the Tunebos and their culture. Although the three visitors slept at the mission, they ate with us. They brought in most of their own food that I cooked for them. They were quite surprised to meet North Americans so far from civilization and were even more astounded when we told them that we planned to spend a good part of our lives there. "You're going to spend twenty years of your lives here?" they asked incredulously.

One of the Peace Corps volunteers was Catholic and attended the daily mass the local priest celebrated. The priest took notice of the fact that the man attended mass and also ate with us. One evening, we invited him to have supper with us and the visitors. It was the first time in his life he had eaten with a Protestant. He was aware that at Vatican II the previous year, it had been decided that Protestants were to be considered "separated brethren" rather than "heretics" as they had previously thought. I think it impressed him that we were dedicating our lives to this work with the Indians. He began to see us as brethren. At supper, he told Paul he was leaving early in the morning for another village to see a Tunebo who had been injured by a falling tree. He invited Paul to take the trip with him.

After our guests left that evening, we wrote a letter to our director explaining the improved relationship with the priest. In the letter, we reiterated our desire to move to the village to actually live in the house the Indians had given us. We took the opportunity to send the letter out to be mailed with the Peace Corps men.

The Director's Visit with the Priest

About a month after we sent the letter to the director, Paul came down with a severe ear infection. He was extremely dizzy and could hardly get out of bed. I talked by two-way radio to the office in Bogotá. They in turn talked to a doctor who insisted he needed to see Paul. We made the difficult decision to return to Bogotá to get the doctor's diagnosis. The Indians expressed genuine disappointment to see us leave again so soon. The chief said he wouldn't let us be gone for over two weeks. We requested a JAARS flight to pick us up.

The priest didn't seem want us to leave either. He checked on Paul to see how he was doing. He said to him, "Put you finger in your good ear." Paul dutifully did as instructed. Then the priest shouted in a very loud voice. "Can you hear me now? Can you hear me now?" Paul could hear him, and although we were touched by his concern, we felt we should follow the doctor's orders.

By this time, the director had received our letter telling of the improved relationship with Padre Builes. We radioed and asked Clarence Church to come out on the plane, which was to pick us up, so he could talk to the priest. We wanted him to broach the subject of our moving to the village. We were hesitant to mention it again ourselves since the priest had previously been opposed to the idea. Clarence said he would come. The priest agreed to accompany us to the airstrip to meet our director.

Because the airstrip was a very marginal short mountain strip, the plane could only take off with a limited load. Paul and I flew out on the first flight to a longer strip at the foot of the mountains, leaving our director and the priest time to talk. As they talked together, the priest said to Clarence, "I have never met two more charitable people. I think Paul got sick from walking back and forth in the rain to the village every day. They need to move to the village." Clarence didn't even have to bring up the subject— God opened the door.

We were overjoyed when Clarence relayed to us what the priest had said. We would be able to live right among the Indians. We felt especially blessed to realize that our prayers of many months had been answered.

When we arrived in Bogotá, Paul was able to see an ear specialist. The doctor determined that the ear drum was not broken, but there was an acute infection. Paul was in danger of permanent hearing loss. The doctor gave Paul a number of medicines to fight the infection. He responded well to the treatment—another answer to prayer. As a Bible translator, it was especially important to hear voice inflections, decipher tones, and recognize other unique word distinctions.

Our first thought was, *We can't afford to pay the cost of the flight to go and return from Cobaría before the upcoming conference and workshop*. But with the promise of moving to the village, we decided we had to go back regardless of the time or expense. We were thrilled at the possibility!

Our director confirmed our decision. He definitely advised us to return to the village as soon as we had the doctor's release. He thought it was important to make the move up to the village as soon as possible. At long last, we would be living among the people! No more walking up the mountain every day in the rain!

Now the people could bring us some of their sick instead of our always having to go to them. Every waking hour would allow for language practice and cultural observations.

Cobaría—settled in the Village, House Built

At the end of October, as soon as the doctor cleared Paul, we went back to Cobaría. We did not spend another night in the school teacher's house but moved immediately to the little leaf hut the Tunebos had given us in the village.

Crowded as it was, we were thankful to be in the first house we could call our own. I was surprised how I, who love order, managed to live, eat, sleep, cook, and keep all our food, medicine, clothes, and firewood in a room about eight by ten feet.

We moved the shelves Paul had built for the other house as well as the storage boxes he had made in Bogotá. These served as cupboards and helped me get organized. For a few days, I cooked over an open fire with three rocks on the floor. Later, we made a mud stove with iron stove plates we brought from Bogotá.

At last, we were living in the Tunebo village right among the people! Early in the morning, the neighbors across the stream called out to us, "It has dawned. We are going to the field." In the afternoon, when they came home with heavy loads of firewood or food, we'd hear them calling "Are you there? We are back." And at bedtime, "Sleep well." If they asked a question and we didn't understand, they asked the same question again and again. We would try to imagine what they might be asking and might eventually come up with an answer that satisfied them. If I understood before Paul, they would all laugh. Many of our conversations were called out over the small stream between our houses or as we stood visiting outside our house with a passerby.

In the house across the stream (where the chief had stopped to talk before showing us to the house that became ours), there were two families, Wanisa, and his sister, Riwusia, and their respective spouses and children. On the other side, a single mother, Ahbata, lived with her mother and children. Frequently after dark, they would slip quietly through our door and sit down on the floor with us for a long visit. One evening, I asked Ahbata's mother how people were related. She gave me the names of each of the chief's children and their mother's name. It turned out that half of the children had one mother and half had another mother, the woman that we knew as the chief's wife. Coming from my cultural background, I was taken aback by this information. We knew the other woman too, but not as his wife. She lived in a little house near the ceremonial house where the chief lived with the woman we knew as his wife. Later on, stories he told confirmed to us that our dear friend had two wives.

The Indians decided to build us another leaf hut to provide additional space to study and entertain visitors. They built it right next to the one they had given us. Even though they were preparing for the final and biggest ceremonial dance of their yearly cycle, as important to them as Christmas is to us, the men worked when they could. First they brought in loads of leaves and vine. While the leaves seasoned, they brought in the posts and split palm, which they made into a frame. Then to make the roof, which went all the way to the ground, they tied the leaves to the split palm ribbing with vines. They worked all day without eating, with only a few breaks to exchange cocoa leaves to stay their hunger and keep them awake for their all-night ceremonies.

They graciously donated their time, the split palm, leaves, vines, and posts needed for the house. We were very grateful and felt indebted to them. With praise to God for their generosity, we took this as an affirmation of His leading in our work.

Cellulitis

While the men from Cobaría worked on the house, men from the Tunebo village of Tegría worked on the landing strip. They removed trees around the edges of the field and leveled out the ground. With few tools and no machinery, it was quite an undertaking for them and for Paul who had never built an airstrip before. It was also a challenge for Paul to communicate what needed to be done with his limited vocabulary in this domain.

One day we were in the Tegría area near the airstrip on a medical visit. After the visit, although Paul had already complained of a pain in his leg, he went to check on the airstrip. I waited in an Indian house partway down the trail toward home. By the time he returned to meet me, he was sick! While he rested, I took his temperature. It was over 101 degrees.

When we started out for home, Paul's foot hurt so bad he could hardly walk. We sent someone ahead to see if one of the settlers could meet us at a junction in the trail with a mule. They were very gracious and brought the mule as requested. Paul rode the mule the rest of the way home. The next day, his foot was terribly red, hot, and swollen halfway to the knee. His temperature had risen to 103.2 degrees. The Indian Affairs home economist saw Paul and said, "That is erysipelas." I searched the *Merck Manual: A Physicians' Desk Reference*, and sure enough, Paul's symptoms were described as erysipelas (cellulitis). It also described the appropriate treatment. Even with penicillin, sulfa powder, and Terramycin ointment, it was five days before his temperature went down to normal.

Ironically, once his leg was nearly back to normal, one of the Indians insisted on picking at the sore on Paul's leg; he pulled out a fairly thick splinter about an inch long. I had looked for one earlier but hadn't found any. Amazing!

Having an airstrip put us in the awkward position of walking the narrow line of being a friend to both the Tunebos and the white settlers in the area. At times, it was extremely challenging. The settlers asked us to transport coffee for them from the airstrip. We would have liked to do it for them; however, the Indians were strongly opposed to the idea. They had already lost much of their land to settlers and thought they might end up losing more. They didn't want that. Their whole belief system was in opposition to having "outsiders" in the area. At the same time, the airstrip was on the land of one of the settlers, and he had great influence on the other settlers in the area. We needed God's wisdom.[1]

---

[1] For practical reasons, it never worked out to fly coffee out for the colonists. They accepted that, and the immediate crisis passed.

8

LIFE AT THE CENTER

A Tunebo Accompanies Us to Lomalinda

BEFORE WE KNEW it, we had to pack up everything in the house again to go to Lomalinda, the SIL center. The Tunebos would soon migrate to their fields in the lowlands, as was their custom several times a year. We followed their pattern and "migrated" at the same time to Lomalinda. We established a procedure for our packing to save time when we were leaving as well as getting set up again each time we returned. We had to protect the things we left against humidity, bugs, and animals.

At the Lomalinda center, we could concentrate on study and analysis of the language in a way we couldn't do in the village with all the daily interaction with the people, medical work, visiting, cutting hair, and playing games with the teenage boys. There we could also get the expert consultant help we needed. This time we would be there for the group conference and the phonology workshop.

José promised he would go to work with us at the center, but we weren't sure he really would be able to go. He worked the soil and planted corn just as all the others did. During the time in the lowlands, they also hunted, gathered food, and made some woven articles which they took out to town to sell so they could buy salt and a few clothes. If José went with us to Lomalinda, some of these activities would be left undone.

The night before we were going to leave, we were informed that José was not going to go with us. He had arranged for his nephew Manuel to take his place. Manuel was one of the few Tunebos who spoke some Spanish. He had been to Bogotá before, so he was comfortable with the idea of accompanying us. Even though he spoke Spanish, he used the Tunebo language almost exclusively when speaking to us, a real asset in a language assistant. This gave us opportunity to continue gaining fluency speaking Tunebo, but we could use Spanish to elicit words in Tunebo if needed.

When Manuel left Cobaría, he left behind his taboos, including the prohibition of eating anything that had been cooked on our fire. Although corn and bananas were the main things he ate at home, at Lomalinda, Manuel ate and apparently enjoyed everything we ate. He was especially fascinated with ice and popcorn. When he heard popcorn popping in the pot, he was astounded. When they toasted their corn, maybe one or two kernels would pop. He also left his coca behind, which seemed to make him very hungry. When we ate in the group dinning room, we would gather leftover food from the other tables to help fill him up. After a few weeks, he seemed satiated. He was congenial and liked people, and everybody liked him too.

Occasionally, we were able to take a little break from work and the responsibility of entertaining Manuel. Our second anniversary was one such occasion. To celebrate, we borrowed a small dugout canoe from one of our colleagues to go for a paddle in the moonlight on the lake at Lomalinda. Even though there were alligators in the lake, we enjoyed leisurely paddling in the moonlight. Paul had used a little imagination to make it special. But there was something extraordinary he had not planned. As we headed in to tie up the canoe and go to shore, it began to get darker. We looked up, and saw to our delight, the full moon was beginning to eclipse. We stayed out longer and enjoyed the spectacular event God had planned for us after our first year living with the Tunebos! We never forgot that anniversary.

To accommodate all the Colombia SIL members who came together for the conference and the workshop, the work crew had quickly set up these roofs with metal frames. They stood six-foot sheets of asbestos cement roofing on end for walls. There was a huge open space between the top of the wall and the roof. We lived under Schauer's roof with two other couples, Stan and Junia Schauer and Rich and Karis Mansen and their baby. Every word could be heard from one "room" to the next. When the rain came with a wind, we had to rush to cover our bed, language materials and whatever else we could with plastic.

Once the intensity and time demands of the annual Colombia SIL group conference and the Christmas holidays were over, we were able to establish a work routine. During the next month and a half, I managed to study around five hours a day on Tunebo grammar while Paul studied almost eight in preparation for the upcoming phonology workshop. During the workshop, he would have to write up a description of the Tunebo sound system in order to develop a scientific alphabet. He recorded examples of where each sound occurred in the word; initially, medially, or finally. With what other letters did it occur in contrast? For example he discovered that the [r] sound never occurs initially or after [n]. In initial position and after [n] it sounds like [dr]. Since [r] and [dr] were never found in contrast, for the alphabet, we could just use the letter [r] for both. His study also included figuring out stress, tone, and length. He recorded all the words necessary to have examples of each sound on tape. Manuel patiently repeated the same words as many times as needed. We praised God for his help.

While Paul worked on phonology, I was enjoying grammar study. For me it was like discovering gold to learn what a verb affix meant, such as there is no time affix in a negative verb. "I am not going," "I didn't go," "I won't go" are all the same "No go."

The phonology workshop started in mid-February. A consultant with her PhD in linguistics came down from Mexico to lead the workshop. We were motivated by the guidance of this knowledgeable consultant who confirmed what we had analyzed correctly and identified what problems still remained. She said we needed more data to prove or disprove some of our tentative conclusions.

Manuel stayed with us at the workshop until nearly the end of March. We didn't feel we could ask him to stay any longer. It was planting season, and if he were away longer, it would mean missing meals later in the year. We sent him on ahead. He had the equivalent of one hundred dollars in Colombian pesos in his pocket when he left. Four years later, Paul happened to see him counting his money. He still had fifty dollars. Obviously they were a self-sustaining culture and not dependent on goods from the outside.

On arrival back in the village, before Manuel could live with his family again or eat from their fire, he went through the required four nights of ceremonial purification by the shaman. The shaman blew over his sacred egret feathers on Manuel and everything he had brought back with him while chanting to the spirits to appease them. After that, he could no longer eat with us, touch us, or sit in our house.

9

NO DOCTORS

Early Medical Ministry

He sent them out to proclaim the kingdom of God and to heal the sick.

—*Luke 9:2 (NIV)*

THERE WAS NO medical doctor in the Cobaría area. Even in the town of Cubará, two days' walk away, there was only sporadically a doctor serving his required rural year. I was soon treating a large number of sick people each week. When people came to me with their aches and pains, I felt compelled to try to help them. We treated malaria, diarrhea, parasites, infectious diseases, injuries, pneumonia, infections from tropical insects, and many cracked feet from walking barefoot on the trail. I spent many evenings studying the *Merck Manual* and other books to determine how to treat the conditions of the people I had seen that day in preparation for the next day's visits.

On one occasion, I gave a lady some medicine for intestinal worms. She ended up being sick in bed for three days after taking the medicine. Anxious about my diagnosis, I prayed for her continually and was extremely thankful when she finally recovered.

Those opposed to our work strongly discouraged the settlers from bringing us their sick, but Diego's mother was more worried about her son, Diego's little brother, than any possible repercussions of receiving our help. The little boy had put a kernel of corn up his nose. After a few days it expanded from the moisture and was firmly stuck causing him great discomfort. His mother brought him to me. I prayed as I worked trying to dislodge the corn without causing him too much pain. The irritation caused him to sneeze and out flew the kernel of corn. We all breathed a sigh of relief. It was one more way God used to cement a relationship with Diego's family.

On another occasion, a young settler came to me when his wife had been bleeding for some time from a miscarriage. I insisted she needed to go to the hospital in the city for a D&C. I explained that she needed surgery to stop the bleeding as well as blood transfusions to replace what she had lost. She was in no condition to make the two-day hike over the trail followed by a long arduous day on the bus. We offered to ask for the JAARS plane to come and fly her out to the city. The young man asked us to request the flight against the wishes of his in-laws who were worried about how much all this would cost. The night before the flight, I tried to give her IV fluid, but she had lost so much blood I was unable to find a vein to insert the needle. I could put it in and pull it out and not a drop of blood came. She passed out on the bed. I wondered if we would lose her. I gave her the fluid subcutaneously. By morning she roused enough to sit on a mule to get to the airstrip. In the plane, she passed out and was unaware of the rest of the trip to the hospital. At the hospital she had a D&C and blood transfusions just as I told them. She recovered, and for years she visited me each time we were in Cobaría to thank me for saving her life. Her parents were grateful too. Some of our missionary friends helped pay the expense of the flight.

Medical work could be very tiring. It wasn't necessarily the number or nature of the illness or injury; the wearing part was getting from one home visit to the next over steep slippery muddy trails, especially during the rainy season.

We usually finished our language work for the day about the same time the Tunebos came home from the fields. Many times a Tunebo would come by to say, "Please come to our house this afternoon. My mother (baby, brother, sister, or whoever) is sick." And off we went on medical visits.

One typical afternoon, I restocked my medical bag, put on my boots, raincoat, and hat, and headed out on the narrow overgrown trail to visit and care for medical needs. My first stop was the chief's home. His son had been suffering with an infected foot. Although still quite swollen, the foot seemed to be somewhat better, and the boy was experiencing less pain. I was encouraged by his progress.

My next visit was at a house located on another knoll. I walked through a pouring rain to see a little girl who had been sick with a very high temperature the day before. But the doors were tied shut, and no one was home. I could only hope she was improving and the family had gone on about their routines. However, I returned home reluctantly, disappointed and discouraged.

Once home, I was asked to go see a family living below us who was very ill. The trail to get to their house was almost straight down, and although I knew it was dangerously wet and slippery, I felt I had to make the effort to determine their condition. The people usually didn't ask for medical help until they were so sick they could hardly walk or even get out of bed. I have to confess I had mixed feelings when I arrived and discovered the family was resting well and their panic and the sense of urgency had passed.

We were in bed reading one Sunday evening with the rhythmic sound of the Tunebo ceremonial dance in the background. Suddenly we heard, "Edna! Edna! Heal me." We jumped up to see a ten-year-old girl with a long machete gash from almost the corner of her mouth back to her ear. We were getting ready to stitch her face when another girl about sixteen came with a five-inch cut on her arm at her elbow. Somehow we got them both taken care of. The people were bewildered and ashamed that someone would actually strike someone else with a machete. Things like this normally didn't happen at the Tunebo ceremonies.

Another Sunday, the chief's brother sent for us. He and three of his children were sick. When we went back on Monday, he was gone, but his wife was there and she was sick too. What a time! While I was trying to give one of the children a penicillin shot, she kicked and squirmed so much I couldn't hold her and inject the medicine at the same time. Paul came to help, but by that time, the medicine had stuck in the needle. When I forced it, penicillin went shooting out all over my face. The worst of it was we had to stick the little girl all over again.

"My baby is dead! My baby is dead!" Our neighbor, Ahbata, called as she came running. She handed me her baby who had stopped breathing and was turning blue. I cleared her airway and did CPR. She started breathing. Her color returned. Ahbata happily received her baby and returned home. This happened three times during an epidemic of whooping cough that spread over the village in April 1965. The last time it happened, Ahbata was so sure the baby had died she just left her. After some time of CPR, the baby miraculously responded. I was able to return the baby to her mother.

The whooping cough epidemic continued. At least three babies died in just one week. Our hearts were heavy as we wept for our Tunebo friends who lost children in the epidemic. We were distressed as we learned each grieving mother went out all by herself to bury the baby. No one accompanied her to lend support or comfort. They were saddened but were forced to continue on in their normal pattern without showing any grief. Open grief might indicate to the spirits that she wanted to accompany the baby in death.

After we learned the language, I was able to do some health teaching in the area of tropical diseases through demonstration and by explaining hygiene practices while treating the sick. The main change that I noticed was that they started to use soap to wash their clothes. I wrote a booklet in Tunebo on the prevention and treatment of parasites and another on the prevention and treatment of malaria.

When the whooping cough epidemic subsided in Cobaría, the people again migrated to the lowlands to clear and plant their fields there, and we went to the SIL center. Epidemics were devastating in all the indigenous areas. During the time we were at Lomalinda, Jim and Jan Walton, working with a group in the Amazon jungle, called in by radio. There was a case of smallpox in the area. None of the Indians had been vaccinated. SIL personnel acquired vaccine in the city, a service flight was arranged. They needed a nurse, and I was chosen to go along. We vaccinated most of the two hundred people in this small group. The team had not had medical training, so it was rewarding to be able to help them.

While there, I noticed a stark contrast between these warm, outgoing jungle people and the reserved mountain Tunebos who would never allow me to hold or play with their babies.

10

CHALLENGES AND LESSONS IN VILLAGE LIFE

I have become all things to all men, that I might by all means save some.

—*1 Corinthians 9:22b (NIV)*

Slippery Mud on the Airstrip

THE FIRST[1] TUNEBO primer we wrote, which taught the five Tunebo vowels and four consonants, was approved on a provisional basis. We worked long hours at Lomalinda to get it mimeographed so that we could take copies with us when we went back to the village in August.

Although we were chomping at the bit to try out the primer with the people, we knew the first job was to do some concerted work on the airstrip. We had been told that unless we greatly improved the airstrip, JAARS could not continue to use it. We didn't know how urgent those repairs were until the plane landed and got covered in mud. The pilot managed to control the landing in the slippery mud; however, he couldn't take off again until some of the mud had been cleared off the field. After many

---

[1]   It would become a series of six primers.

hours of work clearing mud from the runway, the plane took off successfully. We breathed a sigh of relief and a prayer of thanks.

We were also thankful that Dave, a college student who had come to work for the summer, was with us to continue improving the airstrip. He worked with Paul alongside a few Indians using just a couple picks, shovels, and a wheelbarrow. They picked to loosen the grass and remove it along with top soil off the strip in order to get down to a harder surface. They filled in one particularly low spot and made a ditch on the upper side to create better drainage. Each night when they came to the little shack near the airstrip, where I had a hot meal waiting, they plopped down exhausted from the backbreaking labor in the miserable weather. To this day, we remember Dave by his oft-repeated phrase. "Guess what?" The answer was always the same: "It's raining."

After Dave left, Paul and I went back with some Indians from Cobaría to work a few more days filling low spots. The Indians were good workers with a "Let's hurry up and get this work done so we can go home" attitude. To prevent cattle from grazing on the airstrip grass and turning the surface into a mushy slime, Paul made a contract with the Indians to put some fence posts around the airstrip. We had some barbed wire brought out the next time we scheduled a flight and hired someone to string the wire between the posts. With the drainage ditch to help reduce the water problem and the fence to eliminate the cattle problem, we anticipated many safe landings and takeoffs.

With the airstrip in better shape, we were free to test the primers on a few of the men in the village. They quickly learned the five vowels and four consonants and the syllables made up of the letters introduced in the primer. Before long they were able to sound out the words made with those syllables. They frequently played a matching card game we made to introduce the nouns in the primer. Even the man next door who had no previous contact with school or written words grasped the idea. The chief went through the first section of the primer in just two sessions. He had apparently learned to read in Spanish when he was young but said he had forgotten.

In August 1965, although the airstrip work went well and the primer testing was progressing, there were obviously some people who were not in favor of our being in the area. Rumors were going around that something bad might happen to us. Two of the settlers came and expressed their concern for our safety. They said, "If anyone comes around to bother you, send for us immediately." The intent of the rumors seemed to be to frighten us into leaving the area. José was also receiving pressure for teaching us the language. His sixteen-year-old daughter fell off a pole bridge into the rushing mountain stream below and died. She was epileptic, so we surmised that she may have had a seizure while crossing the bridge, which caused the fall. Someone told José, "God is punishing you for teaching Paul the language." As a result, he didn't come to teach us for a number of weeks. About that time our director came to Cobaría to see our location and encourage us in the work. We explained to him our difficulty in getting regular language help. We aren't sure what Clarence said to José; all we know is that José came back and helped us again much more consistently.

When José came back, we started to translate Old Testament stories with him. Translating stories was easier than straight Scripture because we did not have to include every detail. Stories teach the attributes of God and who He is in longer narratives that can be grasped. These stories were essential for the Tunebos to understand the New Testament.

José enjoyed the challenge of helping us to find the words needed to express biblical concepts. We translated the Creation story, the Garden of Eden, Cain and Abel and started work on the story of the Flood. The Creation was the hardest because of the difficult concepts; especially the concept of light. Some of their own taboos also made translation of God's Word hard for them. In Genesis 1:28, God gives dominion over the animals to mankind, and in verse 1:29, He gives them all the seeds, plants, and trees. When I checked the Creation story with Manuel for comprehension, he told the story back in his own words. When he came to the part, "God gave us every seed-bearing plant," he could hardly choke out the words. His father was the shaman who conducted the ceremonies related to the spirit of a sacred tree. The Tunebos believe that spirits are the owners of trees and plants as well as all living creatures. They think that they have to perform rites and ask permission from the spirits to eat the fruit of certain trees or to kill animals. However, we were encouraged when José said, "We didn't know some of these things about God until you came here with the Bible."

Don't Loan Fire!

I had to learn one cultural lesson the hard way. Many times when they asked for medical help, the Tunebos were close to having pneumonia and needed a shot of penicillin. After giving an injection, I would throw the used alcohol cotton ball into the cooking fire. I was always puzzled when they would quickly reach in and take the cotton out of the fire. Sometimes they would do it very obviously, and sometimes they tried not to let me see what they did. I thought, *Why do they do that? Isn't burning the best way to get rid of contaminated material?* That is a very true statement from my worldview, but not from theirs. I had read earlier about some of their beliefs about fire, but I didn't believe them. I would soon have another lesson that would remove all doubts about their worldview about fire.

Busucayá, a lad of nine, returned from the field in the pouring rain with his little brother and sister. His sparse clothing was dripping with water. His dad and mom wouldn't be home for another hour or two. He must have tried rubbing the sticks together to start the fire, but to no avail. He came to us. "Can

I borrow some fire?" I remembered what I read about Tunebo fires being sacred and them not using other people's fires but we had seen little evidence of it. So with a little boy standing there shivering, I did the logical thing; I reached in my mud stove and took out two pieces of burning wood and gave them to him. He quickly ran home to his leaf house across the stream from ours. Using the burning wood he started a fire in their fire place.

But then it happened; his mother came home! We heard her arrive before we saw her. I peeked out the door to see what all the commotion was. I saw his mother yelling and kicking Busucayá, kids crying, and the rocks from the fireplace, the leaves, and mud that held them in place were all rolling down the side of the hill to the stream. The mother dragged the kids down to the stream and bathed them in the cold water. She washed all the clothes in the house. This normally gentle woman had reached the limit! I had inadvertently "contaminated their whole house" with my fire. I didn't see it at the time, but in retrospect, I am sure they had to have a shaman[2] come that night to blow across a ceremonial feather and perform a ceremony to purify the house so they could continue to live there.

Suddenly I understood what I had read and experienced. I realized that we were facing a culture whose worldview was different from ours in many areas. In their worldview, fire can be contaminated. In mine, fire purifies. They consider their fires sacred. Each fire has its own purpose and is started by rubbing sticks together. There are many taboos regarding who can eat from whose fire. I stopped using their cooking fires to dispose of contaminated materials, and I certainly didn't give children burning firewood ever again. *To the Tunebos, I became as a Tunebo that by all means I might save some.* Fire was just one area. What other deep cultural differences was I missing?

---

[2]   The word *shaman* is used today as more politically correct. The term *witch doctor* was used at the time this story transpired.

One Sunday the man who lived just up the hill from us got a small deer in one of his traps. We learned that they don't try to preserve the meat but rather they cook all of it at once. They steamed it in a big clay pot with greens in the bottom. When it was cooked just right, they served the people who had been arriving. We weren't sure just how word got out or who was welcome, but many people showed up. Even among themselves, not everyone could eat from everyone else's fire. The man's own son-in-law couldn't eat with them. Their taboos didn't allow them to give us their cooked food (or accept ours), so we didn't get any. We could only observe while our taste buds were awakened by the aroma emanating from the steaming pot.

Where Did the Mail Go?

Even with the airstrip in good condition, the plane only came either to take us to the area or to pick us up. From the village, we were able to communicate with the Lomalinda center by two-way radio. Occasionally our prayer partner would call on the radio and get news to write a short note to our parents. We still wrote letters regularly and looked for ways to get them mailed. Once, we sent a Tunebo the two day's walk to the town at the foot of the mountain to get our mail. He came back with nothing. Apparently the air force plane had not made its usual stop in Cubará. We had sent out a lot of letters with him, so we were consoled that it wasn't a completely wasted trip. Later we found out those letters never reached their destination. After several similar disappointments, we gave up trying to get mail in or out from Cobaría.

Without mail and newspapers, we were able to keep up on world news by listening to our Zenith Transoceanic Radio that we had received as a wedding gift. We listened to the Voice of America news every night. We were thankful on a daily basis that HCJB, a Christian shortwave radio station in Ecuador, broadcast programs that provided a source of spiritual refreshment. Listening made us feel we weren't quite so alone.

Washing and drying clothes was a problem with the incessant rains. For a while, I even tried ironing with a Coleman gasoline iron to finish the drying process. That didn't last long. Paul eventually put large sheets of clear plastic over the clotheslines outside and additional clotheslines inside upstairs over the stove. After wearing myself out washing in the cold stream water, I trained the neighbor who frequently visited after dark, Ahbata, to wash clothes. She was slightly more relaxed about the taboos and fear of outsiders. Her help gave me an extra day a week to work on the language. She faithfully did our wash for years, even with people asking her repeatedly, "Don't you get sick from handling their clothes?" She became one of our closest friends.

November 6, 1965, was a good example of a typical day in Cobaría. We slept until about 6:00 a.m., had devotions and breakfast. (Often there were people there before breakfast but not that day.) Paul kindly did the dishes for me while I ran to the neighbors to give their little baby some medicine for a terrible diarrhea.

When I returned home, I translated some of our grammar material into Spanish to help teach a young priest, recently assigned to the area, who was very interested in learning the language. These lessons were the start of a small book, which eventually became the *Simplified Tunebo Grammar*. It had the main points of the grammar and some dialogues of typical situations to memorize. He came at 9:00 a.m. as he had done for a few days. After the lesson and a little snack, he left. Then I read some background material about Tunebo that another priest had written in 1926.

To round out the morning, I restocked my medical bag, revisited our neighbor to give the baby more medicine, and fixed lunch. Most of this time two little boys had been around asking, "What is this? What are you doing? Give me this." We nicknamed one of them *Icuri Yaqui* (What are you doing?) because he asked it so often. The neighbors on the other side of us had just returned from being up at their field for several days, so we called back and forth a bit. A typical Tunebo way of communication in the village with deep ravines and wet trails was to shout from one house to another since they were close by the way the crow flies but much farther to walk. After lunch, we went up the hill to see a new house our neighbor was building.

When we got back, our language assistant was waiting. He and Paul tape-recorded the story of Cain and Abel they had been translating for some time. José did well as he told back what they had translated. He said they had never heard anything like this in their language. Later that afternoon our neighbor came so we played it for her, and she seemed to understand and enjoy it.

While we were listening, one of the women settlers arrived a bit out of breath after walking all day. She told me she wanted to buy medicine for parasites and malaria to have on hand for herself and her six living children. She had lost four. She confided in me how her family and the other settlers had come to the area from a small town four day's walk away to escape the violence in the 1950s. They sometimes went for months without salt and other supplies because there was no place to get it.

The afternoon ended with one more visit next door to give the baby another dose of medicine, supper preparations, and a visit from Manuel, who had just come back after living in his field. After supper we chatted about the day with Ahbata and her family sitting on the floor.

Exhausted, we crawled under our mosquito net, thanking God for the opportunities to minister through medicine, teaching, translating, and building friendships with the young priest, the neighbors, sick babies, the little boys hanging out, Tunebo leaders, and the colonist lady. God was giving us brothers and sisters one hundred fold.

11

ROUTINE: COBARÍA–LOMALINDA

Another Night Waiting for the Plane

THERE WERE ALWAYS uncertainties associated with our seasonal moves between our home among the Tunebos in Cobaría and the center in Lomalinda. November 1965 was no exception. The weather was bad at both ends. We were ready to leave on Thursday morning. The plane didn't come until Friday afternoon. Some Indians went ahead and met the plane to get our incoming supplies. Ahbata and her mother accompanied me on the trail and carried some delicate clay pots. We met the Indians returning with our supplies. It really touched my heart to see the chief and the second chief carrying our packs, but when I saw the chief's wife carrying one, I almost cried. It took courage for her to venture out like this, but she wanted to see the airplane. Paul stored the things in the house then met me at the airstrip.

Just as we were ready to get in the plane to take off, a dark cloud filled the mountain pass. This precluded our departure. We walked the thirty minutes to Diego's parents' house to spend the night. They gave us a good supper of eggs, beans, and boiled green bananas. Our pilot added canned tuna and sardines to the meal.

That night we shared our bed of planks with the pilot as well as with the fleas; neither Paul nor I slept well. The weather was nice in the morning. We got off to an early start and arrived at the Lomalinda center in time for lunch.

We were amazed at the progress on the development of the center. The children's home was already completed. More buildings were started, and others were finished. We stayed in the radio operator's guest room, with no place to cook. We ate each meal in a different home until the dining room opened.

Conference

Paul was coordinator for the branch's annual weeklong conference. At the conference, we were recognized along with others who were made senior members of Wycliffe. We especially enjoyed hearing reports of work with the Indians from each of seventeen translation teams. We learned that some of our colleagues had language assistants who were educated enough to read and write and even type—a real advantage to their work. Marianna Slocum and Florence Gerdel were translating for an indigenous group where there were many Christians who were motivated to have God's Word. In addition to the reports, we were challenged and encouraged by messages from the pastor of a Presbyterian church, in Cali, Colombia. Conference was also a time to conduct group business and elect officers for the executive committee.

After conference, we were able to rent a house from another couple who returned to the indigenous village where they worked. We cooked for ourselves and concentrated on the work of making primers. It was restoring to be living on our own after having been in the village with Indians in our home much of the time watching our every move. We started planning our own house at Lomalinda. We consulted with the director, and he gave us permission to start building. Each afternoon after work on the language, Paul went to the lot and made a cement pillar in preparation for laying the floor joists. It was an arduous process doing everything by hand. In March, Ralph Hoffstetter, a carpenter who had come from Oregon to build a house for one of the pilots, approached us and offered to stay longer to build our house. We were thrilled!

Primer Series

The Tunebos were 99 percent illiterate. If they were going to benefit from the translation of the Scripture, we realized at least some of them needed to know how to read. We needed more than just the initial primer. We worked diligently on the next three primers in the series introducing new letters, syllable patterns, and words along with simple stories. A colleague, Mardty Anderson, drew pictures of Tunebo cultural objects and activities to illustrate the primers. She also did the layout. We were excited that the branch got a mimeograph machine. We bought fifty reams of paper for the printing. The books turned out beautifully in our eyes with their orange, yellow, and blue covers. We carefully packed them for the trip to Cobaría, praying all the time for a good reception of them by the Tunebos.

In March 1966, we returned to Cobaría with the newly printed primers. We were excited to have them and eager to teach the people to read. Because our regular language assistant was away, Manuel helped us a few times. One Monday our language study with Manuel turned into a reading class with four men as students. On Tuesday there were only two, and then the next two days only Manuel. He indicated a serious interest in learning to read. A year previously at the center, he had started learning to write numbers. He proudly pointed out numbers on the calendar. Although he had never been exposed to books, he learned quickly, which was unusual for someone starting to learn to read as an adult.[1]

---

[1] The interest shown was short-lived, and we never had the opportunity to see Tunebos of Cobaría become truly literate. A big disappointment to us.

I treated a lot of cracked and infected feet; many times I soaked them in a pail of warm salt water. One man took advantage of the time he sat with his foot in the pail to play a prereading game we made for the Tunebo. He said when he finished clearing his field, he would return again to learn to read. It was hard to ask people to study reading when to do so could mean that they wouldn't have enough to eat at harvest time. We tried to take advantage of the off seasons when they had more free time.

Interest in reading was stimulated by a young election official who came to Cobaría to monitor the national election. When he heard about some of the Tunebos' problems, he wanted to help them. He told them that they would do much better if they would learn to read. This gave them a real incentive to start learning.

In addition to encouraging reading while in Cobaría, both Paul and I concentrated on grammar analysis as we were preparing for a grammar workshop to be held in October (1966).

In the midst of a week of miserably rainy weather in March, my day was brightened when a Tunebo boy, about ten years old, brought me a dozen beautiful orchids, the national flower of Colombia. It was a rare treat for us in Cobaría. We gave the boy a peso (about five cents). He did not know what it was as he had never had any money of his own.

In contrast, in April, there was no rain and almost no clouds for ten days in a row, which was quite a record. On one of those beautiful days, we went up into the woods and watched Wanisa and his wife firing pots. She had spent days making the pots and a month or more drying them to just the right stage. When we got to the woods, they carefully built up the fire all around the pots. After some time, we heard several pops! Two of the pots burst, leaving a hole in the bottom. They seemed to take it in stride, although I know I would have been disappointed after all that work.

On Good Friday, we walked the two hours over the trail to visit some of the settlers. They received us warmly and prepared a meal of split pea soup and boiled green bananas for us. It was a delightful little break from the daily routine.

Another day we went about an hour's walk to see Manuel's family in the field he was clearing for planting. He had made a simple shelter there to stay for a number of days to avoid the climb back to the village. Staying there gave them more time to cut all the brush into mulch and plant.

Occasionally, someone would gather a group of men to help him clear his field for planting. He paid the workers by having a party afterward. Because the chief was late in returning from working for money on the outside, his wife took things into her own hands; she spent a week preparing an alcoholic drink made of the manioc root for a work party. Then she gathered a big work crew and sent them to the field. We took the opportunity to watch them work in the field. At the end of the day, they all returned to the chief's house for the party. On this occasion, some of the Indians got drunk and had to be escorted to their homes. However, normally, we saw very little drunkenness in Cobaría.

When the Tunebos finished clearing and planting their fields in mid-June, they migrated to the lowlands, and we returned to the Lomalinda center. Ralph had worked industriously on construction of our house. We were excited to see the house was going up so fast! It had a roof, two walls, and floors. Paul took over the work on the walls while Ralph began work on the kitchen cabinets. We hired a Colombian worker to dig the septic tank. Before long, we had a bathroom! Hooray!

In August, when we returned to Cobaría, we noticed an improvement in the people's attitude and some real breakthroughs in our rapport with them. The facade that the people initially portrayed to us as outsiders began to be replaced by a genuine sincerity. Many of the things about their culture that we had read or heard from outsiders previously had been hidden from us. However, at this point, the people began to allow us to observe their customs openly or candidly.

For example, Manuel told us when twins were born, they were abandoned in the forest. The father and mother were required to follow rigorous taboos in order to appease their god. We had heard about this custom before, but never by the Indians.[2] Although saddened by the practice, we felt quite pleased that Manuel would tell us this so openly with all the details. He knew that most outsiders didn't practice the same thing and, indeed, looked upon it with scorn. We told him that it was not our custom. Later we learned that they believe one of the twins is the child of an evil spirit who would do harm to the people. Since they don't know which one of the babies is from the evil spirit, they abandon them both.

This not only showed their confidence in us (and we hoped made them more open to the message we brought), but it also gave us the kind of information that allowed us to understand their thinking, actions, fears, motives, and hopes. Knowing this enabled us to relate and communicate with them more effectively. We looked forward to the day when they would understand God's power to protect them from evil spirits.

September 10, 1966, Paul wrote in a letter to my parents:

> It has been hard for Edna to watch Wanisa's wife be sick and not improving for several weeks. She was not willing to take our medicine. Several times, Edna was ready to go over and try to persuade the sick woman to take medicine, but the Lord gave her patience. She knew she had to wait

---

[2] In 1999, this became known nationally in Colombia when a Tunebo mother had complications with her pregnancy and ended up in the hospital. When twins were born, the couple abandoned the twins in the hospital. Later, the leaders wanted to get the twins back, and there was conflict because outsiders did not want to have them abandoned in the forest (Meléndez, Diego Enrique, Enviado especial a Saravena, Colombia por El Tiempo, Periódico de Bogotá, Colombia 20 de febrero, 1999).

for the woman to request help. Our prayers were answered and Edna's patience was rewarded a few days ago when Wanisa asked us to come over and treat her. "This is what we have been waiting for," I told Edna. She went over and gave the neighbor a penicillin injection. That was Saturday.

We prayed that she would improve. However, Edna felt that in any case she should give another injection Sunday. When she went to give it, she intentionally told them what she was going to do (the shots really hurt). Both Wanisa and his wife said, "Fine." She was improving, and they now seemed to have a real confidence in our medicine. It was a relief to feel acceptance rather than resistance, as well as to see our friend up and around again. We thanked God.

November brought the end of the rainy season and the beginning of the dry season in Cobaría. It was the time of year when the trees began to bloom. We enjoyed the purple-colored flowers that dotted the mountains but missed the beautiful fall colors of Minnesota. Dry season also meant it was time for the Tunebos to migrate to the lowlands where there was more water. We followed their pattern and went to Lomalinda. Wisa, Manual's brother, an ordinary hardworking Tunebo husband and father, went with us to help us with work on the language. He was completely monolingual, which required us to communicate in Tunebo and made him depend on us for all his communication with others. He was not able to use Spanish to give us meanings of words or phrases in Tunebo.

12

A PACKAGE

Joy's Adoption

WE HAD CONSIDERED adoption for some time. I had had one miscarriage and medical testing and had been told that even with surgery, it was doubtful that I would be able to get pregnant. When we decided we did indeed want to adopt a child, we asked Marion Price of WEC (Worldwide Evangelization Crusade) clinic to look for a baby for us. When she had found a good match for us, she was to send us a radio message that she had a "package" for us. A few months later we were in Cobaría when LaVerne McClendon, the radio operator at Lomalinda, relayed the message, "I have a package for you." Our hearts jumped with excitement.

After our time in Cobaría, we returned to our own house in Lomalinda and made arrangements to go to Villavicencio to pick up our precious baby. She was at the Paraiso Infantil, an orphanage, run by two Christian nurses from Florida. After discussing with them the various legal aspects, we were able to the watch the baby as she amused herself on their living room floor.

That evening we happened to run into LaVern McClendon, who had come to the city to do shopping. She asked, "Some months ago I passed a radio message to you about a package Marion Price had had for you for five months. Did you ever get it?" We avoided the question. We went on to the hotel and prayed that we would make the right decision. We discussed the idea and dreamed of how wonderful it would be to have a baby.

The next morning we returned to the orphanage to pick her up. Afterwards we proudly took the "package," Joy Ann, a seventeen-pound year-old baby girl with dark brown eyes, brown hair, and two teeth, to show LaVerne. "This," we said, "is the package Marion Price had for us."

Then we took Joy the three-hour taxi ride to Bogotá to begin the paperwork for her legal adoption. We held her the whole trip up the mountain to Bogotá and back down the next day and then home to Lomalinda from Villavicencio by JAARS plane.

While at the orphanage, we observed that Joy constantly rocked back and forth when she sat in her crib. She rocked when she was on her hands and knees too. After holding her in our lap and showing her love on the entire two-day trip, she never rocked like that again.

When we got home, I dug into the barrel and sorted through baby clothes which we had taken with us when we to went Colombia. Disappointingly, most of the things were for a boy as we had gotten them from my brother who had four boys. However, two days later the ladies at the center gave me a baby shower. We got a lot of darling little girl things. It was hard to believe all the gifts people came up with in a place where there were no stores. I especially loved a white dress with red smocking made by one of our friends. I had the time of my life trying everything on our sweet baby Joy! She looked like a little doll in the pretty dresses I put on her almost every day. Life changed quickly.

Wisa, a father with children of his own, was still with us. He loved Joy and helped care for her. Our friends all chuckled one Sunday when he quietly carried her out of church, putting her baby bottle in his back pocket.

Parents Visit

Paul's parents came for a visit in December. It was a huge undertaking for them; they planned for months ahead of time, even before they knew they would have a new grandbaby to see. The thought of holding Joy in their arms added to their anticipation of the trip. They came loaded with gifts for her.

His parents also looked forward to meeting the Tunebos. When the time came, they were eager with expectation as we all crawled into the small Helio Courier airplane, designed for landing on short airstrips. We had told our Tunebo friends we would be bringing Paul's parents to the airstrip to meet them. As we flew up the valley over the lowlands, the Indians heard and saw the plane. José said to the others, "There go Paul and his parents. I'm going up to the airstrip to meet them." His parents couldn't make the arduous walk over the trail to the house in Cobaría, but they met José and a few other Tunebos, saw the area, and a Tunebo home near the airstrip. That satisfied them!

Mom and Dad Headland stayed for the holidays. Christmas in our small half-finished four-room home at Lomalinda was quite a stretch for me: with a new baby, a Tunebo language assistant, and my in-laws. For the first time, I realized why my mother never got all her Christmas gifts wrapped. I was too busy with all the cooking and everything else that goes with Christmas preparation to wrap gifts. Although Paul's folks had come loaded with presents and we had received a package from my folks, Joy was attracted to a little plastic hammer that we got her. Wisa made and even wrapped a file box for Paul. He was very proud of himself.

I made my first Christmas dinner of two stuffed chickens. Thankfully, it turned out tasty. It was a wonderful day with Paul's parents; the only Christmas we ever had with Paul's dad.

Shortly after they returned home, we received word that Paul's dad was in the hospital with a serious heart attack. We were sad to receive the news but thankful it hadn't happened when he was out on the airstrip several hundred miles from a hospital. While there, he had become quite winded when we hiked up the mountain to a Tunebo house. We were also thankful he was home and not in Bogotá, where I had noticed that his color was not good in the 8,600 foot altitude. He recovered from the heart attack but was forced to take an early retirement as he continued to suffer from a congestive heart condition.

13

LITERACY

Help from an Expert

IN JANUARY AFTER Paul's parents left, a literacy workshop started. In addition to making Tunebo books to teach reading, Paul was coordinator for the workshop, which added to his responsibilities. Our goal was to complete the primer series during the six-week workshop. We still had a lot of grammar analysis remaining, but we put it aside while we worked on the literacy materials.

The literacy consultant gave valuable suggestions of things that we had not considered. Earlier branches of SIL had gone through the development of primers on a trial-and-error basis, but now we had consultants from Mexico and Peru to call on for advice and guidance, thereby avoiding some of the pitfalls. During the workshop, we finished the series of five provisional primers. In addition to the work on the primers, Wisa told us stories about animals and how to process the fique plant to make hammocks and bags. He listened with us as we transcribed and helped us edit stories collected on tape from others in Cobaría. We compiled these into a small book, which we later read to people to motivate them to learn to read. A typical reaction from those who heard was, "Yes…yes…uh-huh….That's right."

"Who taught you that?"

We explained, "Wisa did, at Lomalinda. He is learning to read too."

Some were surprised, and all were pleased as they heard us read about these aspects of their daily life. Animal stories were among their favorites.

Joy made a lot of friends in Cobaría. She sat in the doorway for hours at a time, saying hi to everyone, anyone, or at times, no one. They all wanted to help the new little girl in the village learn to say *tetú* (daddy); *abú* (mommy), and a few other key phrases.

Although a month was altogether too short a time to spend in the village, we felt good about all that was accomplished. It seemed as though we had just begun to work when it was time to leave for Bogotá for a temporary assignment. It was a frustration to be away from the Tunebos for the time it was necessary to be in the city. The chief, José, was reluctant to give us permission to leave Cobaría. Our neighbor, Wanisa, said, "When you leave, we'll all be sad, but when the plane brings you back, we'll come back to the village again too. Then we can live together." It was their way of saying, "We love you and want you here." We didn't want to be away too long.

Support Roles

Translators are asked to take on various support roles from time to time. These included duties in areas of buying and shipping supplies, communication, children's education, and government relations, such as filing reports, helping members obtain visas, and arranging for international shipments.

Paul had been called upon several times previously to help in the Bogotá office of SIL relating to different government agencies for a month or more. This assignment was for three months. He assumed full responsibility for the office while the director was at SIL's international conference in Mexico.

Recruiting people specifically to do support roles was a new direction in SIL. There had always been a desire to have administrators who had come up through the ranks and had linguistic and translation experience in an Indian village. The Colombia branch was getting more personnel to fill these support roles. However, it took time to orient the new people to the job and the Colombian language and culture. With the new personnel arriving Paul hoped that this might be the last time he would have to fill a support role in the Bogotá office.

Nevertheless, he was thankful for the time he had in the support role. His Spanish had improved greatly as high government officials courteously corrected his mistakes. Not only did his Spanish improve, but he also learned to relate better with Colombians. The time in Bogotá also made it possible to complete some of the legalities of Joy's adoption.

Time for our home leave was fast approaching, so as soon as we were released from our responsibility in the city, we returned to Cobaría to study with José. He was a busy man. In addition to all the other duties of the chief, he was responsible for the ceremonial dances. Even at that, he came to help Paul as faithfully as possible. He told stories on tape and patiently repeated phrase by phrase as Paul transcribed them for grammar analysis. They began translating the Easter story from the Gospel of Mark. It was challenging to translate concepts basic to the Christian faith, such as *cross* or *forgive*, that didn't exist in the Tunebo language and culture. Both Paul and José enjoyed the challenge. José indicated he would like to translate more when we returned from home leave.

We felt our increasing rapport with the people. Joy won their hearts with no effort. We were touched when Wanisa, seeing Joy fussing out in front of the house, came across the stream from his house, gently spoke to her, and gave her his hand. The two of them came into the house hand in hand. (He made a rare exception and broke the "don't touch" taboo). For our whole first term in Cobaría, we lived and studied in the leaf huts with dirt floors. With hopes of having another child, we realized the need for more space. In addition to taking care of the family, we wanted to have adequate space to work on translation, to play literacy games with the young people, to tutor those who wanted to learn to read, as well as to entertain Tunebos and settlers. We began to think of building a lumber house in the village.

Several of the settlers in the area knew how to cut lumber from logs, but we had a dilemma. We weren't sure if they would help because people in the area who opposed our being there made trouble for anyone who helped us. God had His ways of solving our problems. In two situations, He used women to influence their men to help us with our project.

The first, Doña Evarista, the wife of the most prominent settler in the area, came to see us. During her visit that afternoon, there was a rainstorm to beat all storms. The rain came down in sheets, and a blustery wind blew. Water came into the house through the leaves on the roof, through the doors, and through the split palm wall on the end of the house. The dirt floor became a big mud puddle. Doña Evarista sat through it all, huddled in her shawl, trying to keep dry. She was concerned for "these young people living so far from home." She had asked us previously what our parents thought about our living in this remote area. After the storm let up, she went home. I wish I could have heard the conversation she had with her family that night; I only know she convinced them to saw a big portion of the lumber we needed.

When it was time to leave, we had used up our supplies and were scrounging for food and rationing white gas for the lantern. Even so, we felt positive about our time in Cobaría. We had had good help on translation and good relations with the Tunebos, as well as the possibility of getting lumber sawed.

On December 17, we flew to Miami where my parents and sister Lois met us and drove us back to Minnesota for the start of our seven months of home leave. They had several days in the car to get to know and love Joy.

14

A SON

Waiting in the Rain

AFTER A BUSY seven months in the States speaking in churches, contacting partners, and visiting family, we returned to Colombia. We were again given support assignments in Bogotá: Paul in the office and me in the group house. We had other plans first. We wanted to adopt a baby brother for Joy. We also wanted to have a brief visit with the Tunebos.

On the way out to visit the Tunebos, we stopped in Villavicencio at the Paraiso Infantil orphanage where we chose a precious little baby boy. We had to leave him there for the three weeks we would be in Cobaría. We made arrangements to pick him up on our way back to Bogotá. We spent those weeks dreaming about having this dear baby as part of our family.

I'll let Paul tell the story from here:

> Finally the day came, September 12, 1968. We were set to leave the village early. The radio popped and crackled, notifying us that the plane was on its way. We locked the door and started the three-hour hike down and up the steep trails to reach the airstrip before the plane arrived. One of the Tunebos, Manuel, accompanied us as he wanted to go to Bogotá. Unbeknownst to us was the fact that the plane developed a problem and returned to the

Lomalinda center for repairs minutes after we left the hut we called home.

Our eager anticipation turned to disappointment as the waiting stretched on into late afternoon. The Tunebos who were to carry some equipment and materials back to our house grew impatient. They all left, including Manuel, promising to return the next day. Finally, just before dark, we walked to Diego's family's home to spend the night.

Our hosts gave us their best plank bed. We spent that night, tossing and turning, fighting off the fleas. It seemed morning would never come. But it did come and brought with it rain; it rained all day long. We never left the farm. We waited; we spent another night looking for soft spots on the plank bed, scratching the evasive fleas. It seemed the planks were even harder that night.

At last day broke, sunny and beautiful. We hurried to the airstrip, skipping breakfast in the rush. When we arrived, the pilot was unloading the aluminum roofing we had ordered for the new house. It was a slow process getting it out of the small plane because it was so long. It took up precious time while the weather was good.

For the plane to take off from our short strip, it would require two shuttles. I remained behind, as Edna and Joy took all our things on the first trip to a larger airstrip only fifteen minutes away. The pilot was to come right back. So every piece of baggage went on the first trip, the lunch, the extra clothes, the rain gear—everything. The plane took off nicely and turned the corner around the mountain. Manuel and the carriers returned as promised. I sent the carriers off with as much roofing as they could carry. They promised to return the next day to take the rest.

It should have taken only an hour at most before the plane returned for me. However another storm moved in, forcing the pilot to land with Edna at an airstrip in a town a little farther away. Meanwhile I put up a few sheets of roofing to keep dry. Why didn't I at least keep my raincoat? The rain grew worse, and the wind came up. As the sky was darkened by the clouds, a puff of wind peeled off the sheets of roofing over my head, and I ran through the drenching torrent to an open shelter ten minutes away.

With some effort I got a fire going and stripped off my wet clothes and hung them near the fire to dry. Sundown brought clear weather but no plane. Discouraged, I left the airstrip and walked the twenty minutes to impose once again on Diego's family's gracious hospitality.

As I walked along, feeling dejected, I thought of the Tunebos on the other side of the canyon. They were rejecting anything I said about Jesus Christ. Most of them refused to even listen. Was it worth it all?

Then I thought of José. He had spurned the strict practice of forbidding outsiders to learn the language. Rather, he had patiently taught us words and phrases and helped us translate some Bible stories. He had even arranged for us to live in the village. No outsider had ever lived in their village before.

I thought of twelve babies and young children who died of the whooping cough and of many others who might have if Edna hadn't been there. I especially thought of Ahbata's baby whom Edna had resuscitated three times and is now growing as any child. I thought about all the sick she took care of daily. What would happen to them?

And I thought of the message of hope found in the Word of God, "Perfect love that drives out fear" (1 John 4:18, NIV). Who will tell them if we leave?

"Yes, it is worth it all," I said as I walked to the farm, hoping tomorrow would bring clear weather and the plane.

Getting Ronnie

While Paul was on the airstrip above, Joy and I were on a larger airstrip in the town of Saravena. We sat inside the plane the whole day while local people milled around on the outside. They were curious and wanted to see the small plane and the Americans. Joy was sick with what I thought was scarlet fever, so I was trying to be careful not to expose the people. Finally it became apparent the pilot wasn't going to be able to go back and pick up Paul that night. He locked up the plane, and we walked the few blocks into town to find a "hotel." I am not sure what was happening in town, but the hotel was full, actually overflowing. The kind owners offered me a small cot right in their own room where Joy and I slept together on the cot. We were so tired we fell asleep in spite of the light being on and the music blaring. I awoke in the middle of the night, hoping this would be the only night we would have to spend in this place and that the next day we would, indeed, be able to pick up our baby boy at Paraiso Infantil as planned.

At the crack of dawn, the pilot went to the airfield and readied the plane. As soon as it was light enough, he took off to fly up into the mountains to pick up Paul. This time there were no problems on the short flight. The pilot and Paul were soon back to pick up Joy and me for the flight into Villavicencio.

When we got there, Paul stayed with Joy in town. We didn't want to expose the children in the orphanage to Joy's fever. Manuel, the Tunebo who was traveling with us, went with me to Paraiso Infantil. He wanted to know where the children in the orphanage came from. "How did the people in the orphanage get the children? Were they taken forcefully from good loving parents?"

Nancy Tappan, the director of the orphanage, carefully explained how desperate mothers abandoned their children on the streets in Bogotá. The police took them to a large hospital to be cared for while they searched to see if someone would claim them. After a period of time, if no one claimed the children, they were released to orphanages. When Nancy had space, she would go to the hospital in Bogotá and receive children.

While Nancy explained all this, I held our new son in my arms. After some photos and a few more instructions, we were on our way with our special bundle. We met up with Paul and

Joy and took a taxi up the mountain to Bogotá. We thanked God. He had once again shown us that He was able to work out all the details in our lives. His grace was sufficient to help us through the difficult times, and He was also with us in our joyful times.

When we arrived at the group house apartment in Bogotá, I put our baby in a high chair. He didn't have the strength to sit up. He slid right down in the chair. I tried laying him on a blanket on the floor to play with toys. He was too weak to hold up his head.

Paul wrote to his mom and dad September 18, 1968:

> Here is the news you have been waiting for: Ronald Blake Headland, born December 5, 1967, came to live with us September 16. He has a sweet smile to go with his dark hair and eyes. He is somewhat anemic and not as strong as he should be at nine months—but he is now getting the personal care and attention that he needs. Joy is really excited about him. She shows a little jealousy, but mostly concern and the thrill of having him with us. Now our family is complete, and we are on cloud nine!

A week later, we were able to write, "Ronnie is getting stronger every day. He can sit up and roll over."

When Nancy Tappan from the orphanage visited a month later, Ronnie was standing by the couch pushing a little car, saying "Burr." Nancy was so amazed she exclaimed, "Oh, Edna, I need to get all the children in homes right away!"

15

HIS WAYS ARE HIGHER
THAN OUR WAYS

WHEN WE RETURNED to Cobaría, we learned Evarista's sons had indeed sawed the lumber. They were, however, concerned about the people who were opposed to us. So to avoid trouble for themselves, they sawed the lumber secretly in the forest above their house, an hour-and-a-half walk from ours. That created a dilemma. How were we going to get this lumber back to our house? Although we planned to pay the Tunebos to carry the lumber, they ignored our requests for help.

The chief's wife was the second woman God used to influence her man to help us. In the midst of this predicament one afternoon, I decided to pay her a visit. I took Joy and Ronnie and walked down the precipitous trail to her house. We went in and sat down on leaves. I said in the Tunebo language, "I am tired of sitting in my house so I came to sit with you in yours." An innocent statement, but in Tunebo "to live" and "to sit" are the same word. She must have thought I meant, "I am tired of 'living' in my house, so I have come 'to live' in yours." She was not about to let that happen, and she must have told her husband so. The men were stirred to action. Over the next few days, they walked the one-and-a-half-hour trek over the trail to carry the lumber home for us. They brought it all!

One day we went to the forest about twenty minutes away with José and his wife to fire pots. While there, José offered to give us the huge tree that he was using as firewood. It was beautiful wood and enough for the other half of the boards needed for our house. We were able to arrange with another settler, who wasn't afraid of those opposed to us, to come and saw the boards there. The short distance made it easier to carry the lumber to our building site; a real blessing. Even so, we built the upstairs of the house first so the Tunebos wouldn't think we were finished and didn't need the additional lumber.

Back at Lomalinda, we talked to Bob Paden, a carpenter, who agreed to go to Cobaría with us to help Paul finish the house. The plan was for his whole family to go. All summer, Joy went around telling everyone, "Padens are going to the village with us." Both we and the Padens were looking forward with great anticipation to their help and an experience in the village.

The day before we were all to leave for Cobaría, the JAARS pilot decided to fly over our airstrip and check on some work that was being done. It had been raining very hard just before they flew over. The rain made it look like there were deep gullies in the airstrip that would make it impossible to land. Our scheduled flight was cancelled. We made a quick decision. I would stay at Lomalinda with Joy and Ronnie and the Padens' two little girls. Paul would go with the Padens and their boys by commercial transportation to Cubará and walk in the two days over the trail.

Of course, we were all disappointed and didn't understand why this happened. I wrote letters to supporters, "'For my thoughts are not your thoughts, neither are your ways my ways,' declares the Lord. 'As the heavens are higher than the earth, so are my ways higher than your ways and my thoughts than your thoughts'" (Isa. 55:8–9, NIV)

I didn't know it at that time, but God was working out the circumstances to have me in the right place at the right time. Ten days after Paul and the Padens left, I received a radio message with the shocking news that my younger sister, Lois, had been killed in a car accident. I was able to make arrangements for someone to care for Ronnie and the Padens' girls. Joy and I got a flight to Minnesota. I was out of the country for two days before Paul made radio contact with the center. He didn't know my sister had died or that I had left for the funeral. If I had been in Cobaría, I would not have been able to go to be with my family at that difficult time.

God worked out the circumstances as well to make it possible for me to take Joy with me. (Ronnie's papers were not in order for him to go.) Joy had been in the States on a green card when we were on home leave. The green card was only good for one year and renewable for another year. Paul had made a special trip to Bogotá to renew it the previous month. Joy was able to enter the States on the green card. While we were there, I was able to finish her citizenship papers, and she became a US citizen. Indeed, His ways are higher than our ways.

A week after returning to Colombia, our family went to our new twenty-by-twenty-foot house in Cobaría. It seemed like a mansion to us. I was thrilled with the nice work Bob and Paul had done. We were so happy to have an adequate place to live and work. One corner of the living room had upper cupboards for medicines and a lower cupboard for "layaway" for the things we traded with the Indians for firewood. They left the things there until the required purification ceremony that would then allow them to have the things in their homes. Another corner had a bulletin board and a book rack for the Indians, as well as a shelf for View-Masters and puzzles.

The Indians enjoyed the house too. For the teenagers it was a place to go when they got done with their day's work in the fields. For many it was a clinic. For some it was a hotel while they waited for the purification ceremony when they returned from being in town or working on a white man's farm.

Alvaro (one of the Tunebo leaders), his daughter whom he just brought home from the mission boarding school, and a small boy were the first of many who stayed in our home over the years. They stayed with us for six days while they waited for the shaman to start the required ceremony before resuming life with their family. When they left, Alvaro said, "I stayed six days and didn't go hungry. You have a good heart."

Paul began working on translation of Scripture in earnest with José in his new office. It was off the porch and had a separate door he could close when he was working. The people knew to come to the front door when they came. Occasionally, Ronnie slipped into the office. He would go right up and put his head on José's lap while they were working. Because of their belief system that we were contaminated, Tunebos normally did not touch us, but José seemed to kindly overlook being touched by our baby son.

16

SPIRITUALLY BLIND

Therefore, my beloved brethren, be steadfast, immovable,
always abounding in the work of the Lord, knowing that
your labor is not in vain in the Lord.

—*1 Corinthians 15:58*

Sight Restored

BÚSWARA ALWAYS USED a long stick as he gingerly walked along the trails. He was rapidly losing his sight. Being very social with a lot of time on his hands, he was a frequent visitor in our home in Cobaría. On one of his visits, we suggested that an eye doctor in Bogotá might be able to help. He agreed to go. After receiving the go-ahead from his family, we made arrangements with Marion Price for Paul to take him to the WEC clinic (hospital) in Bogotá.

From Cobaría, the kids and I went back to Lomalinda, and Paul took Búswara, accompanied by Wisa, to Bogotá. The doctor discovered that one eye could be operated on; however, he said Búswara would lose his sight again in a few months. The other eye was already beyond hope. The operation was performed, and Búswara recovered his sight. Because of the generous help of WEC clinic and the doctor, the bills were less than $50. The living expenses in Bogotá were high, so Paul and the two men went to Lomalinda as soon as Búswara was released by the doctor.

With two kids and two monolingual Indians, there was never a dull moment in our lives at Lomalinda. Búswara was delightfully outgoing while Wisa was stable and serious. They taught Joy to speak a little more Tunebo. At the same time, Ronnie learned to speak a word of Tunebo, a word of Spanish, and a number of words in English.

Paul worked hard with the two men on the translation of some stories from the Gospel of Mark. He asked them questions to make sure they understood the correct meaning of the passage. He also incorporated the suggestions made by the consultant. Paul was pushing to get these stories done to be put on records when the representative from Gospel Recordings came to record. We also translated and practiced singing a few hymns to record. Tunebo-style music only used three notes and a rather different rhythm. Búswara and Wisa sang about a word behind Paul, which was another aspect of their style. It sounded like authentic Tunebo music, but the words clearly contained the message of Jesus.

Larry DeVilbus from Gospel Recordings (now Global Recordings Network) came and recorded the stories of the Prodigal Son, the Calming of the Sea, a number of Jesus's healings, and a story entitled "Are You Afraid?" telling of Jesus's power over evil spirits. Including music, they recorded material for six records. Before leaving, Larry gave Paul a tape recording of the work to use while they made the records.

While Paul worked on translation, I worked on the primer series and storybooks as fast as I could to be able to teach Wisa and check the content with him. Each evening, we gave him reading and writing lessons. We were encouraged to see his progress.

Along with many others, we prayed that Búswara would not lose his sight again in a few months. We also prayed that both men would open their hearts to Christ. Búswara and Wisa showed some interest in learning about Jesus, but they seemed to be afraid to make a commitment to Him. God worked a miracle in answer to the first prayer. Several months after the surgery, Paul took Búswara back to the eye doctor. The doctor said that it was a miracle. He saw real improvement in both eyes since the operation. The progress was contrary to his own prognosis that Búswara would lose his sight again in four to six months. He instructed Paul to bring him back if there were any changes.

It seemed that the miracle of opening his physical eyes was easy in comparison to the miracle needed to open the spiritual eyes of the Tunebos. The Lord showed us the physical miracle to renew our faith in His power.

During the time we were at Lomalinda, many of the Tunebos in Cobaría were very sick. Some died. Among those who died was Alvaro, one of the leaders and a powerful shaman of the village. His death caused the Tunebos great fear since he did the incantations to appease the spirits. With Alvaro gone, they feared the spirits all the more. Their fear of evil spirits made them adhere more closely to their taboos. Normally, the one exception they made in their rigid taboo system was for medicine. Most people received it without question. However, when we returned after Alvaro's death, they were adhering strictly to their taboos. They included medicine in their prohibition of receiving anything from the outside. Even though many were sick, they were afraid to take medicine.

We had eagerly anticipated them listening to a tape recording of gospel stories and songs in Tunebo we had made, but their fears kept them from coming. Very few came. We prayed earnestly for the Lord to take away their fear. We asked specifically that they would listen to the gospel stories and songs with open hearts and that some would make clear decisions to follow Christ. We also prayed for love and wisdom in all our dealings with the Tunebos. God has chosen to work in response to prayer, so we urgently prayed for His working in their lives. God has also given people the right to do their own will, and He did not force this closed people to listen against their will.

We frequently looked at the verse we had posted above our kitchen table to remind ourselves God had called us to this work. It was not futile. "Therefore, my beloved brethren, be steadfast, immovable, always abounding in the work of the Lord, knowing that your labor is not in vain in the Lord" (1 Cor. 15:58, NKJV).

Although we had few visitors, we continued working. We wrote more music and hymns in their language. I finished the work on the primer stories, at least until I could test them by teaching someone else to read to see if more changes would be needed. Wisa came one morning, and we got him to help us check and put accent marks on one of the primers. I spent some time typing up new words to bring the Tunebo/Spanish dictionary up to date. I took advantage of fewer visitors and less medical work to spend more time with our kids.

We still had some medical work. We were called to take care of a baby with severe diarrhea, dehydration, and sores on his tongue. He was sicker than most of the babies I treated. I felt the heavy responsibility of his care. I was able to talk by radio to Dr. Altig, the medical doctor who had arrived in Lomalinda to take up work with SIL in Colombia. He had served with SIL in Peru for several years, so he was familiar with tropical diseases. He was also aware of the difficult problem of transportation and communication as well as the reluctance on the part of the Indians to receive certain kinds of help. It was an encouragement to be able to confer with him about difficult cases.

With so few visitors, we were surprised one morning when the main shaman actually came inside our house for the first time since we had come to the village six years earlier. He came with Manuel, his son. Both were friendly and chatted with us as Manuel showed him things in our house including "the other land," the name they had given the View-Master. We hoped and prayed this might mean a breakthrough, but the shaman didn't come back.

I started to plan for our next village stay. It took time for me to learn to plan months ahead so we would not run out of provisions. As our family grew, so did our need for supplies of food, but at the same time, with more body weight in the plane, there was less weight available for supplies. How much faster did we use up food with two more mouths to feed? Our chocolate, cinnamon, baking powder, and margarine were all gone. We only had about a cup of oil, and our cereal ran out long before it was time to leave. We had to eat more bananas.

When migration time came, we anticipated going to Bogotá from Cobaría. Joy remembered stores in the city. She prayed that she could go to the store and buy some bubble gum. She was also anxious to see the "talking people" in the group house in Bogotá, meaning those who spoke English.

The plane that came to pick us up brought a pile of mail. I quickly went through it and found that Joy's US passport officially stamped with her Colombian visa had arrived. Ever since I had returned to Colombia after my sister's funeral, I had been concerned. Although we had Joy's US citizenship papers in hand, we had been anxiously waiting for her US passport with a Colombian visa. When I had tried to get a visa for her in the consulate in Los Angeles, they didn't see any reason to give her one since she was Colombian. They wouldn't give it to me. There was nothing I could do but use her Colombian passport when we reentered Colombia. By Colombian law, this was fine, but by US law, a naturalized citizen has to give up all previous citizenships. At the same time, we rejoiced to have received Ronnie's final adoption papers.

When we returned to Cobaría after our time in Bogotá, we took the finished Gospel Recordings records in Tunebo. We gave the shaman a Phonette hand-crank record player and a set of records. His son Wisa's voice was on the records, so we thought that would make him more desirous of having them.

We were surprised when someone came with a message from the shaman that we were to go and pick up our things. He had performed a purification ceremony on them, and they were ready for us. We explained that they were a gift for him, but he wouldn't keep them or purify others for Tunebos to keep in their homes. It was a big disappointment.

The taboo of taking medicine relaxed again, and some Tunebos started to come with their medical needs. Treating tropical diseases among the Indians was an ongoing challenge. A young couple brought their two- or three-year-old malnourished daughter to us for treatment.

The little girl had the appearance of a premature baby. I thought it was just a case of malnutrition, so I tried to give her a bottle right away. She choked and vomited three round worms. We gave her worm medicine, and that evening she expelled about one hundred worms. Unbelievable! The next morning the mother told us her daughter had expelled about that many again. The young family stayed with us from Monday afternoon until Friday morning.

A week later the mother came back for more medicine. The baby seemed to be improving and was beginning to eat a little. We were learning that prayer for cases like this is as important as medicine. And I was reaffirmed that God does answer prayers!

On Saturday evening, the day after the couple with the baby left, Miguel came to tell us his father had been bitten by a snake while in the lower village. Miguel's father, Saŵira, was a dear friend of ours. He was also Búswara's father-in-law. We put a few things together including antivenom serum. Paul and Miguel left before 6:00 a.m. on Sunday morning. They hiked about a six hours down the mountain to get to Saŵira's house. Saŵira was better by the time they arrived. Paul observed him for some time, and explained to him he felt God was sparing his life for a reason.

Sunday afternoon, after Paul left, a settler woman came for a visit. I invited her to stay overnight with me. She readily agreed and took the time to give me a cooking lesson. She baked bread and some very tasty little corn cheese cakes. Paul savored her yummy treat when he arrived home Monday afternoon, worn out from his trip.

Another Emergency Trip

We had returned to Lomalinda in late October 1970 when we received word that Paul's father had died of a heart attack. Paul left immediately to be with his mother to comfort her and help her with the arrangements for the funeral. I was left at Lomalinda with Joy, six; Ronnie, almost four; and Rayotá, a Tunebo who was there helping with translation and learning to read, as well as a crew of Colombian workers who were putting an addition on our four-room house.

One night I noticed a light was on in the language helper's house in the middle of the night. I asked Rayotá in the morning why the light was on. He said, "The mosquitoes were bad, so I turned it on to chase them away." He associated the light with fire, but didn't realize it is the smoke that chases away mosquitoes, but they are attracted by light.

With Paul gone, I felt the need to make contact with family. I took advantage of the opportunity to do so through ham radio, a combination of radio and telephone contact. It was an effective and economical way to make voice contact with our loved ones in the States before the days of Skype and cell phones. I talked with my parents and Paul. What a comfort to hear their voices. What a wonderful service of ham radio operators!

While Paul was gone, I put away Ronnie's crib and set up a roll-away bed for him. Ronnie was "all boy" with a cute shy smile that won hearts. At the same time, he teased Joy to death. She cried like a baby even though she was two years older. He constantly found ways of getting himself dirty. One day, I had him all ready for nursery school. Five minutes later, I went to see where he was, and he was covered with cement! On another day, he had the cement bag over his head. If it wasn't cement, he was covered with red mud, a kind of mud that was hard to wash out of clothes.

A Mother's Commitment

Paul brought his mother back with him after the funeral. The workers didn't finish putting the boards down on the living room floor until a few days after they arrived. I could finally have Joy's birthday party that I had delayed because I didn't want the kids to fall between the joists. Paul's mother enjoyed the party while Paul kept the kids entertained with games.

She was grieving as she began to realize her husband of thirty-nine years was gone. Undoubtedly she was thinking how alone she would be without her husband with both of her sons on the mission field. We asked, "Who will be there to help you?" The idea of either of her sons coming to help was not an option in her mind. She had already decided that she did not want us to leave the mission field on her account. She and Paul's dad had gone forward in a mission's meeting, giving their sons to God to serve as missionaries. Even at this difficult time, she did not go back on her commitment.

17

A Change of Locations

A Fleece

AFTER SEVEN YEARS in the village of Cobaría, we felt that the Lord was leading us to move. This was not a light or easy decision. We had only lived in our new lumber home for a short time. We cared for the people. Many were special friends. The Cobarías had helped us learn the Tunebo language, but when we started translating the Scriptures, willing helpers became scarce. It appeared that someone was pressuring the people not to help us in any way. Normally, we had an abundance of firewood that the men or boys brought in exchange for used shirts, but no one wanted to bring us firewood. We prayed about the situation for some time, and finally we put out a fleece. We prayed, "If no one brings us firewood for a week, we will take it as a sign that You are telling us to move." Not one person had the courage to face whatever pressure was being levied. No one brought us a bundle of firewood. We took that as God's answer to look for another place to work on the translation.

Paul explored another area to find a new location to complete our work. He found a few dozen Indians who were apparently more acculturated to Spanish culture than the Cobaría people. They spoke some Spanish as well as Tunebo. However, because it was such a small group and they were somewhat bilingual, Paul wasn't convinced it would be a good place to work.

In Cobaría, we had sought feedback on the clarity of our translation of the Scriptures. We read portions to the people and asked them to explain what they understood. Often the only response we received in Cobaría was, "Paul, I didn't hear a thing" (meaning, I didn't understand anything). We thought our translation was unclear until Paul met Ernesto, a Tunebo from San Miguel area in the town of Saravena. When Paul read a story from the Gospel of Mark to him, he listened. His eyes lit up as he said, "Why! Paul, I can hear that!" (Meaning that he could understand.) Then Paul realized anew that the Cobaría people simply did not want to hear the gospel. Ernesto bought a hand-crank phonograph and a set of the Tunebo Bible story records.

Paul visited Ernesto a month later in San Miguel, a small settlement of less than fifty people in widely scattered houses. Paul sat in Ernesto's yard, praying and seeking the Lord's will. "Is this the place?" he asked. "Can it be, Lord, that you want us here, in a settlement of less than fifty, when there are over four hundred in Cobaría?" Previously, when some people from the San Miguel area had invited us to live there, Paul had said no because we would not be able to work there except certain months of the year. However, Ernesto and his family did not migrate like the others. Ernesto wanted Paul to come. He promised to be available to help at any time. Paul reconsidered his decision. We had prayed for such an invitation, and this seemed to be it. Paul told them he would be back in a month with the family.

We made plans. Before moving completely, we would go back to Cobaría for a short time to read the Bible stories to the people and sing the choruses to them. Then we would pack up, close up our house, and say our good-byes. We prayed that in this short time, their hearts would soften to God's Word. We considered rotating between San Miguel and Cobaría in our tribal stays, still hoping and praying that the resistance they showed to the gospel would break down.

We asked our partners to pray with us for the move. Moving was never easy. The dialect was slightly different, and we would need to adjust our ears to it. We began praying for Ernesto as he promised to help us in translation. Thus he would be exposed to the gospel more than anyone else. We prayed that someone from this new area would receive the Lord and carry the message to the Cobaría people.

In April 1971, we went to San Miguel as a family. Although the San Miguel Tunebos speak the same language, hold many of the same beliefs, and had the same customs, our month's stay with them was very different than our times with the Tunebos in Cobaría.

The San Miguels wanted to learn to read! Five students completed the first primer and started the second one. Only with constant nagging had we persuaded just a handful of Cobarías to even try to learn.

Often we overheard the San Miguel people playing the gospel records or even discussing the stories. We overheard one man tell another man about the stories, "This is not man's thought, it is a message from God." The people were listening. Some seemed quite interested.

After our month in San Miguel, we were scheduled to go to Bogotá to do group service. Paul filled in for the government relations man while he was gone for a few months. While there, I had my first operation for endometriosis, which had caused ovarian cysts that needed to be removed.

More Changes

In August, we returned to Cobaría. The people seemed glad to have us back and were friendlier than they had been on the previous visit, although they still did not show an interest in the gospel. We raised José's pay, and he worked more and better with

Paul on translation. At the end of the time, we closed the house more securely than normal and said our good-byes.

We planned to take Búswara, the man who had had eye surgery, to Bogotá to see the doctor because he was having some loss of sight again. At the last minute, his wife wouldn't let him go.[1] In the meantime, we had arranged for Pablo, a bilingual Tunebo, to accompany Búswara. Even though Búswara didn't go, Pablo did. Pablo had lived in town for some time when he was younger and learned Spanish there. He wanted to learn to read, and we envisioned him being trained to help Paul with translation. His twelve-year-old nephew, Warawaná, accompanied him. Pablo had always seemed less energetic than the other Tunebo men. At Lomalinda we took him to see Dr. Altig, who discovered he had serious heart trouble. Dr. Altig prescribed digitalis, and Pablo noticed an improvement. However, he found it hard to accept his limited activity ordered by the doctor and became homesick. Learning to read was also much harder for him as an adult than it was for Warawaná, his very bright nephew.

We prayed that Pablo would come to know Christ and receive peace. We also prayed that he would be happier and feel a sense of satisfaction in learning to read. God answered part of those prayers. Although he did not receive Christ, in time, he felt happier with us and his reading. Both Pablo and Warawaná also enjoyed participating in Spanish, math, and carpentry classes offered by other center personnel.

During that period, a major milestone was reached. Paul finished checking the Gospel of Mark for faithfulness to the original, with an SIL translation consultant. He then worked with Pablo and Warawaná to make the changes suggested by the consultant. The next step was more proofreading and finishing all the details necessary for the printshop. Finally our part was done.

While they were with us, Pablo and Warawaná had the opportunity of a lifetime for a Tunebo. They would see the

---

[1] Sadly, Búswara did lose his sight.

president of Colombia! The Tunebos often discussed their desire to talk to the president about their need for protection of their traditional lands. Now it would become a reality. The president planned to celebrate the Day of the Indian with a big meeting where Indians from all over the country could present their problems.

The big day came to take the bus to Bogotá. We borrowed the center jeep, and I dropped Paul and the Indians off at the road to catch the bus. On my way back home I thought, *It feels good to be alone with the kids and not have any Indians to worry about.* I prayed for Pablo. He was so quiet and didn't talk much to our friends at Lomalinda. In Cobaría with his own people, he was outgoing. I prayed that he would be at ease with the president.

When they came back to Lomalinda, I learned Pablo and Warawaná shook hands with the president. They were thrilled. The total group of Indians presented their concerns, so Pablo was satisfied.

When it was time to go home, Pablo wanted to take ice cream for his family. He apparently didn't realize that with no refrigeration, it would have been sour liquid after the four-day purification ceremony it would have had to go through. Paul took them back to their home area in mid-November. After leaving them, he went on to San Miguel to see about having a house built for us there. The Tunebos cleared a little spot for our house and put stakes in the ground to mark where it was to be built. Paul reiterated to the people in San Miguel that he would be back with the family in January.

San Miguel

Cecil and Treva Gorsch accompanied us on the trip to San Miguel in January. The trip turned out to be quite complicated. We had to split our shipment between three airlines. Two of our trunks and a barrel containing our mattress, didn't arrive. We had two days delay along the way. Finally we were on the last leg of the trip. We had four riding animals and nine cargo animals transporting our stuff. Quite a mule train!

When we arrived in San Miguel, the Indians hadn't done one thing on the house. However, they rallied to the job the day after we arrived. Cecil pitched right in with the rest of the workers. Although the house was more rustic than the one we had in Cobaría, it was larger. It provided additional space for a picnic table on the porch for the Indians for reading lessons and other activities. They put it up in record time. It was started, finished, and ready to be occupied in less than two weeks. Being just a shell with a tar paper roof and dirt floor sped the process. Later, some young boys went out and split bamboo for inside partitions.

In San Miguel, we had five boys for reading lessons in the first few days. A few girls also began learning to read. Joy sat with them and sometimes helped them with a word. Ronnie played close by with a bow and arrow one of the boys gave him. One day he prayed, "Help me use the bow and arrow." He learned to shoot it that very day. Oh, to have the faith of a child!

We were encouraged. The printshop had supplied us with ten advance copies of the first primer to bring with us. By the time we needed more material, the second and third primers arrived by mail. The oohs and aahs of the students were priceless. One of the boys had studied five weeks with us the year before. He was now well on his way to reading. The phonemic alphabet made learning to read in Tunebo much easier for a beginner than beginners learning to read in English.

We had a range of students: four big boys, three were new, one had come before; two little boys, one of them was new; and a little girl. Because of their different skills and learning levels, it was like giving each one private tutoring. That multiplied the preparation work involved. They liked to study on the weekends, so that meant we had someone coming for reading lessons every day of the week.

One morning Paul had already given a reading lesson by 8:00 a.m. We didn't always get such an early start, but we tried to fit into the people's schedules. The older boy student was going off to work for a week, so we told him to come in the morning before he left. We prayed for the salvation of those learning to read as they were potentially the leaders of the future.

Paul translated Old Testament stories by day. In the evenings, he read our draft copy of the Gospel of Mark to the people. It was a rather grueling schedule. At times, Paul found it a challenge to do the exegesis and prepare a draft of the passage before working with his language assistants. However, they were able to make progress. They completed a number of stories from Genesis and were ready to start the story of Moses during that stay.

The San Miguel Tunebos showed real interest in the Gospel of Mark. The second time reading through Mark to the people, one of the men commented to another man, "I am beginning to learn this material now." They seemed to grasp the meaning of the message as well as being more open to the gospel than the Tunebos in Cobaría. We continued to pray for a breakthrough.

We still needed a good translation helper. Our regular language assistant didn't correct our grammar mistakes in the draft or give ideas to make the translation sound more natural. He just said, "That's fine." There were a few others who did make suggestions, but they didn't work on a regular basis. We knew we needed more input on the translation from a mother tongue Tunebo speaker. We called out to the Lord for help.

18

SARAVENA ESCAPE

Pure religion and undefiled before God and the Father is this,
to visit the fatherless and widows in their affliction

—*James 1:27 (NIV)*

A General Strike

I̶T WAS A warm day as we started on the trail for the five-hour walk from San Miguel to Saravena where there was daily commercial air service. Paul had arranged for mules to take us over the trail. We had to stop several times along the way as Ronnie was sick with vomiting and diarrhea. When we finally reached the "road" leading into town, we left the mules with their owners.

We were all tired, and Ronnie was even more miserable. We were able to prevail on a man to take us to town in his jeep. The narrow rutted road was just tire tracks with only enough clearance to drive a truck through.

As we entered Saravena, a group of men stopped the jeep at a roadblock. We were puzzled but didn't think too much about it. We were exhausted and grateful to be on our way within a few minutes. When we arrived in town we went to the local hotel, a humble one-story structure. Each of the ten small bedrooms opened onto a dirt courtyard. The one lavatory, shared by all the guests, was often without water. After Paul unloaded all the gear from the jeep, he rushed off to arrange for travel on the bush airline while I got the family settled in our meager hotel room. Here's how Paul remembers the events of the day.

There were a lot more people gathered on the square than usual. Many of them were wearing arm bands with some kind of insignia. When I got to the Avianca Airline agent's office, operated out of his home, I asked my friend Carlos when I could get a flight for my family to Villavicencio.

"Pablo," he said, "we have no more flights out of here."

"What's happened? Last month there were sometimes three flights every day."

"Well, they say it is the poor runway. It's hard on the airplanes. But if you ask me," he lowered his voice to a whisper, "I think it's the influence of the antigovernment people here. Did you have any trouble getting into town?"

"We were briefly stopped in a road block."

"I don't suppose they would cause problems on that road, but the protesters are controlling every road in and out of town. No one can leave until they give the word."

So that's what the arm bands and the crowds are about, I said to myself as I headed back to tell Edna the frustrating news.

After we prayed together about the situation, we decided that, if necessary, we could stay for a day or two. But we needed to leave by the end of the week when Pastor Churchill of Minnetonka Community Church, one of our main supporting churches, was coming to visit. That afternoon, I revisited Carlos.

"Carlos, you know this town and everyone in it. I have to be back at our center in a few days. There has to be some way to get out. Who can help me?"

"Pablo," Carlos responded, "go see either Dr. William or the colonel at the military post. But don't let one know you saw the other. You're a gringo. I'd say the colonel is your best bet. But I wouldn't hold much hope if I were you."

The next day I was talking with the army colonel. I never did see Dr. William who was known to practice more political propaganda than medicine. The shouts and marching in the town square became more boisterous as the national anthem of Colombia blared out over a PA system.

The colonel gave me new insight into Colombian political philosophy: "We believe in freedom of political opinion here. We let them have their rally. That's the way they express their desires to the government. Unless they have this strike, the only road into this area will never be improved. But we have made it clear that we will not stand for property damage or personal injury to anyone. If it comes to that, then we step in and..." He snapped his fingers.

Then he went on to confide, "There is a village near here which has a military post and an airstrip." Just then I heard the *putt-putt-putt* of a helicopter. It circled and began to descend sixty feet away. Before it landed, a crowd appeared like a flash flood running toward the gate of the compound. Without a moment's hesitation, the colonel stood up and shouted, "No ONE COMES IN THAT GATE!" He gave instructions to some lesser officers as tension dominated the scene. Almost immediately, it became obvious that the crowd would respect the gate and there would be no incident. A messenger came out of the helicopter and saluted the colonel.

If only I had the family and our duffels with me, I thought. *It would be so easy to get aboard the helicopter and be out of there.* But I knew I could never get through that crowd and back in time.

About a half-hour later, the colonel and I were talking again. "I can get a truck to take you to the river. From there you will have to get to the military post, where your plane can land. Beyond the river, the strike is not in effect."

Early the next morning we were bouncing along in a truck with all of our duffels toward the river. Because there was no bridge, we got out of the jeep and arranged for a canoe to ferry us across the river. Two young soldiers carrying automatic rifles accompanied us. The driver gave them one last word: "Don't let anything happen to these Americans."

Across the river, there were none of the usual jeep-taxis. There was only one direction to go now. The army truck had returned to the post. We got some cokes at a makeshift hut nearby and asked about the frequency of jeep-taxi service. No one really knew. Edna and I began to pray. With two children and the duffels, walking was out of the question.

Finally a jeep came. "I'd like to go the military post. How soon can we leave?" I asked.

"This jeep isn't in service today."

"Oh, come on. I'll pay you well. I'm in a hurry."

"No. There is a strike on. They'll beat me up and take my jeep away."

I knew the threat was real. I certainly didn't want to cause the man to lose his livelihood, a father trying to support his family in difficult circumstances.

I relayed the information to Edna and the kids.

She prayed silently while I went back and talked to the man. After more discussion about our families, I pleaded with him.

"Listen, I don't want to make problems for you. But I have a dilemma. I really need to get my family to the outpost," I pleaded.

"Get your things, and let's go," he said.

We boarded the jeep. He delivered us safely to the military outpost, charging only the normal rate for his service. That was a real blessing.

God provided us with another miracle. A JAARS plane was in the area that day en route to another location. The JAARS pilot took us to the nearest town, where we got a commercial plane for the next leg in our journey, Villavicencio. We met Pastor Churchill there and flew to Lomalinda together. We shared with him the exciting story of God's miraculous timing in working out so many details over the last forty-eight hours. His grace is sufficient!

While in Lomalinda, we shared our concerns and prayer requests with Pastor Churchill to communicate with the church. He had been a missionary who was evacuated from China, so he was very understanding of our situation.

After the Churchills left, we participated in a workshop to further examine and write up the analysis of the Tunebo grammar. Paul had written it up several years earlier. We thought then we had submitted it to the consultant for the last time, but he sent it back with more suggestions. We dug in again and rewrote it in a form that would be more acceptable.

During the workshop, Paul's ear started bothering him. We were thankful that we were working on grammar. Most of the data was written, so he didn't have to listen to sounds on tape like he did for the phonology workshop. But of course, he would need to be able to hear the Tunebos to work on translation. We prayed that his ear would clear up and that he wouldn't lose any more hearing. The doctor gave him ear drops that cleared up the immediate problem.

While Paul worked on a more technical grammar description, I continued the work I had started with the young priest on simplified grammar lessons to help Spanish speakers learn the Tunebo language. There were some evangelicals around the town of Cubará who also wanted to help reach the Tunebos. One of them, Marcos, wrote asking for materials. We sent him the Scripture portions we had translated into the language. His interest further motivated me to work on the simplified grammar. We envisioned Marcos and others like him using it to learn the language and being used by God to help reach the Tunebos.

Joy fit right back into school at Lomalinda although she was a little behind after being in San Miguel. At the school awards program, she received a citizenship award for classroom conduct and courtesy. We were so proud of her. Her teacher told us that Joy was always the first one to follow her instructions and helped the other kids put their chairs up, etc. There were nine kids in Joy's class. The following year, they were anticipating eleven, a big class for Lomalinda compared to only three in the eighth grade graduating class. When school let out for the summer, a lot of families left for the States: some for longer home leaves, some just for the school vacation time.

Life at Lomalinda sometimes gave unexpected opportunities. A group of twenty-six students studying linguistics at a university in Bogotá came to have some classes with our linguists. Two girls stayed with us, which gave us opportunity to share with them the way we were using our linguistic training for Bible translation.

After the grammar workshop, we had the privilege of having Dr. Sarah Gudchinsky, a leading literacy expert in SIL, come to Colombia for a seminar. Her lectures were excellent. She shared from her wealth of literacy experience working in many countries. She quickly came to understand how the Tunebo grammar and alphabet functioned and was able to communicate with us clearly. She helped us revise the series of primers using a tested and proven method.

Measles

When the workshop was over, we returned to San Miguel. We arrived there safely after a fairly easy mule trip. We only had three pack mules this time. The kids rode on a mule together. They had quite a scare when one of the pack mules tried to pass their mule on the narrow trail squeezing their legs between the mules.

We were shocked to find our kitchen cupboards and our large medicine cabinet pretty well emptied out. Our plates and bowls were gone as well as the food we had left. The thieves left several cups and glasses and a few spoons, or we would have been eating with our fingers. We improvised by using some cookie can lids for plates and tin cans for cereal bowls.

Ernesto and all the Indians who lived in the same clearing we did were gone when we returned. It was a sad time. The measles had hit the area just prior to our return. Two of the three women in the family that lived next to us had died. Other families in the area were affected too. They were all very fearful. One of the shamans was the first to die. They believed that it was his departed spirit that caused the others to get sick and die. They had left to get away from the death-causing evil spirits they dreadfully feared.

One Saturday a Tunebo man came from several hours away to ask for medicine for his son who had measles. His pretty daughter of about fifteen years old had died just days before. Paul went home with the father. Together they brought the boy, his mother, and a baby back to stay with us until the sick boy got better. He needed to be kept warm and eat, as well as take medicine. We wanted to make sure those simple things were done. The Tunebos had a custom of putting anybody who they thought was going to die out in a little shelter in the woods. They were not given food cooked on the family fire. Although the boy was fairly sick, when we gave him food, liquid, and medicine to keep his fever down, he improved. The family took him back home, thankful they had not lost another child.

The day they left, Ucuácuba, Ernesto's son-in-law who lived in the same clearing as we did, came back with the family he still had after losing his wife, oldest daughter, and four-year-old daughter to the measles. His eight-year-old girl was very sick. We called the doctor at Lomalinda. With his advice, we gave her an antibiotic, and she improved. We praised the Lord for that! Ucuácuba had already lost too many precious loved ones. He, along with the others, seemed to really be obsessed with fear of death. To make matter worse, they all came down with bad colds or flu. It was quite discouraging to hear them sitting around talking about dying and being afraid.

The Gospel Recordings story entitled "Are You Afraid?" was God's message for the Tunebos at that time. We had adapted it to specifically address some of the things that they feared. The recording started by asking several questions about things they feared. When people came back, they attentively listened over and over again as they heard that, "Christ is more powerful than the evil spirits." They still needed, however, to step out and trust Christ above their fears. But their fear held them back. We prayed fervently and asked others to pray for them to trust Christ.

With so much sickness and death, Paul had no language assistants to help on translation, nor did my best student come for reading lessons because his mother had died. After a few weeks, most of the sick people got well, and their fears gradually began to subside. They slowly returned to some of their normal activities such as hunting. Ronnie was excited one day when he went with them to butcher and cook an animal they had killed. He even got a taste of the meat.

For us, it was a time of ups and downs, of joys and disappointments. In addition to the serious illness and deaths, Satan seemed to be using every annoyance he could think of to get us discouraged. We found scorpions in our shoes more than one morning. I found a snake coiled under a cookie can. I opened my medicine cupboard and saw a snake eyeing me from the top shelf. Another one was hiding behind a kids' game. There were cockroaches, fleas, and lice. We were at a very low point in our lives.

We found a few places in San Miguel to get away from it all in the midst of the measles epidemic. We occasionally went to a rocky beach some distance from the house for a picnic and to roast canned wieners on a stick. We frequently went to a small stream for a cool afternoon dip. Ronnie and Joy each caught their first fish in the same stream. These outings provided Paul and me the much needed opportunity to talk while the kids played.

In July 1972, we wrote our supporters, "In reviewing our work, it seems it is more appropriate for us to go to the United States on home leave this year than to wait until next year. We feel the need of rest, spiritual strengthening, and encouragement." It was a hurried decision as we hoped to get there in time for Joy to start school in the fall.

You What?

One day after we made the decision to go on home leave, Paul was off visiting with other Tunebos. While he was gone, I was approached by Ernesto and his wife, asking me to take care of Queú, their very sick great-grandbaby (the grandson of Ucuácuba). Queú's mother and grandmother had both died in the recent epidemic. I didn't want Ucuácuba to suffer more loss. I had the idea in my head that we could take the baby to our friends who had an orphanage. They would nurse him back to health while we were on home leave. When he was well, we would take him back to the great-grandparents. It seemed so logical I was sure Paul would agree. So I said to the great-grandparents, "We will see to Queú's care for a year and bring him back when he is healthy."

When I told Paul what I had promised, he was not at all pleased. He responded, "You what? Did you forget I'm planning to make a trip back to Cobaría directly from San Miguel? You will be traveling back to Villavicencio and Bogotá by yourself with the kids. How are you going to manage a six-year-old, a four-year old, and a baby? What are you going to do with that baby?"

We were going on home leave because we were exhausted and emotionally drained. But I had given my word and didn't want to go back on it. He let me go ahead and take the baby, but as I got on the commercial plane, he said, "I don't want to see that baby again!" In other words, I better get him placed in the orphanage before he got back. It was a long flight in what was more like a cargo plane than one for passengers. It stopped in four or five towns before we got to Villavicencio, the city where the orphanage was located. When we arrived in Villavicencio, the airport was more crowded than I had ever seen it. It turned out there had been a big land slide, and the road was closed. In the crowd were some of our Lomalinda colleagues who were trying to get a flight to Bogotá. Tía Altig, the Lomalinda doctor's wife, said she would accompany me to the orphanage. We got a taxi and were on our way. We came to a large bridge close to the orphanage and found it had been washed out. No cars could go across. We had to get out and cross the river balanced on a single steel beam. There I was with a sick baby, a four-year-old, a six-year-old, a dignified doctor's wife, and baggage to get across the bridge on the narrow steel beam. Once across, we walked about a mile to reach the orphanage.

Somehow, we made it. But that wasn't the end of my difficulties. I didn't have any papers for Queú. He was so sick he looked like he might die at any moment. Even though the woman who ran the orphanage was my friend, she couldn't risk having a baby with no papers die in her care. In addition to that, she told me, "The orphanage doesn't take in kids to give them back; we put them up for adoption." She wouldn't take the baby.

We spent the night at the orphanage. I tossed and turned, wondering what I was going to do with Queú, afraid to face my husband in Bogotá. Even though it was totally clouded over in the morning and I knew there would be no flights out very soon, the doctor's wife was anxious to be on her way. So we left early, once again carrying the baby and taking Joy and Ronnie and our things back across that washed-out bridge. We got into the city where we spent the day and another night—this time in a hotel. We were able to meet up with colleagues and fly to Bogotá with Jerrie Cobb, a pilot with her own plane, who was a friend of SIL.

In Bogotá, I took Queú to the WEC clinic. The director, Marion Price, another friend of ours, was willing to intern him temporarily. At least if he died in the clinic, not having papers would not present the same problem as at the orphanage.

When Paul arrived in Bogotá, the baby was still in the clinic, so he didn't have to see him. God took care of me even when I may not have used the best judgment, promising to take the baby without Paul's input. In consultation with our director and others, we were able to work out with a short-term support couple, Bud and Shirley James, to take Queú for a year. They lived in our house at Lomalinda while we were on home leave. They were delighted. Although Queú had an unusual parasite that was hard to eradicate and drained his strength, he improved dramatically after several treatments with the appropriate medicine. He gained weight. His color, skin tone, and energy level improved in a short time.

We went back to Lomalinda to make home leave preparations. We packed up our language material to take. Packing was never my favorite thing, although we did it so often that I used to say, "If we fail as missionaries we could go into the packing and moving business." Getting ready for home leave was no different. I bemoaned in a letter home. "It just gets so hard at times to decide what to leave and what to take. Our things fade so badly from the sun that they probably look terrible when we get away from here." A sale of my clothes for the cleaning girls from the various houses on the center was a big hit. We sold just about everything in a half hour. We saved most of the kid's and Paul's clothes for the Indians.

On July 29, 1972, we flew to Miami and on to Los Angeles. In the morning before we left the house, when Paul explained to the kids we were going to take a long hard trip, Ronnie asked, "Are we going to ride the mules?" He was probably remembering how sick he had been.

Paul's mother met us at the Los Angeles airport and drove us to Fallbrook, where we spent the next six months.

Paul and Edna Engaged

Arrival in Cubará

Mountain Ranges We Climbed to Get to Cobaría

Cobaría in the Distance

Miraculous Gift!

House the Tunebos Built for Us

Language Learning, Visiting, and Medical Work

Cobaría from the Air

Village of Cobaría with Ceremonial Dance House in the Center

Typical Cloudy Day in Cobaría

Ceremonial Dance

Blowing Ceremony

Joy and Ronnie

José and Wife

Starting Fire

Making Pots

Translation

Lumber House in Cobaría in the Midst of Tunebo Fields

Good-byes Are Hard

Radio Contact with Kids

Airstrip as Seen from Cobaría

Plane at Airstrip Near Cubará   Diego and Siblings

Landing at Our Airstrip

Teaching Reading

Joy and Friend Putting Together Literacy Books

Translation Workshop

Bob and Dee Ricker's Visit

Paul on Bridge

Edna on the Trail

Tunebo Scripture and Literacy Books

Writer's Workshop

Saddle Sore!

Guerrillas Vandalized Our House

Nina with Marion Price

First View of Printed Tunebo New Testament

Printed and Delivered Tunebo New Testament

Dedication

19

MATERIALS FOR THE TEMPLE

Home Leave 1972

WHILE ON HOME leave in California, I had the opportunity to attend Bible Study Fellowship. We studied the life of David. I remember the day we studied the passage about David not being allowed to build the temple. He really wanted to build it. He wanted to see the structure completed. From a human perspective, it seemed like a wonderful thing to do. Even Nathan the prophet told David to go ahead and build it. However, that night, God spoke to Nathan and sent him back to David to tell him he wasn't the one to do it but rather his son Solomon would be the one to build the temple. David was, however, allowed to gather and prepare materials for it.

> Then David said, "The house of the Lord God is to be here, and also the altar of burnt offering for Israel."
>
> So David gave orders to assemble the foreigners residing in Israel, and from among them he appointed stonecutters to prepare dressed stone for building the house of God. He provided a large amount of iron to make nails for the doors of the gateways and for the fittings, and more bronze than could be weighed. He also provided more cedar logs than could be counted, for the Sidonians and Tyrians had brought large numbers of them to David.

David said, "My son Solomon is young and inexperienced, and the house to be built for the Lord should be of great magnificence and fame and splendor in the sight of all the nations. Therefore I will make preparations for it." So David made extensive preparations before his death. (1 Chron. 22:1–5, NIV)

The leader of the Bible study asked, "Is there something that you are willing to do in the background for God, even if you never see the final results?"

I prayed, *Lord, you know I really want to see a thriving church among the Tunebo. I am disappointed not to have even the beginnings of a church after eight years' work. But I commit myself to preparing the translation and literacy materials for the Tunebo church even if I never see a church among the people we so desire to see come to know you.*

That prayer was not prayed lightly. It was a deep commitment at a time I needed it.

We were still in California when we received word that the measles epidemic had spread to Cobaría. It deeply hurt us to receive the disturbing news that sixteen children and one adult had died in the village. These were people we had lived alongside of and ministered to. It was hard not to think, *Things would have been different if we would have been there to treat them.* We had to give our concern for the people to God and trust that we were where He wanted us to be at the time. He was more concerned for their loss than we were. We desperately prayed that this calamity might cause the Tunebos to turn away from their superstitions and turn to Christ.

After six months in California, we spent six months in Minnesota, seeing family and supporters there. Time away from the rigors of living on the mission field, encouragement from family and friends and regular worship with other believers refreshed us, and we felt ready to return home to Colombia.

As we began to get settled back into Lomalinda life, enjoying lemonade from two trees loaded with fruit in our yard. It was hard to believe that only a week before we had been in Minnesota. I quickly readjusted to using a wringer washing machine and was thankful for an unusually beautiful day for drying clothes in the midst of the rainy season. We hired a man to cut the overgrown grass. It always lifted my spirits to see the freshly cut grass.

The baby we had left in the care of the James family looked healthy. He was running around and smiling. He had a sweet, quiet temperament. After a few days of settling in, Paul and I left to take Queú back to San Miguel. Since Joy and Ronnie weren't anxious to take another mule trip and we only planned to be gone for about two and a half weeks, we left them in the care of friends at Lomalinda while we were gone.

Singing in the Rain

We traveled by commercial DC-3 air service to the town of Saravena. In the afternoon and evening, we visited friends and spent the night in a frontier hotel. In the morning, we got up early and took a jeep-taxi to the end of the road where we contracted for mules and their driver. Except for the rain and getting soaked, we had a good trip. Queú loved the mule ride, rain and all. In fact, when we got on the narrow trail and the wet branches hit our faces, he started to sing. It was like he knew he was going home. It seemed God was answering the prayer we had prayed every night that he would go back to his people without difficulty.

When we got to San Miguel, we found a Colombian wood sawyer and his family living in our house. We waited a few hours until they moved out. They moved into an abandoned Indian house nearby. It made me feel a little bad to put them out even though they had no right to be there.

Everything we had left there was stolen except the furniture, and even some of that was gone including our bedding and mattress. I was glad we had brought along two sleeping bags we got in Minneapolis; otherwise, we would really have been in bad shape. I had taken a cooking pot, but I couldn't use it without something to set it on; the grill had been taken. I borrowed a pot from the people living in the house to do my cooking. I washed dishes in the same pot.

The wood sawyers had moved out, but they didn't take the roaches with them. Thousands of cockroaches had taken over. We had no poison to kill the nasty roaches. I tried putting a chicken in the cupboard one day to see if it could eliminate the pests. It didn't work. We couldn't even sit down to eat without roaches crawling on the table, until one night we woke up with roaches in our faces (our mosquito nets had also disappeared). We discovered the roaches were trying to get away from an army of ants that was passing through our house. We got out of bed and went out to the porch where we sat on top of the table until the ants were gone. After that, the roach population was greatly diminished.

One little girl came the first morning with her book ready to study. It was really encouraging to see how she had progressed while we were gone.

The great-grandmother was very happy to see Queú. We still had him staying with us, but we sent him over to visit for short times with them. He seemed to like them. We learned Ucuácuba, his grandfather, had remarried and was living a day's walk away from San Miguel. Someone went to tell him to come and get Queú. We had some anxious days wondering whether he would really come back for his grandbaby. What would we do with this sweet child if he didn't come? We had learned that they ask the spirit of snakes if it is all right to go to this place or that. Was he waiting on a snake spirit for guidance? We never really learned the answer to that question, but after a few days, the great-grandfather came back from town and said he had seen Ucuácuba and that he would be coming the next weekend. It was hard to wait not knowing if he would actually come or if he would take the baby.

Queú's grandfather did come as he said. He was thrilled to see that the sickly baby whom he had sent off with us, thinking he might die, was now a beautiful healthy little boy running around and laughing. We put Queú in the loving care of his grandfather and great-grandparents. After a few days, we said our final good-byes and returned to Lomalinda.

20

NOW WHAT?

Return to Cobaría

THE SETTLEMENT OF San Miguel had disintegrated. The people who held the site together had died. Their relatives had moved away. Our things had been stolen, which meant we would need to start setting up all over again. We were in a bind. Returning to Cobaría seemed the only logical option. Was God really leading us in that direction? Did He only want us to leave for the brief two years we had been gone? Was His answer to our fleece just for that short interval? Was it to test our faith? Two years earlier, we had thought maybe He was telling us to "shake off the dust of our feet" (Luke 9:5). However, we were reminded that our initial reception in Cobaría had been unbelievably miraculous! Something only God could have done. They had given us a house in the village when we had been told they would never let outsiders live there.

As we prayed about the situation, we felt God was leading us back to Cobaría. We followed His leading and made preparations to return there.

Paul went on ahead by commercial plane to do government relations and to make some face-to-face contacts. He needed to establish credibility and create a better image of the work we were doing with the Indians. He stopped in several towns along the way where he met with local officials as well as the Roman Catholic bishop of the area. It was amazing how face-to-face contact built trust. He also stopped at the Roman Catholic mission station, where we had spent our first month, and visited the nuns. From there, he hiked the two days over the trail to Cobaría.

When the kids and I joined Paul in Cobaría, the people readily received us back. Some people began calling Paul *werjayú*, meaning "elder," a term of respect. They noticed that our conversational ability in the language had improved.

Just two weeks later, the plane returned to take Joy back to Lomalinda for school. It was a hard day when I said good-bye as Paul started down the trail to the airstrip with Joy to put her on the plane. She was only in second grade. She was going to stay in the children's home for the first time. Ronnie stayed with us in the village, and I taught him kindergarten. He visited in the neighbors' homes. They weren't sure what to do with the active healthy child compared to their own, who were lethargic from parasites. The first thing he learned were all the negative commands, "Don't touch! Don't run! Don't play!"

Although the Cobaría Tunebos welcomed us back, translation work did not go as well as we hoped. José, the chief, and Búswara, the blind man, came on alternate days to help with translation of the book of Acts. However, they seemed to lack the motivation to really make it clear. That left more of the responsibility to Paul. He was not able to reach the goals he had set for translating the book of Acts during that period.

We recorded more gospel stories on cassettes and played them for everyone who came to the house. They listened with attention to the stories. Some even invited us to take them to their homes to play. We longed for them to apply what they heard to their lives, but their hearts seemed closed.

When it came time for the Tunebos to migrate to the lowlands, we went immediately to the SIL center to be reunited with Joy.

Two Tunebos, in their late teens, Rora and Rayotá, went to Lomalinda with us for the season. Rora was strong willed.

His father was a leading shaman. Rayotá, from Sinará's humble family, was a follower. He had been with us at Lomalinda before. We had three goals for these three months: to teach them to read, to finish translating the book of Acts, and to give them more exposure to the gospel. We found we had our hands full with the two of them. They didn't hesitate to remind us that God didn't give books to the Tunebos. This attitude seemed to come from José who had decided reading was not for them. They were also forthright in expressing their thinking about the Scriptures. They liked to argue with us and frequently told us something the Tunebos believed that was contrary to the Scriptures. Our prayer was constantly that God would change their hearts and that they would realize there is only one way of salvation, through Christ, for both the Indians and others.

Rora finished the fourth primer. Rayotá, who had started learning to read on a previous trip to Lomalinda, finished the fifth primer in the series. That completed all the lessons in Tunebo. The sixth primer was a transition primer that taught the letters in Spanish that were not found in the Tunebo alphabet.

They took their books with them when they returned to Cobaría. As always, they and everything they had with them went through the purification (blowing) ceremony before they went home to live. Apparently, the shaman would not purify Tunebo reading books. One day I unexpectedly found Rayotá's books in among the Bibles and commentaries in Paul's translation office. To avoid making us feel bad, Rayotá had secretly slipped them onto the shelf. Previously others who had taken books home from Lomalinda had told me, "I lost them on the trail." We prayed they would one day be allowed to bring books and the Scriptures into their homes, so that they would understand the message of the gospel and claim the promises of God's Word.

21

TRIALS

LOMALINDA (MEANING PRETTY hill) was located in the rolling hills of the plains of central Colombia. It was spread out over a large area so the houses could be located on top of the hills to get the benefit of the cool breezes. In the dry season, strong winds blew across the open fields of the plains surrounding Lomalinda. Each year, the local ranchers burned off the old dry grass on these fields to get new tender grass for their livestock. The wind carried sparks from the fires for long distances.

One Sunday afternoon in mid-February 1974, sparks got into some boxes in the attic of our friends Frank and Jerri Morgan's house. They quickly burst into flames in the tinder dry conditions. I stood helplessly on the hill in front of our house and watched from the distance as their home burned to the ground. The asbestos cement roof popped and exploded, flying into the air. Within twenty minutes, the house and all their possessions were gone. Paul and all the other men were fighting the fire, which covered much of one side of the center. Although they weren't able to save the Morgan's house, no other houses were lost.

The following Sunday evening in our service the Morgans and another couple sang "He Giveth More Grace." It was a real testimony and reminder that God's grace is sufficient even in the face of a great loss. What a blessing and encouragement the message in song was to all of us at the center.

He giveth more grace when the burdens grow greater,

He sendeth more strength when the labors increase;
To added affliction, He addeth His mercy;
To multiplied trials, His multiplied peace.
When we have exhausted our store of endurance,
When our strength has failed ere the day is half done,
When we reach the end of our hoarded resources,
Our Father's full giving is only begun.
His love has no limit; His grace has no measure.
His pow'r has no boundary known unto men;
For out of His infinite riches in Jesus,
He giveth and giveth and giveth again! [2]

Just two weeks later, very early on Sunday morning, March 3, we got a telephone call from the prayer chain. One of Gerry and Nancy Gardner's three-year-old twins[3] was having difficulty breathing. At 7:00 a.m., we got another call that he had stopped breathing. At 7:10, we got the message that he was gone. He had died from croup. It all seemed to happen too fast to believe. We had seen the whole family out in their yard the day before, building a cage for a little animal. In the morning church service that day, we had spontaneous readings of scripture and requests for songs. The song that stood out to me was "Does Jesus Care?" I especially liked the verse that asks

> Does Jesus care when I've said good-bye to the dearest on earth to me,
> and my sad heart aches till it nearly breaks—
> Is it aught to him does He see.
> Refrain: Oh yes, He cares. I know He cares.
> His heart is touched by my grief.

---

2   Annie Johnson Flint, *He Giveth More Grace.*
3   Grady Wilson's grandson.

When the days are weary, the long nights dreary,
I know my Savior cares. [4]

At 3:00 p.m. on Sunday, we were all quietly gathered together for the first funeral service at Lomalinda. I was reminded of so many of the verses that comforted me at the time of my brother Larry's death: Isaiah 40:28–31, Romans 8:33–39, and 2 Corinthians 1:3–4. God comforts us so we can comfort others.

Later in the week, I was able to visit and share comfort scriptures with Nancy Gardner. It made me wish that we had more scripture translated for the Tunebos and more fluency in their language so that we could share more freely of God's comfort with them.

As if the fire and the baby's death weren't enough to discourage the Colombia branch, a few days later, there was an incident with one of the airplanes as the pilot landed. When he slowed down, the brakes failed, and the plane began to veer toward the hill on the side of the airstrip. The pilot did a ground loop. However, the narrow airstrip caused the plane to hit the side of the hill. The tail was damaged. [5] The time required to get the necessary parts and repair the plane put the whole flight schedule and everyone's plans in an upheaval, including our planned trip to Cobaría.

---

[4]   Frank E. Graeff, *Does Jesus Care?* (1901).

[5]   A visitor from a church in the United States recorded the accident with a video camera. This church group spoke to their congregation of their time in Lomalinda, showing the video and telling of the need for a new airstrip. The church raised a good part of the money needed to construct the airstrip. God used the incident to provide for the new airstrip, which gave us many safe takeoffs and landings. God works in mysterious ways. (Taken from a story by Val Hess in *I Was a Stranger*, compiled by Tom Branks.)

When our turn for a flight arrived about two weeks later, one of our close friend's children at the center had German measles. We made last-minute arrangements to leave Joy and Ronnie with other friends until it was sure they wouldn't come down with measles and spread it to the Indians. Ronnie was in kindergarten, and Joy was in second grade, so it was heart wrenching to leave them, but we had seen the death and devastation caused by measles in San Miguel a few years earlier. We knew we couldn't take the risk. The difficulty of scheduling flights extended their time with our friends to more than a month; much longer than we had planned. Finally they were flown out to be with us in the village.

Once back in Cobaría, Joy and Ronnie quickly adjusted to life in the village. One day Paul was working in his office off the porch and I went up the hill to treat a woman. While I was gone, two children from the mission outpost came to deliver some fresh cow's milk. When I returned, Joy had received the milk, poured it in the pan to be boiled, and was washing out the bottle to give it back. Ronnie was serving the children tea and cookies. Our two little kids were growing up and taking responsibility.

Two translation assistants came on alternate days five days a week for about five hours a day to help revise Paul's rough draft translation of the book of Acts. It was challenging for Paul to keep ahead of them, but he was especially grateful for their help since it was the time of year when the people were busy clearing their fields. As Paul progressed in his language ability, he made the first draft of the translation clearer and more understandable to his assistants. They in turn were able to suggest more changes that made it sound more natural in Tunebo. It was a vast difference because for a long time, they merely parroted back what Paul read.

I kept busy with an intestinal flu epidemic that affected many babies including one we were caring for ourselves. In addition, I was helping Joy and Ronnie with the schoolwork sent out by their teachers. We were busy with our life and work among the Tunebos and oblivious of what was happening at Lomalinda.

Tom Branks wrote about the situation there:

> On a quiet Sunday afternoon in May 1974, a large army helicopter landed in front of the children's home while truckloads of soldiers poured from military vehicles into all the public buildings. Residents were put under house arrest. Directed by General Matallana, frogmen spent five days under the surface of Lake Lomalinda peering through the murky water for a glimpse of our legendary treasure.

Since we were totally unaware of the investigation at Lomalinda the week before, it came as a total shock to us when on the following Saturday afternoon we heard a helicopter overhead. The same helicopter with General Matallana and about fifteen military men landed in a small clearing about one thousand feet above our house. The whole crew came running down the hill straight for our house. General Matallana interrogated us with one question after another.

"What are you doing in Cobaría?"

"Why would you leave the conveniences of the United States to live in this remote place?"

Paul answered each question as courteously as possible. He respectfully addressed the general as "major." It was only after he had left that we discovered that he was one of the leading generals of the Colombian army. He questioned our work and our motives for an hour. Then as quickly as they appeared, they left. It was very unsettling.

That night, I couldn't fall asleep as I lay thinking of the implications of their visit. *What does all this mean to the future of our work? Why did they choose to investigate us?* I wondered if they had also gone to interrogate any of the other SIL teams working in other areas or if we had been singled out.[6]

---

[6] We were in fact the only area they visited.

All the external pressures SIL was facing in Colombia prompted Ben Elson, the executive director of SIL and Wycliffe Bible Translators, to visit Colombia. We had the opportunity to visit with him personally. During our conversation, Paul and I poured out our profound disappointment at the lack of response by the Tunebo. Dr. Elson reminded us of the Old Testament story of Josiah (2 Chron. 34:1–3, 14–33). When the priests found the book of God's law in the temple, they read it to Josiah. The young king tore his robes when he heard the words of the book of the law. He then determined to lead his people in obeying the words of that book. Paul and I compared Josiah's story to our work with the Tunebos. We tucked it away in our hearts and started to seek ways to put the Tunebo Scriptures in locations where they would someday be discovered and obeyed by the Tunebos. The meeting with Dr. Elson and the story of Josiah gave us renewed vision to continue with Tunebo work.

22

ANOTHER ORPHAN

Ruiswiya

IN MARCH 1974, Siucayá, a young practicing witch doctor came to us for help. It was somewhat unusual for shamans to seek help from us or anyone else for medicine or medical advice for fear of losing esteem among their people. However, after going through all the traditional healing ceremonies, blowing over a sacred white heron feather, and calling on the spirits to no avail, he was desperate. Since the birth of their sixth child, his wife had been in poor health. As a conscientious Tunebo woman, whenever she was able, she struggled to continue to tend to her garden and take care of the responsibilities of raising the growing family. Her illness affected her natural ability to supply milk for nursing Ruiswiya, the baby, who became very thin. Even though most of the other Tunebo babies were fat and chubby, Ruiswiya continued to lose weight.

Siucayá and his family continued living in the lowlands when the other Tunebos had migrated to Cobaría. His wife had been much too sick to make the trip over the trail. Siucayá had stayed behind in hopes his wife would soon be well again. But she didn't improve; she died leaving Siucayá with a ten-month-old baby and five other children. (The oldest daughter had left home to live and work among the white people.)

Siucayá had a major dilemma. How was he going to manage? Would his twelve-year-old daughter be able to assume the responsibility of most of the cooking, bringing in the food from the fields, and some babysitting? How could he leave his seven-year-old to care for her younger brother and baby sister while the twelve-year-old was out in the field?

Siucayá's oldest son, our friend Warawaná, had come ahead to Cobaría. He told Paul and me about his mother's illness and death and the condition of his baby sister. He said the baby was very thin. We kept our eyes open for Siucayá and the rest of the family to return to Cobaría, knowing they had to pass by on the trail just outside our door. When they passed by, we talked to Siucayá about his loss. We saw how weak and thin Ruiswiya had gotten since we had last seen her.

Moved by compassion, Paul suggested, "Siucayá, would you like us to take care of the baby until she can manage a little better at home without a mother?"

"I will have to think that over," he responded. He was being cautious as he was concerned that his oldest daughter had gone to live with whites and hadn't come back to live at home. He didn't want to give up another one of his children to whites.

Ruiswiya cried almost constantly for two or three days. It was not an easy decision for Siucayá to make, but the crying and lack of sleep was getting unbearable. Siucayá decided to accept Paul's offer. He was afraid that the baby would die, and he would lose her permanently. He sent his son Warawaná to tell Paul to come and get Ruiswiya.

When we went to bring Ruiswiya to our home, I saw tears in her sister's eyes as she put her baby sister in my arms. We promised to return her when she was strong enough. When we reached the trail, Ruiswiya must have sensed our love. She stopped crying. Once home, I gave her a warm bath and dressed her in a soft gown and a diaper made from a towel and plastic pants invented from a plastic bag. She soon learned to drink from a bottle. We converted one of our shipping trunks to a crib, but most of the time, she ended up sleeping in our bed.

We had no idea the misery we would soon experience; Ruiswiya had scabies (a parasite under the skin, otherwise known as seven-year itch), and I got it too, especially in the bend of my arm where I cradled her head. She also had intestinal parasites, which cleared up nicely with medicine, contrary to the scabies, which hung on even with treatment. She ran a fever and was fussy every time she cut a tooth. She suffered from a bad flu. Then as would happen to Indian people who are not accustomed to the common childhood diseases of our country, she became very ill when she got the chickenpox. The unexpected blessing was that the high fever she ran burned out the scabies. Even with all of the illnesses, she soon became fat and healthy. Joy grew very fond of her and enjoyed taking care of her.

We prayed a lot for little Ruiswiya. Our prayer was twofold: first, that the time would come when she could be returned to her family and second, that God would use this experience to help bring her people to Christ. The first part of the prayer was answered, when after five months, we returned Ruiswiya to her family. This time, when I placed Ruiswiya in her sister's arms, the tears were in my eyes, not her sister's. Ruiswiya went right into her sister's arms without crying.

Only time will tell how the second part of the prayer will be answered. One day, however, when talking to the neighbor lady, I asked, "Can your people take a baby of another woman who has died and nurse it?"

She responded, "We can't." She went on to say, "We're bad."

It is unusual for these hard-working people ever to admit they do anything wrong, so maybe in some small way, that prayer was being answered. The Tunebos might have begun to realize they were not perfect. They do need Christ to free them from their sins and from their taboo system.

When Ruiswiya reached home, she went through a purification ceremony. After that, she could no longer take even a cookie from us because of the taboo that all things cooked on an outsider's fire carry disease.

23

NEW PLANS

Dialect Survey

IN AUGUST 1974, Steve Eglund, a survey specialist, came to Colombia to help the translators with dialect surveys. These surveys determine which language groups would need separate translations and define for the government how widely the education materials in each language can be used. Steve went with Paul to visit eight different Tunebo locations. Here is how Paul described it in a letter to his mother.

> The dialect test works like this: we made audio recordings in each area and then played them in the other areas, asking questions to determine the people's understanding of the recording. We were able to do recordings in eight Tunebo locations. We need to return to seven of the eight areas to test for intelligibility.
>
> We did test Agua Blanca the most divergent dialect against the nearest dialects including Cobaría and found it does need another translation. A Roman Catholic nun, María Elena Márquez, is translating in that dialect.

In May 1975, Paul went with Roger Van Otterloo, another SIL dialect survey specialist, to do the testing for understanding needed to complete the survey. Roger summed up their results this way. "Paul and I were able to confirm that Tunebo Indians living in ten areas speak one of three dialects. Separate translations will be needed for each of these three dialects."

Information Load

In the fall of 1974, Dr. Robert Longacre, a leading linguist well known for his work in discourse analysis, led a workshop in Colombia for twenty translation teams. Previous to that time, linguists had concentrated mainly on how words were made up and a little on sentence structure. Dr. Longacre was concerned about how whole paragraphs and stories interconnected. During the workshop, we made some significant discoveries about the Tunebo language.

I had remembered something that Dr. Mildred Larson, my grammar teacher at the Summer Institute of Linguistics, said, "There may be a grammar construction possible in the language, but you need to see how frequently it is used. Although a construction may be possible, if it is overused, the translation will not sound natural." I had an inkling that we were putting too much new information in each sentence in the translation. I studied stories the Tunebos had told us to determine the following: How many pieces of new information are given in each sentence? How many times new pieces of information are repeated in a story? What part of the sentence can include new information? Among other things I learned, we were overusing the dependent clause for new information. I discovered the Tunebo language never puts new information in a dependent clause. These discoveries led to a much clearer and more natural translation of the Scriptures.[1]

During the workshop, Paul wrote a paper with Dr. Stephen H. Levinsohn on two aspects of Tunebo grammar. It was entitled

---

[1] "Information Load and Layout in Tunebo," published in Notes on Translation, 1975. Edna Headland, 1976. Estudios Chibchas 1. *Distribución de información en Tunebo.*

"Prominence and Cohesion in Tunebo Discourse."[2] Paul's paper described how the Tunebo language functions to help the listener identify what is prominent or important; that is the theme of a paragraph. Cohesion describes how the various sentences are tied together to form a unit and develop the story.

Bad Press

1975 brought an onslaught of personal disappointments and attacks from the press that threatened to put a stop to our entire program in Colombia. Anthropologists claimed that we were destroying Indian cultures, while the film *War of the Gods*[3] was being shown everywhere…to supposedly expose "who we really were." Our public image fell to an all-time low when a Colombian congressional investigation began with the ultimate motive of putting SIL out of the country. In October, we were stunned to read in the newspaper that ILV was to be replaced by a Colombian linguistic institution. The Minister of Government informed our director that we would receive a letter from the President to terminate our contract at the end of one year.[4]

I remember that day in October 1975. I couldn't hold back the tears when I told our dear friend Wisa that we had heard that morning that we had just one year left in Colombia. We were having our regular Saturday morning time to talk by two-way

---

[2]   Paul Headland and Stephen H. Levinsohn, 1976. Estudios Chibchas 1. "Prominencia y cohesión dentro del discurso en Tunebo."

[3]   A 1971 film directed by Brian Moser partially filmed at Lomalinda, accusing missionaries of cultural genocide.

[4]   Quoted from Tom Branks, "I Was a Stranger: Tales of Colombia SIL," compiled stories from Tom and other Colombia branch members.

radio with our children who had stayed in school at the center. After they finished telling us their news, the radio operator said, "We have been given oral notice that we have just one year to wrap up our work in the country."

Assessment of Our Work

God used the forewarning to get our attention. The possibility of having a limited time in the country caused us to stop and take stock of our work. We had been planting and preparing seed for planting by translating the Scriptures into the Tunebo language. The taboo against having written messages in Tunebo homes was a huge barrier to literacy and Scripture use. If we had to leave prematurely, what assurance would there be that the portions of Scripture already translated would be used? Naturally, we desired to stay longer to continue to minister to the Tunebos and to complete the goal of translation of the entire New Testament, as well as portions of the Old Testament. Even if we had enough time to complete that goal, we wanted to make sure that there would be an ongoing work among the Tunebos after we left, a church planted and growing.

We prayed and evaluated the situation. Due to the urgency of the circumstances, we made a three-part plan:

1. Present the gospel in every Tunebo home in Cobaría.
2. Work through Christian Spanish-speaking settlers.
3. Work with a few Tunebos to become fluent readers.

To present the gospel to every home in Cobaría, we would go to their homes and either read the story of the prodigal son and the verses from the Four Spiritual Laws or play them from a cassette tape. We began to do this immediately, and by April 1976, Paul had shared the good news in the majority of the homes by going to three homes a day and more on weekends.

As we developed the second part of the plan, we realized that if Spanish-speaking settlers were going to communicate the gospel adequately, they would have to do it in the Uwa/Tunebo[5] language. We planned short courses to teach these settlers to read in Uwa and to sing the hymns in the language.

God had started work among the few families of settlers in the heart of a young boy named Diego. Diego had refreshed us with lemonade the first day we arrived in the area. We had become better acquainted with him when we spent many long nights at his parents' house while we waited for clear weather to fly. He had run to meet us each time he heard the plane bringing us back.

One day he volunteered to carry a pack for Paul. Diego wanted to talk about the need he felt in his heart. Carrying the pack, he walked to our house with the pilot, Ron Ehrenberg. Taking advantage of the three-hour hike, Diego asked the questions that he had been pondering about the meaning of life. Ron answered his questions from Scripture and gave him some gospel tracts. Diego read the tracts. On his way back home, he stopped on the trail and opened his heart to Christ. He became a vibrant witness of his salvation. Through Diego, a few other settlers became Christians. These were the people we wanted to introduce to the Tunebo materials.

To initiate the third part of the plan (to bring some Tunebos to the point of being fluent readers) in November 1975, we took Warawaná and Rayotá with us when we returned to Lomalinda. When we arrived we settled right down to work, and they made good progress in reading. In addition to studying the lessons in the primer, we read the Gospel of Mark together. To see the story of Jesus's life through the eyes and ears of someone who had never heard it before was an exhilarating experience. Warawaná

---

5   In the 1970s, the Tunebo began to be known as Uwa (sometimes written U'wa). We use Uwa and Tunebo interchangeably. *Uwa* means *people* in the language. Often we write both Uwa/Tunebo.

was shocked and incredulous when he learned that after all the good Jesus had done for the people, they crucified him.

In mid-November, we were making good when our lessons were abruptly interrupted. Our director called for a day of prayer and fasting. He had learned the cancellation of SIL's official contract was on the agenda of the Colombian Congress. As the senators were discussing what to do with our organization, we were gathered together in prayer. We beseeched our Heavenly Father on behalf of the indigenous groups of Colombia. "Lord, we have laid the ground work of linguistics and language learning. We have started translations in many languages, but we need much more time to finish. Please intervene. You can change hearts and minds." God answered our prayer. He gave some government leaders the courage to speak in favor of SIL. SIL never received the letter from the president saying the contract was cancelled or that we all had to leave the country.

We were able to return to Cobaría. In April 1976, we conducted the first short course to teach the settlers to read in Uwa/Tunebo. About half a dozen enthusiastic young men attended the first course. They had grown up in the area hearing the Indian language all their lives. They had little difficulty learning to read the seven differences between the Tunebo alphabet and Spanish. They were prepared to read the Scriptures in the Uwa homes. Each course participant received copies of the Scriptures translated into Uwa as well as literacy materials. We placed a book case with a number of copies of all the books in the home of one of the settlers.

Although SIL did not receive a letter cancelling the contract, the situation was still tenuous. No new visas were granted for some time. When a visa was renewed, it was only for six months. In order not to jeopardize our visas by being out of the country when they came up for renewal, we decided to take just a short summer furlough in 1976 to spend time with family and our partners in ministry. It was a time to thank them for their part in our work, bring them up to date on what God was doing in

Colombia, and help them understand the situation so they could pray in an intelligent way.

Before leaving, Paul was able to do all the last-minute edits and formatting changes on the book of Acts that he had been diligently working to complete. He turned it over to the printshop with a prayer of gratitude to God that He had given him the strength, the wisdom, and the Tunebo translation assistants to finish the job.

I rejoiced with Paul for a job completed. I was also grateful that I had been able to finish testing a new Tunebo primer that combined all the lessons in one book, instead of five separate books previously used. This was printed later. With those projects completed, we felt ready for the break home leave would provide.

24

DEDICATED SUPPORTERS

ONCE AGAIN, IN 1976, home leave provided the time needed to update our partners in the work. Wycliffe is a faith mission. That means that we trust God to supply our needs through His people. For most of the years of our ministry with Wycliffe, the official policy was, "Full information. No solicitation." We trusted God would lay it on the hearts of those He wanted to be involved. If people directly asked us, we would tell them how we were supported, what our specific needs were, and how they could contribute, but if they didn't ask, we didn't bring up our needs. More recently, the official policy has changed. However, our personal practice has not.

God supplied our needs over the years in many ways. In Cobaría, sometimes it was by means of an Indian giving us beans, bananas, corn, or avocados. Other times, settlers were going to town and brought back groceries. At Lomalinda, missionary friends frequently let us use their tools. Wherever we were, our faithful financial backers in the United States contributed to meeting our needs.

During our first term, we struggled with inadequate support. That was when we learned the meaning of the verse, "All the believers were one in heart and mind. No one claimed that any of their possessions was their own, but they shared everything they had" (Acts 4:32, NIV). Our colleagues let us use their washing machines, store our food in their refrigerators and borrow their tools, and some even shared from their personal support. God cared for us.

Frequently, in those early years and a few times in later years, we received donations from Wycliffe's emergency support fund. Undesignated funds sent to Wycliffe were combined and distributed to missionaries on low support to bring them as close to 80 percent of their determined support quota as possible. We were thankful for that provision.

In 1976, when we shared our work, God raised up new supporters as He had done on our first furlough in 1968 and second furlough in 1972. They joined with the team who was our lifeline of prayer and support to do the work of Bible translation: family, friends we grew up with in our church youth groups, classmates from nurses training and college, and others. In each home leave or home assignment, we traveled from California to Minnesota to renew contacts and thank this team. God used these committed people to bless us, each in their special way. They opened their homes and hearts to us. They met us at the airport, helped us buy a car, hosted us in their homes, listened to our stories and had gatherings in their homes for us to share our work with friends. They supported us with their faithful prayers and backed us financially. Not only did they provide for our material needs, they became cheerleaders and encouragers in our ministry.

We also related to and spoke in supporting churches. My home church, Edina Baptist Church (later known as Grace Church of Edina and now Grace Church Eden Prairie), has been our main supporting church from the beginning. Other churches also became part of the team: my brother Dick's church, Huntwood Baptist (later known as Bay Hills Community Church); Minnetonka Community Church; Upsala Covenant Church; Fallbrook First Baptist Church; and after we settled in Dallas, Hillcrest Baptist Church.

This dedicated team of supporters and prayer partners who gave us the privilege of being on the forefront, working directly with the Tunebos, were an equally vital part of the ministry. They sent us back to Colombia with an assurance of their backing.

25

LASTING POSSESSIONS

Visas Granted

AFTER OUR BRIEF time updating supporters, we returned to Colombia in August 1976. SIL's position in Colombia continued to be shaky. While still in the United States, we had heard that there would be no new visas issued or renewed until the contract was rewritten. Some anthropologists continued to harangue the government about our work.

Our visas were still valid, so we immediately returned to Cobaría. Once there, we settled into a routine. Joy and Ronnie were able to be with us two weeks of the time there. Ronnie, then eight, accompanied Paul on the five-hour trek down the mountains to communicate with the owner of the airstrip land. There had been some misunderstandings with him that needed to be worked out face-to-face. Paul was relieved when the owner agreed to sign a new contract for use of the airstrip for five more years, and another contract to make some improvements.

On the same trip, he was delighted to learn that the church started by the Spanish-speaking settlers was growing spiritually. Some of them continued to show an interest in reaching the Tunebos. They reported a few Tunebos were attending their services. Paul left them copies of the Gospel of Mark and the book of Acts.

At that time, he also met a young woman, María, who was bilingual in Tunebo and Spanish. She spoke both languages and could read well in Spanish. Her father was a settler who had served as the school teacher and had learned the Tunebo language. It was his house we had lived in when we first went to Cobaría. María's mother was Tunebo. María had read the Gospel of Mark in Tunebo, looking for things she could criticize. She confronted Paul, pointing out what she considered to be errors in the translation. She was taken aback when Paul said, "Good. You correct all the errors you find. Send it back to me, and I will pay you." She agreed and read through the Gospel of Mark making notes in the margins. Her husband, Tito, brought us the completed work. Paul sent the payment for her work back with Tito, along with a letter asking her to review the book of Acts. He asked her to insert comments, noting any suggestions she had to make it clearer or more natural in Tunebo. He saw potential in working with her to help speed up the work of translation.

While in Cobaría in mid-October shortly after Tito left, we received word that all SIL visas could be renewed for another six months. This entailed a trip to Villavicencio or Bogotá for each member as their visa came up for renewal. When our time came, we presented ourselves and our documents to a government office in Villavicencio, filled out the necessary forms, and were fingerprinted. With that in place the visa was granted.

His Strength Is Made Perfect in Weakness

In January 1977, we went to Bogotá. Even after two previous surgeries for endometriosis, I continued to suffer from its effects and needed another surgery. After the surgery, we stayed with friends in Bogotá for a few weeks, and I finished recuperating at home in Lomalinda. I experienced some complications. By March 24, when we returned to Cobaría, I hadn't fully regained my strength. I found the trip over the trail from the airstrip to the house exhausting. After walking four hours we arrived at the first house in the village where Rayotá lived with his family. He handed me a scrap of paper with a note he had written. Among other things, it said, "*Anita bar wijacro.*" (Edna has arrived.) That little note greatly encouraged me. After years of waiting for some kind of a breakthrough in the barrier to literacy, it was like a little pinhole in the dam that held back progress. I would soon need that encouragement more than I realized. A few minutes later when we opened the door to our house, we discovered it had been broken into, and many things had been stolen.

Later that same evening, a young boy was brought to us with a large cut on his head that needed stitches. God must have given me an extra measure of His strength to be able to stand and clean his wound and stitch his scalp. Once again, it was a reminder that *His grace is sufficient and His strength is made perfect in weakness.*

A few days later, Paul visited in the home of a settler who was new in the area. While there, he saw some of our stolen belongings. That night, he went to bed still struggling with his attitude about what he had seen. After a night of tossing and turning while he fretted over the loss, the next morning God spoke clearly to him in his devotions when he read, "You sympathized with those in prison and joyfully accepted the confiscation of your property, because you knew that you yourselves had better and lasting possessions" (Heb. 10:34, NIV). It was a good reminder that heaven will be far better than any earthly possession we could possibly have.

Before we left Lomalinda, our friends had made a concerted effort to make sure the primer with all the lessons in one book was ready to go on the flight with us. When we packed, the primer was hot off the press. In addition to the primer, there were large syllable charts with pictures for key words.[1]

---

[1]   It was rewarding to have the primers accepted by educational leaders of schools in the fringe areas of the Tunebos. They did not follow the traditional strong taboo system that prevented those in Cobaría from showing interest in learning to read.

We put the large syllable chart on the bulletin board in our home. Everyone who came to the house looked at it. We were able to give them a brief explanation of how the word in the picture had the sound of the letters. It functioned as a prereading tool. Warawaná came every other day to continue with his reading lessons. He was reading openly when others were around and was able to explain the syllable chart to them.

As a means of stimulating interest in literacy, I wrote notes to Warawaná and Rayotá. They read them aloud for the other teenagers standing around. They responded to my notes in writing, and I read their responses aloud. The young people began to understand that writing is not some magical thing but rather a way of passing messages from one person to another.

Another prereading tool we created was a game of memory using drawings of local objects and animals. We wrote the name of each item on the card so they would see it as they played. It was a popular game, and teenagers would come to play in the afternoons after their day of work in the fields. One of them liked it so much he stole it. Knowing their taboos, we considered this a breakthrough rather than a loss. It was eventually returned.

Paul began translating the Gospel of Luke with José, who was becoming better and better at translation. Paul spent hours in preparation to make good use of the precious time he had with José, who was busy with his own work. Paul studied the passage and wrote a rough draft in his best Tunebo, noting the potential problem areas. When José came, they read the draft to get the whole picture, and then they worked through each verse, changing, adding, and deleting things to make it sound clear, accurate, and natural in Tunebo. Paul kept the tape recorder going during the entire session. Frequently, José would suggest another good rendering while Paul was still writing his previous change. The tape recorder kept Paul from losing those ideas. He was able to reverse the cassette tape and capture everything José had said.

In May 1977, we returned to Lomalinda for Paul to assume a group assignment serving as Assistant Director of Language Affairs for the summer. Warawaná and Rafael went with us. By then Warawaná, was about twenty, married, and soon to become a father. Rafael, one of José's younger sons, was about eighteen and recently married. He was fun loving as well as open to learning. They were there to help me translate Old Testament stories as well as to continue learning to read and write.

One evening after playing a game with the kids and putting them to bed, Warawaná, Rafael, and I were relaxing in our living room. I shared with them that one of the translators they knew was getting married. This opened a discussion of marriage customs. There was a sense of warmness and open communication as the conversation moved from one topic to another. They even brought up some of the shortcomings of the Uwa/Tunebo, which these proud people rarely admitted. They revealed their deep fear of strange people-like beings they see when they go alone into the rain forest. In my heart, I prayed, "What shall I say, Lord?" Warawaná picked up an English Bible to look at the pictures. He opened to a picture of a snake in the reference section. He asked what it was. I was thinking, *Why do they picture such symbols of evil in the Bible?* but I asked to see it and looked up the reference beside the picture. I found it and read, "Do not look at wine when it is red, when it sparkles in the cup and goes down smoothly. At the last it bites like a serpent and stings like an adder. Your eyes will see strange things and your mind will utter perverse things" (Prov. 23:31–32, NIV). I simultaneously translated to Tunebo for them as I read. That was the Lord's answer at that point for the people seeing spirits. It was a lesson to Warawaná and Rafael that the Bible speaks to the needs of their hearts.

Bondage to Satan

In August, when Paul finished his group assignment and the Tunebos returned from the lowlands, we returned to Cobaría once again. One day I visited Isaca, whose baby had died two years earlier. Since then she had been living in a little shelter. As Uwa custom dictated, Isaca had gone to the woods by herself to bury her child. It was the seventh time she had gone through this agonizing process. She had thought this child would live since he had grown and lived a little longer than the others. After burying the child, she trudged back to her hut sad, heavyhearted, and afraid. She wondered, *Why are the spirits attacking me? How can I save the two children I have left?*

Isaca's father, the shaman, had the same questions. He blew over his ceremonial feather, chewed his cocaine leaves, and sniffed his narcotic powder to get visions and an answer. He concluded Isaca and the two remaining children must live in semi-isolation for four years. A small shelter was made for her just above the village. There she was to live, eat, and sleep with her two little ones, without the company of her husband and their father. She was restricted from eating salt and even from going to her mother's house for a meal. During my visit with Isaca, I shared the story of God's power to protect them from evil spirits and the things Uwa/Tunebo fear.

A little farther over on the mountain was another shelter where Cona, the sister of one of our special friends, lived alone. Three years previously, when her brother died suddenly in the prime of his youth, I had visited the family and had wept with those who wept. I felt their grief as I also missed Cona's bright-eyed brother. Her mother confided that her son had been cursed and attacked by a spirit. Cona was singled out to pay the price to prevent another attack from the spirit. Their hope was to appease the spirit by compelling Cona to live alone, following many restrictions in her diet. My heart longed for her to know Jesus and His power over spirits.

26

CEREBRAL MALARIA

Epidemic

IN DECEMBER 1977, the Tunebos were stricken with an epidemic. At the time, we were at Lomalinda, unaware of their plight. Paul was doing exegesis, preparing for translation of the Gospel of Luke, while I drafted Old Testament stories. He was planning a trip to bring Warawaná and Rafael to the center to work with us in mid-February. We put a lot of hope in Warawaná. He was good at translation, open to the Scripture, and was becoming the fluent reader for whom we had prayed, hoped, and planned.

On February 10, the SIL office in Bogotá got a call from the Indian Affairs office. They had received word that Cobaría Tunebos were dying from an epidemic of typhoid. The Indian Affairs director asked SIL to send us out as part of a government medical team. He wanted us to act as interpreters and help vaccinate the people. We were in Bogotá to renew our passports at the time. The SIL Government Relations Director came to us and said, "Nineteen Tunebos have already died in an epidemic. The government wants you to go with their team to interpret for them." It took no time to decide we had to go.

We left Bogotá for Villavicencio on Monday morning, February 13, 1978, to meet the JAARS plane that would take us to the Tunebo area. The plane brought the meager supplies Paul had packed earlier for the trip he had planned. Esther Steen, a dear friend who had cared for our kids a number of times, was also in Bogotá. We looked at this as God's perfect timing as she gladly accepted the responsibility of taking Joy and Ronnie back to Lomalinda and caring for them. We urged our friends to pray for God's mercy to spare the lives of our Tunebo friends and for us as we'd be roughing it in a new area. We needed God's strength and wisdom.

After meeting the JAARS plane in Villavicencio, we flew with Captain Ron McIntosh as far as the town of Tame that afternoon. In the morning, we flew on to Saravena, where we met two doctors, a nurse, and a vaccinator. Paul went with the medical team in a jeep over the road to Cubará. The pilot and I flew over the area to locate the people. We spotted them in the lowlands where there was no airstrip. We returned and landed on the airstrip near Cubará and met Paul.

After getting as many details as possible from a few people in town, we went up to the large Catholic mission to get more information. We were surprised to see Warawaná's eight-year-old sister there. She told us that Ruiswiya (the baby we had cared for) and her fifteen-year-old sister had died within twenty-four hours of each other. She had been very sick herself, and that was why she was at the mission.

From Chuscal, we went on the narrow road (two tire tracks) to the lowlands. It was dry season, so we were able to drive through the shallow places in the rivers. We got fairly close to where the Indians were located and then walked half an hour on a narrow trail the rest of the way.

On arrival, they confirmed that nineteen people had died, including eight men in the prime of life who were heads of families. Several of them were our good friends. Their deaths brought a great hardship on those remaining. They were distressed with concern for their livelihood, as well as living in fear of the spirits, wondering who would be the next one to fall sick and die.

The doctors examined a number of people. We translated as they inquired about the history of the epidemic and the symptoms they experienced. They determined that it was more likely malaria than typhoid. We were all prepared with medicine for typhoid including immunizations, but no one had any malaria medicine, so that night, the doctors went all the way back to Saravena and got malaria medicine.

We spent next the day going from one Tunebo home to the next, translating for the medical team. They tested blood smears from about ten people. It was confirmed to be malaria, not typhoid. Late in the afternoon, the doctors and the others left us with the medicine and instructions. We camped out with the people the rest of the week and treated twenty-two very sick people. We were thankful they all responded to the treatment and were well or getting better when we left. Before leaving, we gave medicine with instructions how to take it to those who had gotten sick the day before.

Initially, we had thought we might be able to take Warawaná and Rafael back to Lomalinda with us as planned. However, we realized Warawaná was devastated by the loss of his sisters. It wasn't an option to take him away from his people. Rafael had to help his dad carry his sick stepmother back to the highlands, so he couldn't go either.

Our hearts were heavy when we returned to Lomalinda. We wondered, *Is Satan using this epidemic to thwart our efforts in translation and literacy?* We asked our friends to pray that the Lord would comfort Warawaná and the others who had lost loved ones and use the suffering to bring them to Himself.

We had seen only a small percent of the people in one location in the lowlands since the others were in a different location between there and Cobaría. We assumed others were sick, so at the earliest possible date in March we knew the Tunebos would return from their migration, we returned to Cobaría. Joy and

Ronnie stayed with Esther Steen again. Our prayer partner from Lomalinda, Ken Cromer, accompanied us.

On arrival, we found many Tunebos incapacitated, shaking with chills, and having high fevers, causing their bodies to ache. They were distraught with fear, wondering who would be next to die. Ken said he could feel the satanic oppression. As we made house-to-house rounds of the village, we found and treated sixty-five more people.

Warawaná's wife was among the critically ill. However, until the shaman had attempted to heal her with his incantations, he would not permit us to administer medicine to her. When we were finally allowed to treat her, the malaria apparently had gone to her brain. The medicine worked temporarily, and she showed a slight improvement. However, it was too late. She died within a few days.

When we heard she had died, we rushed over just in time to see Warawaná finish tying his wife's body in the customary large net bag, which is used for burial. He tied the last knot, leaned against a post, and sobbed. We cried with him. Paul went along with Warawaná and his father-in-law to help him with the burial. He was still in deep grief over the loss of his two sisters. However, he wasn't allowed to show his sorrow nor were others allowed to accompany him for the burial lest the spirits see them grieving and assume they wanted to go with the lost loved one. When Paul came home, our neighbors avoided him for a few days because he had been near a dead person.

After treating the sixty-five people in the highlands, where the mosquitoes that carry malaria from one person to another were not found, the epidemic subsided. However, in the first two or three days after our return, in addition to Warawaná's wife five others died. The disease was too far advanced for them to respond to treatment. People of all ages—men, women, and children—succumbed to the disease. Including those who died in the lowlands, by the first of April 1978, the death toll had reached twenty-six.

While we were in Cobaría, Joy and Ronnie were at Lomalinda for school. We learned of their activities on Saturday mornings as we talked to them by radio. Ronnie told of riding around the center on his bicycle, testing the speed and distance he went with his new speedometer. He put on ninety-one miles in about two weeks. He also reported about the fun he had with the boys in his Sunday school class on an overnight campout. It was worth all the time he spent memorizing Bible verses. Joy described going on the cable car to Monserrate when she had gone with her school class to Bogotá to learn more about Colombian culture. They both mentioned a special banquet that was coming up.

The medical work became less demanding when the malaria epidemic subsided, giving us more time for translation. José was helping me revise the Old Testament stories I had pretranslated. These were compelling stories that were interesting to the Tunebos. They presented important biblical truths that were new to them.

At supper one evening, after I had studied the story of Joseph all day with José, Paul and I reviewed the important points of the story: God was always with Joseph, even in jail. Although Joseph had been treated badly by his brothers and suffered imprisonment, he remained faithful to God's principles, even when away from his father. God worked for good in extremely difficult circumstances. Joseph forgave his brothers. The teachings were imbedded in a story filled with suspense and excitement.

Paul was finishing the first draft of Luke with José. He would like to have had help from Warawaná and Rafael to do the necessary comprehension testing on Luke, but they were not available to help due to the impact of the epidemic. We continued to pray for comfort for Warawaná and of all those who had lost loved ones. We helped them as we could.

God's Gifts in the Midst of Difficulties

After all the loss from malaria, God reassured me of His love through a series of special gifts. The first gift came before breakfast on Mother's Day. I was still in bed when I heard the familiar greeting "Eyariqui," in the Tegría dialect of the Uwa language. Juan and his brother had walked more than an hour to get to our house. He handed Paul a letter from one of the Spanish-speaking settlers who had been in the courses we gave. The letter said, "We have been using your primer to teach Juan and his brother, Aarón, to read. We want you to test them to see how they are doing." I had them read to me individually in Paul's office. They were as nervous as if they were taking comprehensive exams, but they both did well. Juan[1] was exceptional. He didn't make one mistake.

During the fifteen years we had been working with the Uwa/Tunebo, we had been able to get enough help to prepare the primers. However, the purification system and belief that everything from the outside was contaminated created a severe limitation on testing the primers. Now, Andrés and his brother, two young settlers with at most a fifth-grade education and a couple of weekend courses had used the primers to teach two Uwa to read in their own language. It was the proof we needed that the primers worked, a gift of encouragement from God. We thanked God for the demonstration of His love.

---

[1]   Juan went on to finish high school.

A Tunebo Believer

Andrés shared our concern for reaching the Uwa/Tunebo around him with the gospel of Jesus Christ. He had a deep love for the Lord, which grew as he read and studied his Bible guided by radio Bible correspondence courses. When Tunebos went to his house or he visited in theirs, he played the tapes we had given him of hymns and Bible stories in Tunebo. To open up discussion about the story, if any of the Indians could speak some Spanish, he asked them to explain the story. We gave Andrés a copy of the simple Tunebo grammar I had written to help him and others like him learn to speak Tunebo. We were pleased that he had come to understand the need to reach them in their own language. Andrés's help in evangelizing was another special gift from God.

Andrés came another day with news that was the best gift of all. He excitedly told us how he had been teaching the Word of God and ministering to Juan. He took him to services at the small chapel where the settlers worshipped. Juan understood his need for forgiveness and a Savior. He prayed to receive Christ. He was hungry to know more of God's Word. Andrés was thrilled that Juan had accepted Christ into his heart and life as Lord and Savior. It was a day of rejoicing! We sat at the table while Andrés sang hymns, read scripture, and prayed. We wanted to encourage this young believer who was leading others to the Lord. Andrés had a skip in his step as he started down the trail.

Radio Phone Patch

In May, after school was out at Lomalinda, having Joy and Ronnie join us in Cobaría along with two of Joy's school teachers was a special gift. When the Tunebos saw our kids, they were amazed at how fast they had grown in comparison to their own children. They were six or more inches taller than Tunebo children their own age.

Joy's teachers, who were short-term assistants (serving for a year or two), had come to learn more of village life and translation. It was a special treat for Joy and Ronnie to be able to show the teachers the Tunebo village and the way of life there. Ronnie was able to take them to the forest with the Tunebos to bring in firewood and to go hunting. Having the kids with us in the village was another gift from God.

Two weeks after the kids and their teachers arrived, the Tunebos were again preparing for their migration to the lowlands and we for Bogotá. It was pouring rain the day we were to leave, delaying the flight. Finally, the center radioed us to head for the airstrip. After we had walked three hours down and up the mountains to the airstrip, I saw the pilot walking toward me. I wondered what this could mean. Then I saw he had a telegram in his hand. In a few brief words, it said, "Mother died yesterday afternoon." What a shock! Just that morning, I had received radio messages that her condition was stable after her major cancer surgery.

Paul and I briefly discussed the situation. Weight limitations taking off from the short airstrip made it necessary for the pilot to make three shuttle flights to get our family and the two teachers to the nearest town. We immediately made the decision that I would be on the first flight out to Saravena to see if I could arrange for a commercial flight to Bogotá from there. Then I would be able to travel on to Minnesota for the funeral.

When I got to town, I learned there were no commercial flights because it was a Colombian holiday. About 5:30 in the afternoon, when the last load arrived, the pilot said to me, "Do you want to try to call your family?"

I thought, *He has to be kidding. At this time of day with the plane on the ground, all he will get on the radio is static and bells.* But I said, "Sure you can try."

He radioed our center, Lomalinda. To my astonishment we heard them clearly reply, "Lomalinda, 612." From Lomalinda, they called a ham operator in Dallas. Again astoundingly, we heard an immediate clear reply. From Dallas, the ham operator did a radio phone patch to Minneapolis. Much to my joy, my sister Joan answered as clearly as if she were next door. That was another gift, a special little miracle God did for me at that time as if to say, "I know this is hard for you, but I still love and care about you."

Although I couldn't go for the funeral, Joan's son came to Colombia for the summer. He brought all the sympathy cards with him. Reading those helped me feel more in touch with the family.

Gift of Three Roots

There had been one tiny unmistakable glimmer of sunshine that lightened our hearts during the severe malaria epidemic in 1978: bright-eyed six-year-old Enyasa, grandson of the chief. He came almost daily to listen to the Scripture tapes. Even in the midst of all the distractions, Enyasa listened. On some occasions, he brought his cousin to listen with him.

In August, when we and the Tunebos returned to Cobaría, we learned that little Enyasa had been sick for some time with the dreaded malaria. The Tunebos were fasting and strictly adhering to the taboos. These taboos included a prohibition from taking medicine.

By the time these restrictions were lifted, Enyasa was seriously ill. His maternal grandfather asked me to treat him. We gave him the bitter malaria medicine with help from the adults, but with his spitting and crying, we weren't sure how much he actually got. After several days of mounting tension and resistance, we were asked not to continue giving medicine. We respected their wishes.

Weeks later, I saw Enyasa. He had become a mere living skeleton of skin and bones. In his compromised condition, intestinal parasites had taken over. I told his mother I could come to their house in the morning to give him worm medicine that had to be taken on an empty stomach. She acknowledged agreement.

That night, I slept fitfully. Lying half-awake, I kept thinking about Enyasa. In the early hours of dawn, I got up. I faced the chill of the mountain air and struggled down the muddy steep trail to their house. His mother informed me she was going to take him to the witch doctor. I should wait.

I responded, "There isn't time to wait for the witch doctor. Enyasa might die."

We both stood in silence for an uncomfortably long period of time. Finally she said, "All right, if it's good, give it to him, but if he dies, it is your fault."

With fear and trembling, I gave Enyasa the worm medicine. Later, I radioed our center for prayer. It was reported to us he had passed a significant quantity of worms. I followed up with vitamins and iron. However, after a few days, I began to sense resistance, so Paul and I made the decision to commit Enyasa to the Lord for healing and stop any further treatment.

Enyasa's mother was a good friend, but I felt a barrier had come between us. I wanted to clear this up. At the same time, I sensed that if I went to her, she would only think I had come to hassle her about giving more medicine. I reminded the Lord that He could send her to me. Several days later, she came with a gift of three large edible roots. Those roots were another gift from God, a deep reminder of His love and encouragement in a difficult situation.

Enyasa recovered. As soon as he was well, he came back with his little sister in tow to listen to the Scripture tapes. We prayed that someday Enyasa would become a Christian leader among the Tunebo people.

A Song

While we were in the lowlands during the malaria epidemic, we had had a frightening experience that left an impression on us we will never forget. If we ever saw a case of demon possession, that was it. We saw a young man we had previously known as a normal intelligent person lying on the ground with his arms and legs flinging uncontrollably through the air. He was like an animal that had turned on its back and couldn't help himself. His writhing went on for quite some time. We prayed and sang every song we could think of that mentioned the blood of Jesus. It is His blood that protects us from Satan's attacks. The young man finally stopped thrashing and returned to normal.

That experience motivated us to write more songs about the Lord in the Tunebo language. In their ceremonial dances, they sang or chanted from dusk to dawn. Music was their way of passing on their traditions. Their songs enumerated the names of all the mountain peaks and all the animals. The songs were generally in an archaic form of the language that was difficult to understand. We wanted to use their style of music to communicate the truths of God, in a way even a child could understand.

Paul had studied their music and discovered they had a three-note scale. Using those three notes and their type of rhythm, he composed a catchy tune the people liked. I worked on the words. We were not able to write a song that lasted from dusk to dawn, but it did have ninety-five verses! Rather than list mountain peaks, I included names of people by family groups, expressing God's love for each person. After each group of four or five, there was a section saying, "God's son is Jesus. He is powerful. He intercedes before God for people," and then an attribute of God that speaks to them in their culture. These attributes included the following: "He sends the rain,"[1] "He makes the sun shine,"[2] "He

---

[1]   Deut. 11:4.

[2]   Gen. 1:3–6.

protects us from evil spirits,"[3] "He gives us the animals for food,"[4] and "He heals the sick."[5]

We tried to include truths in a way that gently confronted some of their beliefs that are in opposition to the Bible. In Genesis 1, it is clear that God gave man dominion over the animals. In contrast, the Uwa believed each animal species was owned by a specific spirit. In order to placate that spirit, they needed to follow many restrictions or taboos. Some of these taboos included a prohibition against eating salt before going hunting and not allowing the bones of the animal to touch the ground. (We often found bones wrapped in a leaf tucked into the maguey plant in our yard.)

The need to teach these truths had come to light when I translated the first three chapters of Genesis. The concept that all the plants and trees were given to people by God to use freely for their food was beyond their conception. They believed the plants also belonged to spirits that needed to be placated before they could eat the food.

We sang this song and others when we visited the people in their homes in the afternoons when they came home from work in their fields. We also tape-recorded the songs and played them for the Tunebos when they visited in our home in Cobaría. They really seemed to enjoy listening especially when we came to the names of their family. One time, as we were singing, one of the people listening said, "Wow! Paul has become a shaman!" They liked the rhythm and tune. As they listened to the songs over and over, they heard the truth of God's love. More than once, we heard children singing the hymns on the trail. We had found a means to relate to them in a form that they liked and understood.

---

[3]   Luke 7:21, Ps. 32:7.

[4]   Gen. 1:28.

[5]   Mark 1:34.

(While writing this book, I heard that a man who had frequently visited us as a boy still remembered the songs forty years later.)

27

SECURITY DETERIORATES

Threatened by Armed Guerillas

ALTHOUGH IN 1975 activists had tried to stop the work of SIL in Colombia through public opinion in the media and political pressure, in 1979, SIL still had linguist translators in indigenous areas throughout the country. However, the security situation in Colombia had become of great concern in a number of areas in the country especially on the borders.

Dottie Cook and Fran Gralow, a translation team, lived among the Koreguaje in southern Colombia near the Ecuador border. They had been in their jungle location two and a half weeks when on Sunday, January 28, 1979, they were forced to flee for their lives. Fran had left early that morning to go upriver to a town to get supplies they needed. Dottie remained in the village with the Koreguaje.

Shortly after Fran left, two unknown men were seen in the area asking questions about the "white women." Since there had been earlier rumors about guerrilla activities in the area, Dottie was suspicious and radioed our Lomalinda center with this information. The radio operator passed the information on to the director.

Later that morning, while Dottie was visiting with some of the Koreguaje Indians in her house, nine masked men suddenly rushed in and at gunpoint ransacked the house, taking anything of value—money, tape recorders, typewriters, and foodstuffs. They also took the two-way radio, which was Dottie's only means of contact with our center. Before leaving, they told Dottie they would have killed her on the spot if she had been a man and threatened to kill her if she and her coworker remained in the area.

Meanwhile, shortly after Dottie's radio contact with Lomalinda, the director had sent one of the JAARS planes to bring the women back. As soon as the intruders left, Dottie quickly gathered up a few items and, with the help of an Indian, located a canoe and headed up river and found Fran. Together they continued upriver, to the next town where it might be safer.

By this time, the pilot, George DeVoucalla, was flying low over the Koreguaje village, but he did not see the women. He then flew upriver to search for them. A short time later, he spotted them in the canoe. He dropped a note telling them the plane would be waiting for them in a town further up river. When George radioed the news, the Lomalinda radio operator felt a tremendous sense of relief and gratefulness.

It was dark at 7:30 p.m. when the women finally reached safety. The next morning, they were flown back to Lomalinda, very tired and emotionally drained, but very relieved. Dottie said the Lord kept reminding her throughout this experience of Psalm 56, "When I am afraid, I will trust in Thee."[6]

Two weeks after Dottie and Fran's narrow escape, Paul went to the Tunebo lowland area to get José to bring him to work with us at Lomalinda. This had been arranged two months previously. The Tunebos were on the Colombia Venezuela border at the

---

[6]   Extracted from a letter dated February 2, 1979, and sent to Wycliffe supporters; written by Will Kindberg, director, Summer Institute of Linguistics, Colombia Panama branch.

opposite end of the country from the Koreguajes, so Paul felt confident in making the trip.

On the way to pick up José, Paul had an unplanned contact with a group of four local government officials. It was an opportunity to build positive relations at a time when things were not going well. He gave the men a brief overview of our work. One of them was aware of what we were doing and spoke highly of it as the others listened. That was a real encouragement in contrast to the recent bad press about SIL in the Colombian newspapers.

When we had left Cobaría in November, José had been quite sick with what seemed to be a kidney stone. He didn't want medicine, so there was nothing we could do. It was hard to imagine what we would do without José if something happened to him. We had committed him to the Lord's care. Since we hadn't had contact with him after we left, Paul wasn't sure whether José would be able to accompany him to the workshop as he had agreed.

Many had prayed with us that José would come to Lomalinda to help translate the First Letter of Peter. God answered those prayers. Paul found José well enough to travel. He came to Lomalinda to help with translation as planned. We believed that God had something special for José during his time there.

Each morning during the workshop, the translators worked together with a biblical scholar studying the exegesis, or explanation, of the passage. They also compared notes on potential ways of rendering the selection in the various languages. In the afternoon, each translator worked with his translation assistant on the same verses.[7]

We had hoped and prayed that José might give his life to the Lord while with us in a Christian setting. We thought that his meeting believers from other Indian groups, having daily

---

[7]   Paul suggested different renderings for an accurate translation of a verse in Tunebo. José then helped him make it clearer and more natural.

opportunities to hear hymns and God's Word in his language, and the intense study necessary for the translation of 1 Peter would change his heart. But he apparently couldn't bring himself to make that commitment. He was leader of the ritual dances the Tunebos were convinced kept the world from coming to an end. He also performed purification ceremonies for those returning to the village from the outside. Although he always seemed open to God's Word and enjoyed translation, much to our disappointment, we never had any assurance he accepted the Lord.

Let Down by Friends

In April 1979, after a short time back in Cobaría, we began to realize all was not well in the Tunebo area where we worked near the Venezuela border. It was hard to actually identify the cause, but we sensed tension. April 17, which happened to be Paul's birthday, he was invited to the community action meeting of settlers in Tunebo territory. "I wonder what they might want. It doesn't sound good," I said skeptically. Paul wasn't concerned because they had always been our friends. He thought they probably wanted help with some project. I agreed they had been friends. We had visited in their homes and they in ours. We had treated their injuries and illnesses for many years. They had even sawed the lumber for our house. A number of them were believers and had attended the courses we held to teach them to read in Tunebo.

The leader was solemn as he called the meeting to order. He said, "Paul, we asked you to come because we have some questions to ask you. We want to know what your program is in this area, and second, we want to know what your attitude is about the road that is being built."

Most of them knew very well our reason for being there. It was the second question they were really interested in pursuing. When he heard that question, Paul realized this was not going to be a friendly meeting. He wondered, *Is this part of the tension we are feeling? Are these friends being influenced against us by outsiders?*

They were apparently upset because we had taken Tunebos to the capital city. Some of those had spoken up in government offices against the road that was coming into the area. The settlers wanted the road to take their coffee and other products to town. The Tunebos opposed the road because it would bring in more settlers. They didn't want more people who would clear land thus limiting available forest where game animals thrive. Paul felt caught between a rock and a hard place. He sympathized with the settlers' need for an easier way to bring in supplies and take out their products. At the same time, our purpose for being there was to reach and help the Tunebos.

Paul tried to tactfully explain his understanding of their needs. At the same time, he endeavored to help them comprehend the Tunebo point of view, their need of land for hunting, gathering, and their fields. There were eight hundred or more Tunebos in the area and only twenty to thirty settlers. The settlers weren't convinced.

Someone suggested that Don Juan stop renting Paul the land for the airstrip. Others agreed, figuring that would force him into siding with them. Finally, one spoke for the rest. "Paul, if you don't stop helping Indians oppose the road, we'll close the airstrip." They knew we wouldn't be able to come in or bring our supplies to Cobaría without the airstrip. Then Paul reminded them of the five-year contract he had on the airstrip and the improvements he had made to the land. They recanted and agreed he could continue to use it until the lease ran out.

Paul left the meeting wondering what would happen. Without the airstrip, our work would be effectively curtailed, if not completely stopped. Yet he couldn't reject helping the Tunebos in one of their areas of need—protection of their traditional lands.

That summer, we were scheduled for a time in the United States. We looked forward to a break from the political pressure, the demands of translation work, and of village living. It had been a year since my mother had died, and I still hadn't seen my dad or the rest of the family. Paul's brother was home from his work with SIL in the Philippines. It had been years since we had seen him and his family. They were in California with Paul's mother. At the end of the school year in May, we flew from Lomalinda to Bogotá in the JAARS plane, from there to Miami and on to California. The kids fit right in with their Headland cousins. Missionary kids share a lot in common. Sometimes they are called third-culture kids because they are neither really culturally American nor of the country where their parents serve. They often feel more comfortable being with each other than being with kids from their parents' home country.

All too soon, our time with the Headland family came to a close. We started early in the morning from Southern California to cross the desert before it got too hot. We were on our way to study at the Summer Institute of Linguistics in Oklahoma. By 9:00 a.m. Paul was burning hot, not just from the desert heat but also with a fever of over 104 degrees. We stopped in Indio, California, and got a motel room. We had some penicillin with us, so I naively went to a drug store to buy a syringe. They wouldn't sell me one. I remembered somewhere in our luggage we had a glass syringe, so I went to the Goodwill store looking for something I could use to boil the syringe. I found and bought an old-fashioned popcorn popper. Back in motel room I filled it with water and boiled the syringe. By this time I was on edge, hoping no one would see me and think we were taking drugs, but I managed to get the penicillin mixed and injected into Paul's hip. His temperature was normal the next morning, and we traveled on to Norman, Oklahoma.

At SIL that summer, we took advanced courses to improve our translation skills. We also took guided studies with experienced linguists. I felt honored to be mentored by my hero, Dr. Mildred Larson, a leading translator and scholar who worked in Peru. Paul was encouraged to be directed by Dr. Joe Grimes from Mexico SIL. Paul and I each analyzed different aspects of the Tunebo discourse grammar.[1] These studies resulted in articles that were later published.

At the end of the summer course in Oklahoma we went to Minnesota. It was hard to go home for the first time after my mother died. The rest of the family had had more than a year to feel the loss of our mother firsthand, but I was at a different stage in my grief. I hadn't seen my dad without her. I hadn't felt the emptiness of home without my mother being there to run excitedly to the car to meet us. She had always been a servant waiting on all of us, fixing and serving our favorite foods. God comforted me in my loss.

Jean Smith, "Mrs. Missions" of Grace Church Edina, blessed us with her sacrifice. She moved out of her home into one room at a friend's house so we could have her whole house to ourselves. Her unselfish act did not go unnoticed. Jean's generosity proved to my brother-in-law, Cully Arneson, that Christianity is real.

Later that fall, with Paul's guidance, Cully made the decision to receive Christ as his Lord and Savior. He was changed and became a vibrant witness. It was a day we will never forget.

Joy and Ronnie attended public school for two months. In all of Ronnie's years of school through twelfth grade, that was the only time he attended school in the States. (Joy had been there for first grade). During their fall break, they enjoyed the unforgettable experience of traveling across part of Canada in a train with a number of families from Grace Church. Both Joy

---

[1]   Edna Headland, "To say *said* or not to say *said*," Quote Margins in Tunebo. "Forma, posición y uso de fórmulas citativas en tunebo." Publicado en "Artículos en Lingüística y campos afines," Número 10. Instituto Lingüístico de Verano (1979); Headland, Paul, Notes on Translation. "Words that get people to do things: Translating imperative meanings" (1997).

and Ronnie were baptized as a testimony of their belief in Christ as their Savior by Pastor Ricker at Grace Church.

By the end of October, we had shared our burden to see the Tunebos open their hearts to Christ with our supporting churches and many individual supporters. Once again, the Lord used His people to bless us with their hospitality, words of encouragement, prayers, and gifts. After saying good-bye to family and friends, we were on the way to Colombia.

28

FOILED PLANS

Planning in Uncertainty

AFTER SETTLING IN and getting the kids back in school, the next thing on the agenda was doing the necessary paper work to once again renew our visas. This entailed a trip to the city to be fingerprinted. We went with photos and documents in hand and soon had the necessary visa stamped in our passports.

Immediately following that, we attended planning sessions. A year previously, while Paul was in administration, the branch had established a new requirement for all translators to make finalizing plans for their work. To consider our work complete, we needed to answer among others the following questions: What conditions should be in place to assure the translated Scriptures would be used? What literacy materials did we still need to produce to prepare students to read and teachers to teach to assure that materials would continue to be used? Had we written the linguistic articles and dictionaries to fulfill SIL's contract with the government? Were there believers who could and would use the Scriptures to teach others? As well as finalizing plans, we were to make monthly, yearly, and three-year plans in each of these areas: literacy, translation, linguistics, and scripture use.

We found it particularly challenging to make a plan to finalize our work, which included assurance of enough literate people and believers to guarantee the use of the materials we were producing, especially the New Testament. Even the monthly and yearly plans were difficult with the uncertainty of the availability of Tunebo translation assistants and people interested in learning to read and in teaching others

On faith, we made a plan to hold a two-month course from May 15 to July 15, 1980, to teach Warawaná, Rayotá, and Rafael or Juan how to teach reading. We planned classes to teach them beginning teaching skills as well as to increase their fluency in reading and writing. Part of the plan was to bring in a beginning student for each of them to work with. We requested prayer for God to work out all the circumstances necessary to make this plan a reality, especially that the Tunebos would actually go to Lomalinda for the course.

In addition to formulating these plans, we both began work on proofreading the books that had been laid out for printing in the printshop while we were gone. Paul went through the book of Luke while I proofed the summary of Genesis, Job, and Exodus. We were thankful the work had continued while we were gone. We were part of a larger team, each doing their part to provide God's Word to all the indigenous groups in Colombia in their own language. There were printers, artists, pilots, mechanics, radio operators, school teachers, finance people, administrators, and others who served with the same vision as the linguist translators.

Not Even the Last Choice

We wrote our supporters in January 1980: "Pray that Warawaná would be willing, ready and available to come if he is God's choice to work on Galatians. If he is not God's choice pray that José would come." After writing, we began to feel strongly that José would be a better choice than Warawaná to translate the difficult book of Galatians. The week before the trip, Paul prayed, "If it is Your will, God, don't let anything prevent José from coming."

On February 11, Paul, accompanied by Ronnie, made the trip as planned, arriving in the Tunebo lowland area on February 12. The trip seemed to be going like clockwork as he made unusually good arrangements for transportation over the controversial road that was entering the Tunebo area. He found José with no problem and was given an abandoned house to use for the night. But when the crucial issue of going to Lomalinda to work was mentioned, the response was negative. José had been sick and was under a two-year restriction from going to the outside world. Apparently, the shaman related his sickness to his trip to Lomalinda for the 1 Peter workshop the previous year. I felt bad about that because in reality, he had been very sick and weak before he went to Lomalinda. There, with good nutrition and rest, he regained strength and was strong enough to work hard in his fields for several months after he returned to Cobaría. We saw no relationship between his illness and his time with us. Although José would not accompany Paul to Lomalinda, he promised to work with him when we returned to Cobaría after the workshop.

Paul's first thought was, *All is not lost; this is the Lord's way of showing me His choice really is Warawaná after all.* However, Paul learned that just two days before, on February 10, Warawaná had walked down that same road leading to the outside world. He was going out to find work. Paul checked on a couple of others, but they were "too busy."

On the trip back to town, it was hard to say whether the thirty-pound pack on Paul's back or his heart was heavier. No vehicles passed, so Paul and Ronnie had to walk the whole six hours carrying a pack, quite a hike for Ronnie, who was just twelve years old. He did well, enjoying his first trip to the Tunebo lowlands. Paul, at the same time, was questioning in his heart, *Is it really God's will that not even our last choices of language helpers are willing to come?*

One consolation after his disappointment was the opportunity to stop at María's house. She was the literate Tunebo who had been reviewing our translation. Over lemonade, she and Paul began to make plans to work together face-to-face in the future.

Back in town, while Paul and Ronnie waited for the plane, Paul had fun surprising some Indians from another village by greeting them in their language. They had never seen him before and couldn't figure out who had spoken to them. They looked around and could only see white people. When they finally figured out it was Paul, they started talking to him. They were probably testing to see if he could understand more than the greetings. While conversing with them, Paul felt moved to see if one of them would want to help him with translation. Amazingly, one of the young men, Reinaldo, spoke up and said he would accompany Paul. He was willing to drop everything right then to go to an unknown place with a total stranger who spoke his language. Within two hours, he was in the plane with Paul and Ronnie on his way to Lomalinda. He seemed to adapt quickly to sitting with our family at the table and eating our food using fork, knife, and spoon. He adjusted to being at the desk for long hours, giving help with the language as Paul worked on the translation of Galatians. Considering he was used to working in the field, his adjustment was amazing. He enjoyed learning to read.

Although our immediate need for translation help was met by Reinaldo, something had happened to both Paul and me as a result of his trip in February. We had begun to have a feeling our work in Cobaría was futile. We questioned, "How can we ever do an adequate translation without people to work with us? If we translate, who will use the Scriptures if the shaman doesn't allow people to have books in their homes?"

It had been eight years since the furlough when I had studied the life of David in Bible Study Fellowship. I had committed myself at that time to preparing materials for the Tunebo church, even if I couldn't see the church formed. A lot of materials were ready, but the main one, the New Testament was only partially done. Could I turn back on that commitment now?

In submission to God, immediately after the workshop, we returned to Cobaría. Reinaldo was overjoyed to be back in familiar territory. He confessed he wasn't sure he would ever see home again. He said a quick good-bye and started up the mountain to his village six hours away. We never saw him again.

During our first three weeks in Cobaría, José didn't show up once, even though he had promised he would help Paul when we came back. In fact, one day, Paul arranged with José to work at his house. José agreed, but when Paul showed up, he was shocked to hear the usually gentle José say firmly, "Stay out of my house. You have a lot of germs." His son informed Paul he was taking José to the field to live because it was too far to carry firewood to the house. He went on to hassle him about not doing enough to stop the road coming into the lowland area. Paul came back home dejected.

We felt caught in the middle. The settler who owned our airstrip land had recently told us of the pressure he was getting from someone who said, "With that gringo up there stopping it in Bogotá, you will never have a road!" He threw in some other cutting blows like, "What good does it do to make all those books for people who can't read?"

We began to wonder if it would be possible to implement our plan to have a literacy teacher training workshop. Warawaná, who was our prime candidate, was still on the outside working for whites, and hearsay was that he wouldn't be back until August. We feared he might not come back to the village at all. Rafael, who we also hoped would participate in the workshop, had been out in town somewhere for more than a year. No one seemed to know if he were coming back even though he had wife and a beautiful baby. Rayotá, the oldest of the three potential participants from Cobaría, had left his lovely wife and three children for a young girl. He was hiding out since everyone was upset with him. Juan, from Tegría, whom Andrés and his brother had taught to read, was going to school in town. I felt greatly frustrated with the barrier to our work posed by the taboo against paper. Barring a miracle, the literacy workshop was out of the question. Apparently rumors were circulating that we were going to start a school. We had promised them we would not do that unless they requested it.

In our discouragement, we even began to question our medical work. One of José's grandsons was gravely ill with malaria. I was asked to treat him. I gave him the malaria medicine, but when the boy didn't recover immediately, the father was impatient. He said, "I'm going to call a shaman. We will ask the devil to make him better." I strongly advised them not to do that but to wait for the medicine to take effect. But they didn't wait. They called a shaman, who came and prayed to the devil. Meanwhile the medicine took effect, and the boy recovered. The parents were quite pleased that the witch doctor "had healed their boy" and thought the medicine was of no value. It was hardly a fair test, but this boy was not the first to have been "healed by the shaman" under such circumstances.

Medical work had been part of our ministry from the beginning. The people needed it. It was effective, and many lives had been saved through the years. But we questioned, *Is it right to treat people in such circumstances? Is it honoring to God to treat people when they give the shaman or the devil credit for the results of the medicine? Are we just promoting their belief in the power of their spirits? It didn't seem like they were being fair to us by calling in someone else right after they had our help. But would it be right to withhold help?* We didn't have the answer. We considered staying with the sick overnight several nights as well as all day, but that was hardly possible. We were left in a dilemma.

After three weeks, José finally came back to work with Paul. He wouldn't enter our house, so they worked in the open on the porch. Paul was able to work through Galatians with him, comparing the Old Testament laws to the Tunebo taboos and the freedom that comes in Christ. Paul felt certain José understood, but again, there was no open commitment to Christ.

Paul wrote to his mother, confessing he was more discouraged than ever before. He said, "Usually I buoy Edna up, but this time she has buoyed me up." We learned to appreciate the verse, "Two people are better off than one, for they can help each other succeed. If one person falls, the other can reach out and help. But someone who falls alone is in real trouble" (Eccles. 4:9, NLT).

When It Rains It Pours

The end of May, when it was time to leave, was the worst of the rainy season in Cobaría. Sometimes, when it rains, it pours in more ways than one. Joy was graduating from eighth grade on Wednesday evening. We scheduled our flight back to Lomalinda for Monday. It was a rainy day, so we waited at the house until about 1:30 p.m. when they radioed us that the plane was on its way to get us. It was raining in Cobaría when we left the house. Because there were still low clouds when we got to the airstrip, Paul sent the young men who had carried our packs out to the forest to get some firewood and leaves for us to sleep on. The shack where we were to wait was a rather depressing sight; the wet floor with puddles became sloppy mud from the people walking around. Soon we had it covered with leaves and had a nice fire going. I started cooking our supper with hopes of leaving early in the morning. We became even more optimistic when the rain stopped and we could see stars in the sky. We kept the fire going and tried to settle down and get some sleep. We learned that night that mud is soft. We actually slept a little.

The morning was beautiful, inspiring us to quickly fix breakfast over the open fire so we would be ready to leave. But seven o'clock came, then eight, then nine—still no plane. We began to worry and set up the radio; however, the antenna was broken, making it impossible to make contact. By ten o'clock, it was raining, and we settled down to wait some more. We dug into our duffle for some ground corn we were taking to Lomalinda and made soup for lunch.

Around 3:00 p.m., I was sitting on my folded-up sleeping bag when one of the Tunebos casually told me I was sitting in a puddle of water. It had seeped in unnoticed under the leaves on the floor. We quickly hung the sleeping bag over the fire to dry. Shortly after that, all the carriers went back home for the day. Paul and Aarón, who was going with us, went out to find fresh leaves. I threw out the old ones, squatted down and started dipping up water with a cup and bowl. Precisely at that moment, Andrés, one of the Christian settlers, arrived to find me in this terrible mess. He went out, cut, and brought in poles and made a rustic bed frame on which he and Paul laid corrugated roofing. A rather lumpy bed, but better than sleeping in muddy water.

Andrés stayed with us, and we spent the evening around the fire singing. He taught us a new song, "Demos Gracias al Señor," (We Give Thanks to the Lord). He was a blessing sent from God to lift our spirits.

The next morning the weather was still bad. It was now Wednesday, the day of Joy's eighth-grade graduation. After waiting expectantly all day at 4:00 p.m., we realized that even if the plane came, we would not be able to fly to Lomalinda before dark. We were going to miss the graduation. By that time, Andrés was back. He had graciously made the trip to our house and had gotten our good antenna for the radio. We radioed Lomalinda and talked to Joy. Paul, Joy, and I all cried. It was hard to understand why we had to miss such a special event.

Shortly after our talk, we saw some patches of blue in the sky and heard the familiar hum of the airplane. George, our pilot, landed, loaded up, and lost no time making the necessary shuttles to get us to the larger airstrip near town. We spent the night in Cubará. While there, we made contact with a relative of María.

She gave us the book of Acts with the notes María had made. We also tried to locate Warawaná to go with us to the planned literacy training, but he was nowhere to be found.

Our literacy push was now down to Aarón, Juan's half-brother. He was a shy teenager who lived with his mother in an isolated house far up a canyon. We were disappointed he was the only one who came. We were tempted to send him home, but he was so eager to take the course he had valiantly waited with us on the airstrip for three days in the rain. We couldn't bring ourselves to send him home.

Although it seemed like a lot of effort for one person, I taught him classes in reading and writing at several levels, helping him develop skill in sounding out words as well as gain fluency in reading different types of material. Paul taught him Bible using the Gospel of Luke and the Genesis, Job and Exodus summary, which had just come off the press. Ronnie taught him math, and a friend taught him Spanish.

As we worked with Aarón, we realized the need for more simple reading books in Tunebo. As a result, we wrote and made ten copies each of five more small books for reading practice: one on malaria; another teaching where salt, metal, and paper come from; one of the stories Aarón wrote; and two were stories of other Tunebos we had recorded on tape. We had a little ceremony for Aarón when he completed two months of study with us and arranged for him to go home so we could have time as a family before returning to Cobaría ourselves.

We went as a family to Bogotá. Joy and Ronnie had earned a rest too. Between classes with Aarón, I had given them typing lessons. They diligently practiced the key strokes using the proper fingers. In addition to helping at home, Joy had babysat, and Ronnie had cleaned offices. They were excited to go to the big city where they could spend some of their hard-earned money. Joy bought jeans and shoes, and Ronnie got cowboy boots. After a few days in Bogotá, we took a family vacation in a small cottage in the mountains near Bogotá. On return to Lomalinda, we settled the kids in school, arranging for them to stay with other families. Paul and I returned to Cobaría.

Not long after our arrival in Cobaría, totally out of the blue, Paul got a subpoena to appear before the judge in town to testify about the burglary of our house six years earlier. Only determination to respect the law made Paul walk the two days each way to and from town to appear before the judge. But when he got there, the judge himself was out of town. This incident served to add to our suspicion that something was going on that we didn't understand.

Even with the undercurrent of things we weren't fully aware of, we continued with our usual activities as much as possible. We worked on translation with Búswara and José, who was coming more regularly. Paul finished translating 1 and 2 Timothy, 1 and 2 Thessalonians and Titus with José and moved on to 1 Corinthians. He reviewed the same portions with Búswara to check for understanding. While Paul worked with one of them, I worked with the other on portions from 1 Samuel.

One day I prayed that we would be able to make contact with Andrés to make arrangements to have the third short course at his family's farm to continue teaching some of the Christian settlers how to use the Scriptures and literacy materials in Tunebo. He lived two hours of hard walking away, and there were no telephones. A few minutes later, I felt like Rhoda in the book of Acts when the disciples were praying that Peter would be released from prison. There was Andrés standing at our door. We thanked the Lord for that evidence of His care. Andrés agreed to attend and host the course although he thought no one would come. We said if no one else came, we would do it for just him and his brother. It turned out that in addition to Andrés, two of his brothers and their pastor participated. The pastor showed interest in working with the Tunebos.

Every little encouragement from the people motivated us. One day after reading Scripture in our friend Sinará's home, he asked me to bring it again the next time I came. That simple request brightened my day. We frequently went to homes and read Scripture to whomever would listen, but there were only two of us. We prayed and longed for the day that some of the Tunebos themselves would go out and read to their friends and relatives.

Young boys came to our house to play memory and other preliteracy games. We enjoyed playing with them and teaching what we could through games, but without any commitment to study and learn on their part, it seemed impossible to get beyond that. While they played games, we kept the tape player going with Tunebo Scriptures or hymns in the background.

Medical work was another area that was affected by the undercurrent. Paul wrote,

> The Lord really spoke to me the other day. I had been giving some medicine to the kid next door. The grandfather got terribly upset and tried to knock it out of my hand. It was so disappointing as I thought I had his cooperation. They had asked us to treat the child.
>
> Later as I walked along the trail after visiting another house, I prayed, "God, my relationship with these people is growing into a battle, not love and understanding. I am finding myself wishing ill to these people instead of good will. Lord, I know the language, and I don't want to quit. But with desires like that, how can I serve? God, give me an attitude of a servant—to be unappreciated but still serving. But, God, please send me to another group of Tunebos. Get me an invitation elsewhere."
>
> Before I went home, I stuck my head into the neighbor's house to say hello. The wife of the man who tried to knock the medicine out of my hand ran across the house and said in a half whisper, "Paul, don't be mad. Don't stop treating the baby. En was here. He would become very upset and angry if we would have let you treat the baby without

opposing you. But we want you to treat him. Give him the afternoon dose when he wakes up from his nap!" All the others joined in to say the same thing.

I had thought the situation was hopeless—the whole village against Edna and me. But God showed me through that occasion that the village was polarized, and there are some who only conformed because they feared the opposition. They are with us. One day they will oppose En openly and hopefully take their stand for Christ. I'm longing for that day and am no longer looking to go elsewhere.

Another day, Paul was sharing Scriptures and discussing them with a young man. They talked about a number of things, including the fact that believers are to expect persecution according to the Scriptures and teachings of Jesus. José was sitting nearby listening quietly without comment. At that point, he spoke up and said, "That is well said." It suddenly dawned on us that José might be suffering persecution for helping us work on translation. We began to wonder, *Is José a secret believer?* We really didn't know, but we certainly hoped so. We also hoped if he were a believer, he would stand up openly for Christ.

Vaccinations

During their fall break, Joy and Ronnie and two of their friends, Peter and Camilla, came to be with us for ten days. Prior to their arrival, we had heard there was whooping cough in an area nearby. We clearly remembered the twelve babies who died in the whooping cough epidemic nearly fifteen years earlier. We didn't want that to happen again. We requested vaccine, packed with ice, to be brought out on the flight with the kids. When the plane arrived, the pilot circled over Cobaría. He airdropped the vaccine. We quickly retrieved it from among the weeds. With the vaccine on hand, we immediately began going house to house to vaccinate the children. Amazingly enough people cooperated that sixty-nine children were vaccinated. We considered that a real success since in the past, the Tunebos had totally opposed vaccinations. None of the leaders openly supported our effort, but José was certainly happy to have his grandchildren vaccinated. We hoped that would be enough to prevent an epidemic. We made plans to give the second shot a month later when the plane came to pick us up.

When the time came, we advised the Tunebos that we would be giving the second dose of the vaccine when the plane arrived. However, for some reason, our flight was delayed four days—time enough for negative rumors to spread. Once again the pilot airdropped the vaccine, and we started to make the rounds of the village. We didn't think too much when we arrived at the first house and found the door tied shut with no one home, but by the time we got to the third and fourth houses with the doors tied shut, we realized they had been intimidated into not cooperating. We were only able to vaccinate fourteen of the village children who had had the first shot and nine new ones. I remember walking home across a pole bridge being angry with God and the whole situation. When we got back to the house, the eight kids who lived in the mission outpost greeted us in English, saying "You are nice. I like you." (For fun, Paul had taught them these phrases some time previously). That was God's consolation prize at a difficult time. I confessed my anger to God and asked for His forgiveness.

The next day, we were up bright and early to start our hike to the airstrip. As I walked down the mountain away from the house, I had the premonition that this might be our last visit to Cobaría.

To our surprise, when we arrived at the airstrip, we encountered Tunebos from Tegría with thirty-one children; they wanted to be vaccinated. Aarón had been at our house in Cobaría the day before and had witnessed our disappointment with the response of the people there. He apparently spread the word about the availability and value of the vaccine. He convinced the people to come. We were touched by Aarón's concern for his people. We vaccinated each of the children before boarding the plane.

On our way back to Lomalinda, we asked the pilot to stop in Saravena in order to see the man in charge of education in the district. Although there were no schools in the villages where we worked, there were some schools on the fringes of the Tunebo area. He was planning an upgrading course for the teachers in his jurisdiction during their vacation from January 26 to February 21. He wanted to include a course on how to use the Tunebo language in their schools. He asked us personally to cooperate with him in this. It was like a dream come true; the opportunity to introduce our materials to those who could teach others. He asked us to plan on coming although he still needed to pass his plan by others involved in the upgrading course.

Safety in a Multitude of Counselors

While the translators were still gathered at Lomalinda after the annual group conference, Paul and I, in coordination with our leaders, called a meeting of all the senior translators. We wanted to present our situation with the Tunebos to get their input and advice. "Where no counsel is, the people fall: but in the multitude of counselors there is safety" (Prov. 11:14, kjv).

We poured out our hearts about the problems of lack of consistent language help, those whom we taught to read and who showed interest in the gospel disappearing from the village, threats of closing the airstrip, pressure from the Tunebos to do more to stop the road coming into the area, and difficulties with medical work. Mostly we were concerned with the lack of response of the people to the gospel.

Our colleagues were loving and sympathetic but at the same time asked difficult questions. One asked, "Are you trying to force medicine on the people?" Another questioned, "Do you take every opportunity to witness?" Someone suggested we study Wayne Dye's work on good news encounters. On the other side, they reminded us that we spoke the language well and that despite the circumstances, we were making good progress on translation. They pointed out that we understood many of the difficult aspects of Tunebo grammar and discourse. Following a time of prayer, the consensus was that we should stay with the Tunebo work at least long enough to complete the translation of the New Testament.

After the meeting, Paul and I discussed what our colleagues had said. We still had ambivalent feelings. Even though we were frustrated with them, we loved the Tunebos we had worked with for seventeen years. At the same time, it seemed futile. After all these years, there were no believers in Cobaría. No one right where we lived had openly responded to the gospel message. Yes, a number of the settlers had become believers and they had led two young Tunebos from Tegría to the Lord. We had written music in Tunebo with Christian words, made literacy books and Bible stories, and recorded Scripture and music on audio cassettes to play for them. But it all seemed for naught. We longed to see more results. We longed for our friends in Cobaría to know Christ.

We acknowledged that our colleagues were right in saying it was logical to continue at this point in time, we were the only ones who spoke the Tunebo language who could do translation. God had helped us make progress on translation despite the obstacles. We prayed and recommitted ourselves to finishing the Tunebo translation. We followed their advice and started to study Wayne Dye's book, *Bible Translation Strategy: An Analysis of Its Spiritual Impact*. In the book, we focused on the chapter dealing with good news encounters. It stressed being alert to using every situation to relate God's Word to them in culturally appropriate ways. Dr. Dye, an SIL leader in scripture use, had studied situations where indigenous peoples had responded to the gospel and found one important factor had been the frequent use of good news encounters.[1]

There wasn't much time to study Dye's work right then as we needed to prepare materials and classes for the upcoming Tunebo teacher training course. We began by working out a schedule for each of the classes. In the process of teaching the teachers to read and write and speak rudimentary Tunebo, we planned to introduce the materials we had developed.

In addition to preparing for the teacher training course, we were taking the very first computer course offered to translators in Colombia. The branch had just acquired the first computer for translators to use. We were thrilled at the advantages working with a computer would provide for our translation work. We were not aware of all the possibilities it would offer, but one that we did know was that we would not have to retype the entire manuscript after each revision. We knew it would greatly reduce the potential of adding new typographical errors with each new typing. While receiving training, we started entering all our recent translation on computer. At that time, the data was kept on cassette tapes.

We were waiting for our personal computer to arrive. Grace Church of Edina was sending us $3,500 for a DEC computer, and JAARS provided the remaining $1,500 needed. We were deeply grateful for the vision the church had and their desire to provide this state of the art tool for our work.

---

[1] In private consultation with Dye, he compared Tunebo culture with a major very closed religion and said it was not likely that they would respond very soon. The more closed the culture the more good news encounters they need.

29

THEY HAVE TAKEN CHET BITTERMAN

These (trials) have come so that the proven genuineness of your faith—of greater worth than gold, which perishes even though refined by fire—may result in praise, glory and honor when Jesus Christ is revealed. (1 Peter 1:7, NIV, emphasis mine)

A Phone Call Changed Everything

AT NOON ON January 19, 1981, I answered the phone to receive an urgent request from the Lomalinda prayer chain. "A man dressed as a police officer knocked on the door of the Bogotá group house about 6:30 this morning. When the door was opened, six men and a woman armed with machine guns burst in. They have taken Chet Bitterman."

I stood in shock and disbelief. What did all this mean? We learned the armed men quickly went around to all the rooms. At gun point, they gathered everyone into the living room, five men, six women, and five children. The mothers sat with their children on the sofas. Everyone else was laid on the floor with their wrists bound behind them and tied to their feet. The intruders were looking for Al Wheeler, SIL's assistant director in Bogotá. He wasn't there. Hoping he would come, they spent over an hour, searching for documents and questioning the guests and residents. The militants then took the two-way radios, records, mail, and valuables, grabbed Chet Bitterman, and sped away using the SIL car.

At our Lomalinda center, there were frequent group prayer meetings and information meetings to update us on the situation and the demands. When we weren't in meetings, Paul and I continued to work preparing for the teacher upgrading course.

By January 24, the M-19 subversive group had identified themselves as the kidnappers. Their demand was threefold: all SIL members were to leave Colombia, to all SIL group and personal assets were to be left for them, and finally, we were to give them good publicity in the United States.

There was no way SIL would meet this preposterous demand. SIL's policy not to pay ransom or comply with demands of kidnappers was clear and firmly established.

Two days after hearing the demands, we were in the Helio Courier airplane on our way out to take part in the teacher upgrading course. We were loaded with books and filled with expectation of what might happen as a result of the course. Two-thirds of the way to Cubará, the plane radio crackled with a message for us. The SIL office in Bogotá had received a telegram that morning. It simply stated our services would not be needed at the course. There was no explanation. I experienced quite a flood of emotions and turned to the Lord to ask Him, "Why? Why? Lord, You know this is what we have dreamed of doing." Right there in midair, the Lord answered me:

> Trust in the Lord and do good;
> dwell in the land and enjoy safe pasture.
> Be still before the Lord
> and wait patiently for him;
> do not fret when people succeed in their ways,
> when they carry out their wicked schemes.
> Refrain from anger and turn from wrath;
> do not fret—it leads only to evil. (Ps. 37:3, 7–8, NIV)

He obviously wanted me to stop my worrying, fretting, and being angry. Instead, I was to trust Him. The whole psalm was comforting and encouraging. Since we had made two-thirds of the trip, we continued on to the place the course was to be held. We received a cold reception. It was reiterated that our services would not be needed.

Although the trip seemed to be futile, it did provide another opportunity to visit María. We found her at the home of a relative, where we visited and discussed the possibility of her further involvement in translation. We made tentative plans to work with her face-to-face when we returned to Cobaría.

The pilot had waited while we checked about the course and visited María. We returned to Lomalinda with him. On arrival, we learned the guerrillas perceived SIL to be a front for the CIA. February 19 was set as the deadline for compliance or Chet would be killed. This deadline was later extended fifteen days.

Tension continued to build as the news wire services persistently followed the story. On February 13, student demonstrators picketed, shouted, and pounded on doors at the Wycliffe headquarters in Huntington Beach, California. On February 26, bombs were set off in Bogotá in front of the SIL guest house and the residence of an SIL member.

Uneasiness and uncertainty hung over the Lomalinda staff as negotiations on Chet's behalf came to a standstill. The clock continued to tick closing in on the fifteen-day extension before the threat on Chet's life was to be carried out.

Friday, March 6, 1981, the M-19 guerrilla group offered a "last chance" to bargain for Bitterman's life. Six hours later, Chet's body, wrapped in a leftist flag, was discovered in an abandoned bus in an industrial residential neighborhood of Bogotá. He died from a single .38-caliber bullet wound in the chest. The bullet pierced his lung. The Bogotá coroner reported that Bitterman died within a few minutes and that his pain was lessened because of the heavy sedative discovered in his bloodstream. By three in the afternoon, the body was released. The coffin was loaded in the DC-3 along with family, SIL leaders, and American embassy officials. Once loaded, they flew over the Andes Mountains to Lomalinda where we all gathered for the funeral. We were a somber group gathered at the graveside in a small cemetery on the edge of the center.[2]

On Sunday, March 8, the wire services carried the story, "Bogotá Rebels Kill American Bible Worker." A statement from Washington, DC, by Secretary of State Alexander M. Haig Jr. read, "The barbaric murder of Chester Bitterman by terrorists in Colombia is a despicable and cowardly act which we totally condemn."

On Monday, March 9, the San Diego Tribune stated, "Police today reported the arrest of an estimated 100 suspects in the kidnapping and slaying of American Bible translator Chester Bitterman."

On Tuesday, March 10, our director, Joel Stolte, came to our house to talk to us. His grim expression and firm stance told us something was up. His words hit us like a bombshell. "You cannot go back to the Tunebo area." It was clear; this was a directive, not an option. He explained that security alerts indicated that the guerillas were active in the area near Cobaría.

How could he be telling us not to go? Hadn't we just been advised by our colleagues that we should continue and finish the translation? Even though he had been elected director at conference a month ago, Joel was also our friend. How could he do this to us? We had studied together. Paul and I had even gone on our first date with Joel and his wife. He was a translator himself; he should understand how important it was to be with the people. We argued with him. We had been in Cobaría just a

---

[2] See the whole story in Steve Estes's *Called to Die: The Story of American Linguist Chet Bitterman Slain by Terrorists* (The Zondervan Corporation, 1986).

few months previously and hadn't seen or heard of any terrorists in the area. We were packed and ready to go. Normally, we were glad for any input from our administrators and respectfully submitted, but this time, it was hard to give in. We had never believed in doing a translation in exile. But Joel held his ground. Our dreams and plans were shattered by this ultimatum.

Was it indeed time to quit? My dad wrote, saying, "I worry about you in South America. I think that you should get out, while you still can. I know it is hard to give up all that work and property. All the news sounds very bad. I am praying for you all the time." My sister wrote saying, "It is really scary. I wish you were safe in the United States, down the block." My sister-in-law wrote, "We are concerned for you and wish you were next door right now! Be careful and please know we love you and wish we knew you were safe!"

A Fragrant Offering

At the time of Chet's death, God answered some of my questions: "But whatever happens to me, remember always live as Christians should … tell the Good News fearlessly, no matter what your enemies may do." (Phil. 1:27–29, TLB). It was like Chet's message to all of us. God also spoke to me through a number of verses from Ephesians 5. I was reminded to "follow God's example, therefore, as dearly loved children and walk in the way of love, just as Christ loved us and gave himself up for us as a fragrant offering and sacrifice to God" (Eph. 5:1–2, NIV). Chet's sacrifice was a sweet perfume to God. God also showed me how I needed to continue the work. "Be very careful, then, how you live—not as unwise but as wise, making the most of every opportunity, because the days are evil. Therefore do not be foolish, but understand what the Lord's will is" (Eph. 5:15–17, NIV).

Our kids were dealing with the events of this difficult time in their own way. In the midst of it all, we got a black curly-haired part cockapoo puppy for Ron. He had wanted a dog for several years, but we had hesitated because of the problem it would cause when we moved back and forth to Cobaría. We finally told him he could get a dog if he could keep it with him in the children's home when we were gone. The children's home parents responded positively. The cuddly dog comforted his heart at this hard time.

Joy often babysat for the Bitterman's children, so she was greatly saddened by the sweet little girls' loss of their daddy. Her heart was comforted when she heard that the three-year-old had pointed to a picture of Jesus in a Bible storybook and said, "My daddy's with Him now."

In submission to our director, we didn't make our scheduled trip to Cobaría in March. We later learned that subversives were apparently watching the airstrip, waiting for our return. God was taking care of us even though we didn't realize the danger.

In May, we were cleared for a twenty-four-hour visit to Cobaría to get a Tunebo to help us with translation. We were ready to go, even though making a twenty-four-hour trip seemed impossible, with bad weather making flying conditions difficult and a three-hour walk each way from the airstrip. We felt we had to give it a try despite the fact that we had no idea who or if anyone would come out with us to help us on the language. We knew José was under a restriction that prevented him from going to the outside. Búswara was blind. We hadn't been able to find Warawaná, and Rayotá really couldn't do the difficult work of translation.

Although it did not seem logical, we felt we should take the opportunity offered by our leaders. We knew the Tunebos would be migrating to the lowlands in a very short time as was their usual pattern. If we wanted to see them, it was obligatory to go at that time, even though we personally needed a vacation.

We were scheduled to leave on Monday. Friday's mail brought a letter from María saying she could come to our translation center to help us on translation in mid-June. We took that as the Lord's leading. We cancelled our scheduled flight and rescheduled one in June to pick up María in Cubará. Isn't it just like God's great love to let us have some sorely needed rest time as a family after the months of pressure we had just been through!

God sent María in June with three of her children. We rejoiced to learn that she had given her heart to Christ five years previously, about the time of Paul's first contact with her. Paul said, "Working with María is like being in air conditioning with a glass of ice water after seventeen years in the desert." She had learned a lot about the Bible from Christian radio. In addition, she was quite bilingual because she had a Tunebo mother and a Spanish-speaking Colombian father. She had five years of school in Spanish. With just a little prompting, she was able to pick up and read the Tunebo materials we had developed. After all these years, you can only imagine what a joy it was to hear someone fluently reading and understanding the Scriptures we had translated.

While María was with us in June, we received a letter from a friend in a town just outside the Tunebo area. He informed us our house had been broken into and ransacked. All the food and medicine had been stolen. The rest of the things in the house had been vandalized. He wrote that although it had been robbed before, this time it was done by rebels or subversives. He went on to say they don't like the gospel and especially don't like Americans. The rumors ranged from accusing us of mining emeralds to dealing in cocaine. He mentioned the airstrip and warned us to be very prudent if we returned to the area. The subversives were watching for us. María confirmed that what he said in the letter was true.

We reviewed the details of the letter with Jim Walton, a translator who was serving as the assistant director of tribal affairs. We discussed the future of our translation for the Tunebo. We asked Jim if he thought this was a sign that God was indeed closing the door to Tunebo work altogether. We weighed the options with Jim. It was clear it would be some time before we could even consider returning to Cobaría. It wasn't the house we were concerned about; nothing in our house was worth anyone risking their life to retrieve. Our language data and translation work were with us in Lomalinda. We could work on that for a time. But then what? We had always felt we needed to be with the people. We didn't feel good about the idea of doing a translation in exile. There wasn't much hope of getting someone from Cobaría to come to Lomalinda to work. If we worked from a distance with a fringe[1] Tunebo, we were not sure how the message would get back to the people in the village of Cobaría and Tegría. María was a good language assistant, but the question still remained in our hearts and minds, *How will the message get to the rest of the Tunebos?*

On the other hand, we could not forget the fact that weighed in favor of continuing the translation program for the Tunebos: most of the people were monolingual in Tunebo. They could not be reached through Spanish. In addition, half of the New Testament was already in various stages of translation.

In the meeting, we considered other options and left the discussion in limbo; Jim, Paul, and I all agreed we would pray about the options. The option we were to seriously consider was finishing the translation away from the Tunebo area with all the new problems that would bring. We needed to consider the following questions: Where should we work? What effect would it have on the Tunebos we would have to take out of their home area to help us? Would we be able to cover the additional expenses involved? Would the translation be accepted?

I remember saying to my prayer partner at the time, "If God clearly closes the door, I will say 'Thank you for sparing us from

---

[1]   We used "fringe" Tunebos to refer to those who lived in areas surrounding the traditional Tunebos who were more acculturated to Colombian farm culture.

a difficult work.'" God must have seen my faith was growing weak. Instead of clearly closing the door, He graciously showed us plainly that He wanted us to continue. Periodically, He did something special—small miracles—to keep us motivated. After seventeen years of working with the Tunebos, we received the first letter that had come through the mail from a Tunebo. Other letters followed arriving precisely at the time we needed the information they contained. When we were desperate for language help, Diego, our faithful friend who had moved to Bogotá, volunteered to make trips to bring people to the center to help us. We responded to God's leading one step at a time. "For we walk by faith not by sight" (2 Cor. 5:7, KJV).

As a result of Chet's kidnapping, the government stationed soldiers on our center to protect us. Ronnie spent all his spare time with them. His Spanish improved greatly by interacting with them. They had great soccer games two or three times a week. While Ronnie was with the soldiers, Joy spent her time with her girlfriends among the missionary kids. In addition to the soldiers at Lomalinda, we had a curfew and other security restrictions.

New Contacts

We began to seek other ways of reaching the Tunebos if we couldn't return to Cobaría. Because the Cuadrangular (Foursquare) denomination had started the work among the settlers, we corresponded with the pastor of the Foursquare Church in the city of Bucaramanga, thinking they might have an interest in the Tunebo people as well as the settlers. Juan Encinales, the pastor, encouraged us to visit a Wednesday evening service. We made arrangements and traveled to the city of Bucaramanga in late August.

When Paul (I stayed in bed in the hotel sick with a fever) arrived at the church, he was amazed first of all to see the size of the building. He was even more surprised when he entered and saw it overflowing with eight hundred to one thousand people. He had expected to find a small group gathered for midweek prayer, but instead, they were in the midst of a celebration of thirty-eight years since the church had been established. Paul was immediately ushered to the platform. He had the thrill of presenting the need of reaching the indigenous peoples of Colombia in their own languages. Pastor Encinales shared his burden to encourage young people to go to the Tunebos. This was the beginning of a long-term relationship with the pastor and the church.

We traveled on from Bucaramanga to Cubará by bus. The first night of the trip, we stayed in Pamplona, a town high in the mountains. I remember feeling the bone-chilling cold in the dingy hotel there. In the morning, we boarded the bus for the long trip over curving mountain roads to Cubará, the small town at the foot of the mountains where the Tunebos lived. We hired a jeep to visit María and a few other Tunebos including Juan. He agreed to go with us to Lomalinda to an upcoming writer's workshop.

We went on to Saravena where we had made arrangements to work with the government official in charge of education in the area. He was the one who had invited us to teach in the teacher upgrading course. He was interested in learning the Tunebo language and studying the pedagogical grammar Paul and I were writing. Our time together was of mutual benefit as we worked through the lessons. The educator learned more Tunebo while we got help editing the Spanish in the grammar. Although I spent much of my time there in bed sick with chills and a high fever, I helped as able. Finally, the JAARS plane arrived and took Juan and me back to Lomalinda for the workshop. Paul went on to a meeting of educators in the area. He presented the primers and other materials we had in Tunebo. Some interest was shown, and at least one person bought a number of copies.

While at the meetings, Paul experienced the same symptoms and fever I had suffered. From the meeting, he went directly to Bogotá to meet his mother who was coming for a visit. Before she arrived, he was diagnosed with typhoid, and spent several days in the hospital.

We had looked forward to his mother's visit after going through such a hard year with Chet's kidnapping and murder and not being able to go to Cobaría. We anticipated receiving motherly comfort and sympathy, but she came with her own set of problems. She had been recently diagnosed with diabetes and was trying to make the necessary adjustments. She was also extremely concerned for her only living brother who had just suffered a severe stroke. We began to learn the responsibilities of having aging parents.

Juan, who had come with me to Lomalinda for the writer's workshop, had completed a year of school in Spanish after the settlers had taught him to read in Tunebo. At the workshop, he enthusiastically wrote stories in his language. One of the best stories he wrote was about a Christian congress for the indigenous people of Colombia. He gave details of the plane trip and the bus ride over steep curvy mountain roads. He described visiting with people from other groups and comparing how they lived and what they ate. He explained the high points of the Bible teaching and other aspects of the trip.

When the stories were all written, he learned how to make copies on a flat-bed mimeo, compile them into books, and bind them together by sewing with string and a large needle.

After the workshop, he stayed another month and helped with translation. He worked with Paul in a workshop on 1 Corinthians. He helped me finish the second volume of the *Old Testament Summary*: the books of Leviticus, Numbers, Deuteronomy, Joshua, Judges, Ruth, and 1 Samuel. I felt a sense of accomplishment and relief when it was turned over to the printshop.

In January, a whole year after Chet had been kidnapped, we were totally surprised to have María's mother, Naomi, and Uriel, a Colombian man who had been ministering to the Tunebos, show up on our doorstep at Lomalinda. We had never seen him before, but he had somehow heard of the Tunebos and wanted to serve them. The day after Uriel and Naomi arrived, Paul left on the flight we had scheduled to pick up María; consequently I was left to give Uriel a crash course in the Tunebo language. It was a challenge as he only had three years of formal education, but what he lacked in education, he made up for in determination. He studied a week, loaded up on Tunebo materials, including Scripture and music tapes as well as books, and was on his way back to the area.[2] Naomi stayed with us.

On Paul's trip to pick up María, he had learned that the government was making a reserve for the Indians. All the settlers were required to leave. That included the Christians we had been training to read the language so they could witness to the Tunebos. They still had many of the books as well as Scripture and music tapes we had given them. These Christian settlers had been our hope in reaching the Tunebos and getting the Scriptures in use if we had to leave. Now they were asking, "What do you want us to do with the materials you gave us?" The government had not paid them for their improvements to the land, so they were still there waiting. We hoped that meant they wouldn't leave at all. But it looked like our vision of the settlers reaching the Tunebos was being dashed to the ground.[3]

Paul came home with María, two of her children, and her sister, Elena. It wasn't easy for María to leave her other four

---

[2]   He worked in a different dialect of Tunebo. We later heard he was killed by the leftist guerillas.

[3]   The reserve did go through, and all the colonists moved off the Tunebo reserve by the mid-eighties. In 1999, the reserve was greatly enlarged to protect the Uwa traditional lands.

children at home, but she said, "What if God was telling me to go and I didn't do it?" All five of them managed to sleep in one room of the house we had in our front yard for language helpers. We converted the other room of the house, which had been our laundry, into a kitchen for them.

María, being bilingual in Spanish and Tunebo with some education in Spanish, and her mother, being monolingual in Tunebo with no formal education, made a great team. They worked together harmoniously, each respecting the other's assets. As they translated with Paul or me, María would turn to Naomi to ask the nuances of meanings of the Tunebo words. Together we made good progress in translation.

When we translated, "I heard the voice of the Lord saying, 'Whom shall I send? And who will go for us?' And I said, 'Here am I. Send me!'" (Isa. 6:8, NIV), I shared with María how that verse had spoken to me in a missionary conference. She in turn shared that one evening, she had asked God, "Can you use me?" That night she saw God in a dream. When she woke up these verses were in her mind. "At the name of Jesus every knee should bow, in heaven and on earth and under the earth, and every tongue acknowledge that Jesus Christ is Lord, to the glory of God the Father" (Phil. 2:10–11, NIV). She was consoled to think that those who had laughed at her would someday have to bow before Jesus.

We taught Elena to read and write in Tunebo as well as to type. As writing practice, she wrote stories, which we compiled in a book for simple reading for the people. Joy, Ronnie, and their friends helped make copies of Elena's storybook. They also helped in a big push putting together booklets of the newly translated Scripture for María to take home with her.

In May, after María and the others left, Ronnie graduated from eighth grade. Following the graduation, we traveled to the States for a short summer furlough to report to supporters the current situation with our work in Colombia. I think I felt more reverse culture shock than ever before. After being used to hopping on a motor bike for a three-minute ride to church on the center, driving for hours on congested freeways at high speeds in California brought stress. Seeing the affluence of huge beautiful homes with two people living in them while thinking of friends in Colombia who lived with five to ten people in a two-room house brought a wave of nausea and confusion. This was especially true when I realized I enjoyed being entertained in these homes. When I found myself converting dollars to pesos in my head to see how much things "really" cost, I wondered, *Where do I belong?*

Our supporters were interested in hearing our story of the events of the last three years: Chet's kidnapping and murder, the threats to our security in Cobaría, and María's help. They were encouraging and caring in many different ways during our brief three months in the United States. One family, the Hoplins, gave Ronnie the wonderful experience of spending a month on their farm in North Dakota with them. The Fallbrook First Baptist Church collected Chex Cereal box tops for us. We used the box tops to get free tickets for Joy and Ronnie on Republic Airlines for the Minneapolis to Miami leg of our return trip to Colombia.

30

LAST STAY IN COBARÍA

A Rushing Mountain Stream

IN LATE SEPTEMBER 1982, special friends Pastor Bob Ricker and his wife, Dee, from Grace Church visited us in Colombia for two weeks. We had the extraordinary privilege of taking them to visit a few of the Tunebo people in the lowlands. The jeep driver stopped at the edge of a rushing stream and said, "This is as far as I can take you." Dee looked at the stream and was ready to return with the driver. I didn't realize her fear of rushing water and said, "We didn't come all this way to turn around and go back." She and Bob bravely went through the stream, hopping from one rock to another as best as possible. From there, we walked on a narrow overgrown path for about forty-five minutes to where we came to a Tunebo woman boiling bananas in a little lean-to shelter. We greeted her and learned the whereabouts of the other Tunebos. A little farther up the path, we were delighted to be warmly greeted by Wanisa and his family, some of our dearest Tunebo friends. We translated back and forth a brief exchange of conversation. It was worth the hike for Rickers to be able to see the people we worked with in their natural surroundings. All too soon we had to return to cross the stream again to get back to the jeep before dark. As we crossed, Dee reached down and got a stone for her altar of remembrance (Josh. 4:7–8).

We had a dinner of fresh fish served by María on her mother's porch. María shared our vision of having more books in Tunebo. She had seen the storybooks Juan and her sister had written. She wondered if more could be done. We began to plan together to have a writers' workshop in Cubará with some of the fringe Tunebos who had learned to read and write in Spanish. The workshop would be a time to teach them to transfer their reading and writing skills to their own language. María would find the people to attend. Her mother could do the cooking.

After singing a few Tunebo songs, Pastor Ricker gave a short message, which Paul translated for the Spanish speakers and I translated for the Tunebo speakers. At bedtime, Naomi showed us to a room with two beds, one for Rickers and one for us. We are not sure where the family slept that night since they gave us their only beds. In the morning, we returned to the airstrip near town where the plane was waiting to take us to Lomalinda.

By October, our leaders felt security in the area was stable enough for us to go to Cobaría. The airstrip was no longer serviceable, so we made arrangements to make the trip from the end of the road by mule. Things were not the same in the area. Our friend who loaned us his mule, came a day late. (That gave us time to finalize plans we had begun to make with María for the writers' workshop.)

When our friend finally arrived with the mule, he sent us off on our own because he didn't want to be seen with us. After the first four hours of the two-day trip, Paul was exhausted from carrying a pack on his back, and I had tears in my eyes from the pain of joggling up and down on the mule. We stopped in a high spot. I pulled out a soggy lunch I had packed three days before. While we were eating, our friend caught up with us and took Paul's pack. As the day wore on and the saddle rubbed more painfully, we adjusted it with towels and a pillow. Finally, we arrived at a settler's home where we spent the night. It had been a long day on the trail. The next day, Paul rode the mule going down the mountain slopes, and I rode going up. We spent that night at another settler's home.

On Sunday, October 24, after four days en route by plane, jeep, mule, and foot we opened the door to our home in Cobaría. The floor was strewn with everything from puzzle and pattern pieces to medicine, ripped-up photos and posters, rags, and spilled paint. Cupboard doors and barrel lids stood open with contents removed. Already being weary from the trail, we were disheartened by what we saw. The natural processes of time in the humid tropics had also taken their toll; the clothesline poles and outhouse were falling over.

The thing that brought tears to my eyes was not the condition of the house, but a box of toys left from when the kids were small. It hurt to think of how much I had expected from my little children. We surveyed the damage and thanked God it wasn't worse as far as destruction of the furniture and the house itself. We were especially grateful that, although the mattress and other bedding were gone, there were two small foam cushions and a sleeping bag that made a pretty good bed. In addition, the mosquito net was still there.

We set about cleaning up the mess. Mice had gotten into the mattress before the thieves so there was shredded foam all over. In addition to the mice, ants and birds had also made nests in the most inconvenient spots. Before we dropped exhausted into our makeshift bed, we managed to get some lunch and supper, picked things up off the floor and swept the living room, kitchen, and upstairs. I picked a pretty hydrangea flower and put it on the table to brighten the dismal house. We fell asleep exhausted without much thought about whether guerillas (subversives) would come in the night.

The first day we didn't have any visitors, although a couple of people passed by and asked us to go to their homes to treat their sick family members. The following day after I got the medicine cabinets cleaned up and put back the medicine I could salvage, we went out to make the requested medical calls. We found whole families of our friends sick with the flu. The sick included the woman who usually washed our clothes.

We came to a point when it was hard to get motivated to do any more cleaning or repairs on the house. A sort of hopelessness set in as we wondered, *Are we coming back? If we come back, what can we do to protect the few things we still have in the house? If we fix it up, will the subversives just come and vandalize it again?* We did the most urgent and left the rest undone.

During the month we were in Cobaría, José came a number of times to help with translation. Other than that, we had almost no adult visitors. We especially noted the absence of visits from the Christian settlers. I felt rejected by the people as they ignored me while I sat at the cold stream washing clothes.

We kept busy with medical work and continued to visit in their homes and read Scripture to them. We also read letters we had translated into the Tunebo language that Paul's mother and my dad had written to them. Wayne Dye had recommended having our parents write letters to the Tunebos because traditional cultures value taking care of the elderly. In the letters, they each explained that others were caring for them and that they were happy that we could be there to minister to the Tunebos. They also expressed their desire for the people to accept the message of Jesus. The people listened with interest to the letters. When my mother had died two years earlier, the Tunebos had begun to realize we had feelings like theirs. We were real people with families. We hoped having a message from our parents would further help them identify with us.

At first I was really happy to see the Tunebo books were still there intact. But then the haunting question came, "What do we do with the books?" The Christian settlers may be leaving as well, so that ruled out leaving the books with them.

When it came time to leave, we packed a duffle bag with the things we didn't want destroyed and left it at the local Catholic mission outpost. It was with heavy hearts we started the trail trip back to town. We stopped at each home along the way and said good-bye to our dear Tunebo friends, realizing that we might never see them again. By nightfall, we reached the home of settlers where we were to spend the night. They graciously shared their meager provisions with us. During the night, I woke up trembling with fever. I had succumbed to the flu that the Tunebos had. Somehow I was able to continue hiking the next day.

Writers' Workshop in Cubará

Finally we arrived in Cubará and set up for the writer's workshop we had planned with María. Ten eager students showed up. We had classes teaching the Tunebo letters that were different from Spanish, the most different being nasalized *w*, which we wrote *ŵ*. To help them transfer their Spanish reading skills to Tunebo, we used the primer, simple story material, and Bible stories from the *Old Testament Summary*. Leah Walter, a literacy consultant with experience in Mexico and Guatemala as well as Colombia, came from Lomalinda to teach the writing portion. Leah stimulated them to write stories of things familiar to them. She encouraged them as they wrote about chickens and wild animals. To broaden their experience, she took them out to visit a large steel bridge over the river. She helped them stretch their imaginations and writing skills to describe it. Leah's enthusiasm was contagious. It was an added blessing to have her there as some days I was too sick with fever to get out of bed. It was like a dream come true having ten students enthusiastically learning to read and write in their own language. Each evening, they sang the Tunebo songs about Jesus with gusto. They compiled about five short booklets of their stories and ran them off on flat-bed mimeograph. Then they hand sewed them together. They all took copies home.

On Sunday morning, I said at breakfast, "I am going to church. Does anyone want to go with me?"

One young boy literally jumped out of his chair and said, "I'm going."

31

A New Beginning

A Family of Seven

February 7, 1983, María, Tito, her husband, and their children excitedly rushed outside when they heard the roar of the plane as it circled over her mother's house. This was the prearranged signal to let them know Paul would be there the next morning with a hired vehicle to pick them up. They had agreed to go to Lomalinda to help with translation for a year. They hurried around making final preparations before the next day's departure.

Paul's heart skipped a beat when he saw María, her husband, their five children ages three, five, six, nine, and twelve, and their cook/baby sitter all dressed in their Sunday best ready to travel. Soon they were at the airstrip just outside of Cubará where they enthusiastically piled into the plane for the two-and-a-half-hour flight to Lomalinda.

Their arrival at the center set in motion one of the busiest years of our lives as we tried to keep two families running smoothly while we spent long hours on translation. The same day they arrived, Paul helped get three of the children registered in government schools. I arranged for the two youngest ones to go to the nursery with the missionary kids on the center. We introduced Tito to Mel Grant, the center manager, who had previously agreed for him to work on the grounds maintenance crew. (Although Tito was full-blooded Tunebo, he had grown up in circumstances where he did not use the language so he could not help with translation.)

In preparation for their arrival, we had done more remodeling to our small language helper house to provide a more adequate kitchen and eating area for their family. The cook/babysitter used the bedroom that also served as a playroom for the children. We were able to arrange for a place for the family to sleep in the house another translation team had for their helpers. Our friends donated clothes for the children, which María and I altered to fit them. María made their school uniforms. We got books, school supplies, and bikes for them. We also had them treated for parasites so they could start school.

It was enlightening at times to see the world through the eyes of a child from another culture. María's whole family attended an open house at the Lomalinda school with us the first week they were there. Motor bikes were the means of transportation at Lomalinda. When the six-year-old saw everyone getting on motor bikes to go the short distance from the grade school to the high school, she asked, "Don't these people have any feet?" Soon she was begging like the rest for a ride. Paul often loaded all five of María's kids on his bike and took them for a ride. One day, her little brother proved Ron had feet. He laid down flat on the floor outside the bathroom door and peeked under declaring, "I see your feet."

By the end of the week, we had begun translating with María. She worked with one of us in the morning and the other in the afternoon. It was a special blessing for Paul and me to have adjoining small offices in the newly finished air-conditioned study building, built by Wycliffe associates. It provided a place away from the distractions of the house and the tropical heat.

Between February and May, while Paul worked with María on translating New Testament books, I completed translating the third and last volume of a summary of the Old Testament with María. The first two volumes had already been published. Even though more comprehension checking with other Tunebos unfamiliar with the text remained to be done, it was a great feeling of accomplishment. I had invested five years working on the *Old Testament Summary.*

Living so close to María gave us the opportunity to observe her personal needs. While we spent all day working over Scripture passages with her, there was opportunity to practice the Apostle Paul's example of discipling Timothy. "And the things you have heard me say in the presence of many witnesses entrust to reliable people who will also be qualified to teach others" (2 Tim. 2:2, NIV). We talked about the application of Scripture to her life as well as how it should be translated.

Each evening all eight of María's family joined us in our living room to read Scripture and sing Christian songs in Tunebo and Spanish. The littlest girl loved a song that included the words, "I am a flower in His [Jesus] garden." It touched my heart every time she sang it. The children often dropped off to sleep one by one as we talked about the application of the Scriptures to their lives.

On Sunday evenings, all the Indians on the center gathered in our home to sing and listen as Paul shared Bible stories in simple Spanish. In these gatherings, we would have each person introduce himself and give a greeting in his language. Sometimes there were people from as many as thirteen different language groups. Different ones often volunteered to sing a special number in their language.

We found the added responsibility for an extra eight people to be a stretching experience. We seemed to go from one crisis to the next—malaria attacks, other illnesses, culture stress for the Tunebos, and backed-up septic systems. Between crises, we had birthday parties for the kids and Saturday night suppers together in the yard with homemade ice cream for dessert.

Tito was restless and needed to be kept busy on weekends and holidays. He wanted to learn a trade while he was there. Our colleagues taught him some mechanics and radio skills, and we often spent Saturdays teaching him to finish furniture, sanding, and varnishing.

There were many others who also sacrificed to help with the *Tunebo New Testament*. Mardty Anderson had been typing our initial handwritten drafts of Tunebo Scripture into the computer bit by bit before we went over them with María. However, piles of revised Scripture were ready for computer editing. In August, we were thrilled to receive a letter from Evelyn Osborne, a widow from Washington State, telling of her plans to come in October to assist with the typing. She asked prayer for these three specific needs: someone to run her realty office while she was gone (it had to be a broker as she had only salesmen at that time), the needed finances for the trip, and someone to care for her house and pets.

God worked out all those details. On September 12, she wrote, "I am planning to come to Lomalinda October 25. My daughter is going to take care of the house, pets and help in the office. I am getting some financial help from church and am selling a contract at a discount to get some money also.

She came down and typed the Scripture manuscripts for us after we went over them with María. We were amazed at the near-perfect accuracy of her typing in Tunebo, a language she didn't know. She had typed code during World War II and had learned to be accurate without understanding.

When I finished the draft of the *Old Testament Summary*, Paul then assigned me to translate the Gospel of John. He reasoned that because we had different writing styles, it would be good if I worked on John's writings while he worked on the apostle Paul's. It was definitely the most difficult translating I had done. I remember thinking with each chapter maybe the next one would be easier, but new challenges came with every chapter. Phrases like "living water," "I am the bread of life," "I am the light of the world," and "I am the gate for the sheep" were unfamiliar concepts to the Tunebos. Together, María and I worked through these passages. By September, we had finished the first draft of the Gospel of John. I then started revising 1 John. Once again it was tough going. In the first few verses, it refers to Jesus in a number of ways without actually using the name Jesus.

At the same time I worked on the *Old Testament Summary* and John's writings, Paul and María accomplished the monumental task of finishing the first draft of 2 Corinthians, Jude, 2 Peter, Romans, Matthew, Hebrews, Revelation, Colossians, Ephesians, and Philippians. On December 1, 1983, the first draft of the entire *Tunebo New Testament* was completed! We all shared in the joy and rejoiced in God's goodness.

Mrs. Osborne edited in the last changes on the computer, and we had freshly printed manuscripts ready to present to Tito and María before they left. There was a simple ceremony in the Technical Studies Department during the morning coffee break. Our fellow translators celebrated with us.

On January 13, 1984, just six weeks after they left, we received a letter from María dated December 24. The letter said her ten-year-old daughter, Nina, had received a severe machete cut while clearing a field. María's sister made a hard blow with the machete to cut down a tree without noticing Nina's hand on the tree. She was in danger of losing her hand. The local doctor, serving his required rural year to become a physician, seeing the extent of the wound, had stopped the bleeding, and stitched up only the skin. He told Tito to take her to the regional hospital. Tito took Nina on the all-night bus trip to the city of Bucaramanga. At the hospital, the doctor on call on Christmas examined Nina's hand. He told Tito she would need surgery so she would not lose her hand. He gave them an order to see a specialist in a month.

Paul and I felt the urgency María expressed in her letter. We quickly decided we had to go meet them in Bucaramanga for Nina's appointment with a specialist. They needed our moral and financial support.

Details as to where to meet them were not included in her letter. We sent two telegrams hoping they would get through and that Maria would pick them up. We said we would meet them at the Foursquare Church Sunday afternoon.

We called a missionary in Bucaramanga referred to us by a friend. She invited us to stay with her. She even went the extra mile to meet us at the airport.

María did not receive our telegrams. She wasn't at the church when we got there. We were faced with a dilemma. Where could we find her in a strange city of over three hundred thousand people?

We prayed.

The next morning, we started off with a list of hospitals and clinics. The first one had twelve floors, and they didn't even want to let us in the gate. We slipped in behind a doctor. We went to the surgical wards on the seventh and tenth floors and peaked in each room. We didn't find them. Someone suggested we try the outpatient department. We finally located it after walking what seemed like miles around the huge hospital.

We must have looked as bewildered as we felt. A nun came up and kindly asked if she could help. She double-checked to be sure she understood us. "You're looking for someone in a hospital, but you're not sure what hospital. You don't know the doctor or the time of the appointment. And they don't know you're coming. Excuse me for saying so, but I don't think you'll find them."

"Pablo! Pablo! Buenos días!" We heard a familiar voice calling excitedly. His eyes were wide with amazement. Tito was shaking our hands. His little daughter Nina clinging tightly to his hand seemed frightened to be in this big hospital.

"Pablo, we lost our appointment for today. We have to return in two weeks," Tito reported. (Actually it turned out he never had an appointment, but rather a doctor's order to make one.) Minutes later and they would have been out the door on their way home. God's timing is perfect!

As Tito arrived in the city at three that morning, he had prayed, "Lord, please send someone to help me." When he saw us with the nun, he knew God was answering his prayer. The nun conferred with me, ran off, and returned with an appointment for Thursday, three days later.

The next couple of days brought promises of help for Tito and Nina from the pastor of the Foursquare Church and Bruce Olson, an independent missionary. On Thursday, after the doctor's appointment and some tests, another appointment was set up for two weeks later. Tito decided to go home until then.

That night before he went to the bus, Tito said, "I want to pray before we go." He thanked God for the help we gave, for that of Bruce, for that of the nun, and then he closed saying, "Y yo quiero entregar mi vida a ti." (I want to give my life over to you.)

Tito was born again. The whole year he had been at Lomalinda, we had prayed fervently for him to make this commitment to Christ. We rejoiced in this answer to prayer. After he prayed, Tito told us that as he entered this big city on the bus, he had asked the Lord to send someone to help.

It warmed our hearts to see how María grew through the experience. She wrote,

> I was very sad because of so many problems, but now I am thinking that as a daughter of God, I have to pass through times of suffering with many concerns as well as happy times. I think these are trials I had to pass through, but the Lord has encouraged me. I am very happy to see that although I have difficulties, He loves me and looked on me with mercy and answered my prayers.

Nina was told a number of times in Bucaramanga to come back two or three weeks later for appointments. We finally moved her to WEC clinic in Bogotá where our missionary friend Marion Price received her. Nina had a number of surgeries to reconnect severed tendons. For her final surgery, we arranged to have an artificial tendon sent from the United States. She stayed in Bogotá a year for therapy. All that year, Marion kept her in the hospital during the week. On weekends she stayed in the home of Rex and Betty Cogar, SIL members living in Bogotá.

After our trip to Bucaramanga, we started the next phase of the translation process. This was to check each book for naturalness and understandability. Again, we needed Tunebos to work with us. Communication and arranging for people to come was a continual challenge. The security in the Tunebo area was such that, not only for our own safety but also for the safety of our friends, it wasn't prudent for us to go to the area. Our friend Diego volunteered to make a trip for us to bring in Tunebos.

María's mother, Naomi, was a good one for "naturalness checking" since she was monolingual in Tunebo and a born teacher. María encouraged her to come by taking care of her farm and animals. She wanted her mother to have the opportunity to know the Lord better by hearing the Scriptures in her own language. Juan came with her. He was bright and was sometimes able to give back most of the material in a chapter of over fifty verses after just one reading. As he told it back in his own words, we got ideas for more natural ways to say things. We also noted that the parts he left out might need more work for clarity.

Naomi and Juan were both delightful to work with and having just two of them was a breeze compared to the eight people of the previous year. The three months they stayed passed quickly.

Once again we were invited to teach the Tunebo language class in the annual upgrading course for all the school teachers in or around the Tunebo area. We were reassured by our friend in charge of education that this time everything had been cleared by the people involved. There would be no decision to cancel our participation. He encouraged us to bring all the Tunebo materials available. We worked with eagerness making lesson plans that would best prepare the participants to teach Tunebo children.

We also planned to have a seminar while we were in the area for the handful of Christian Tunebos and others who had shown interest. Things were fitting into place for a time of building up these new believers.

We were shocked and, I must confess, angry when our own SIL colleague came and told us we would not be allowed to go. He had checked into security in the area and said it was far too dangerous. I thought, *Why can't we just trust God and go anyway?* Once again, our dreams of seeing the Tunebo Scriptures in use seemed to be dashed to the ground. I was somewhat consoled when we received a letter from a friend in the area warning us not to go.

Diego, our pastor friend, realized our disappointment and volunteered to go in our place to hold the seminar for new believers. We spent several days orienting him to the plans and materials. When he got there, María helped him in the language aspects and translation. They used Tunebo Scriptures and sang the songs in the language. Diego returned bearing exciting news. The young boy, who had jumped from his seat saying he was going to church with me two years earlier, accepted the Lord. We were thrilled. Diego brought us letters from María and others telling how they had been encouraged by the Word of God and fellowship together.

Joy Graduates

Along with planning courses, Tunebos coming and going, family life went on. Joy graduated from high school on May 16, 1984. There were parties and celebrations. Paul shared some special things about Joy's life at the baccalaureate service as did each of the other dads about her classmates. She sorted through her treasured possessions and packed up her room. All too soon, it was the end of July, the time for her to say her good-byes to her childhood home, family, and friends and go off to the States, her parent's home country for school. It was a tearful good-bye to Paul and Ron as Joy and I boarded the plane. We were off to

Minnesota where she would study early childhood education at a technical college in Eden Prairie. She would be living with Don and Mary Jane Carlson from Grace Church.

I was facing the hardest thing I had done in my whole missionary career, leaving my child in the States and going back to the field. It seemed like no one understood or cared. They all were busy with their own lives and problems. I visited one friend, hoping to pour out my hurt to her but learned she had recently separated from her husband and needed support herself. The day I actually left Joy was the worst, but a young nephew seemed to grasp a little of how painful it was and took the time to listen to me.

Sunday morning at Grace Church, God spoke to me in two ways. One was a scripture song.

> I know not why God's wondrous grace
> To me He hath made known,
> Nor why, unworthy, Christ in love
> Redeemed me for His own.
> But I know Whom I have believed,
> And am persuaded that He is able
> To keep that which I've committed
> Unto Him against that day.[1]

I had committed Joy to Him. He would keep her in His care.

The sermon that morning by Dr. Bob Smith from Bethel College was on Jesus's temptation. I was still feeling disappointed about not having been allowed to teach the course for Tunebo teachers. I still questioned why we didn't practice our faith and just trust God to care for us in dangerous situations. Dr. Smith read the following scripture:

---

[1] Words based on 2 Timothy 1:12, Daniel W. Whittle, public domain (1883). Music by James McGranahan, public domain (1883).

Then the devil took him to the holy city and had him stand on the highest point of the temple. "If you are the Son of God," he said, "throw yourself down. For it is written:

'He will command his angels concerning you, and they will lift you up in their hands, so that you will not strike your foot against a stone.'"

Jesus answered him, "It is also written: 'Do not put the Lord your God to the test.'" (Matt. 4:5–7, NIV)

Dr. Bob emphasized not deliberately putting God to the test. At last, I had my answer about not being allowed to go to the Tunebo course. God gave me peace.

32

CHECKS, CHECKS, AND MORE CHECKS

WHILE NINA WAS staying at WEC clinic in Bogotá, Tito and María came to visit her. They brought Aarón to work with us at Lomalinda. He was the only one who had come for the teacher training workshop four years previously. Aarón had since married and came with his wife, Eunice, and their baby. One day I read a portion of Scripture to Eunice. When I asked her questions to see what she understood, she did not answer. She sat in silence. Obviously, I had to come up with a new strategy to see what she could grasp of the story. It appeared that, to her, any question she thought I could answer myself was a rhetorical question being asked to make her look stupid. The only questions she answered in the two months she was with us were those about people she had seen since I had seen them. She answered those because she knew something I didn't know.

I had barely started to teach her to write the vowels *a* and *i* when she had to stop to nurse her baby. She began to learn to "read" pictures or recognize things on paper. However, she really wasn't interested in learning to read, so I ended up spending more time just reading Scripture to her. She did learn to sew on a treadle sewing machine and made a shirt for her baby and a dress for herself.

On the other hand, Aarón did better than I expected. He was very helpful with comprehension checking. We were thrilled to learn that he had opened his heart to the Lord. The two months spent on in-depth checking of parts of 1 and 2 Corinthians,

Colossians, Romans, and some of the *Old Testament Summary* were like a short-term Bible course for him. Aarón and Eunice returned to their home in early December.

Another Telegram

Five days after Christmas, we were surprised when we heard a motorcycle pull up to our door as we were eating Sunday breakfast. One of our administrators came to deliver a telegram with an urgent message. My older sister Joan had died on the operating table of an abdominal aneurysm. We lost no time arranging for a flight so I could go to Minneapolis, and soon I was in the JAARS plane on the way to Bogotá. As I sat alone on the plane, I remember questioning why my sister had to die. She was only fifty-one. It seemed God immediately reassured me that He knew what He was doing. Though I trusted Him and stopped questioning, I greatly felt the loss of my sister. Her home was like a second home to us in the States. I remember feeling anger well up when a well-meaning lady tritely said, "She is in a better place." Yes, I agree. Heaven is a better place. But I wasn't comforted by her words at that moment. I wanted my sister on earth for a lot longer.

When I returned to Colombia in early January, we were confronted with more bad news. We received a letter that leftist guerillas in the area had killed a Tunebo while Aarón was in Lomalinda. All the people including our friends were very frightened. They weren't sure if they should continue to come to Lomalinda to help us with translation. In February, we learned some even felt like their lives were being threatened because they had helped us.

On February 9, 1985, we wrote eighty-three letters asking for people to pray for the protection of our friends and that God would send someone to help us with translation. While we waited for help, we made use of the time preparing the third volume of the *Old Testament Summary* (2 Samuel through Malachi) for publication; editing in all the jots and tittles, choosing pictures, and proofreading. God answered the prayers of His people! The day we turned the manuscript over to the printshop, Juan arrived to work on translation for a year. God lets us see His perfect timing sometimes so that we can trust Him more in the unknown circumstances.

The timing also worked out for Juan to register for school in town to finish his primary education. He went to school in the morning and worked with us in the afternoon. He was also able to attend workshops to help him learn more about translation principles and translating songs. We often spent evenings translating songs for relaxation. It was an enjoyable change from the difficult daily work of comprehension checking and making the necessary revisions suggested by the exegetical consultant. The changes needed were usually in difficult sections we had struggled to translate in the beginning. Once I spent two days working on three words!

That summer Nina was scheduled for another surgery. We hoped María would bring her to Bogotá and work with us while she was there. With that in mind and to provide a change for the summer months, we arranged to temporarily rent a friend's house in Bogotá where the weather was cooler. Juan, who was on his school vacation, went with Paul, Ron, and me. While there, Ron had tennis lessons and physical therapy for a back problem. It also worked out to meet Joy when she came back after her year's course in Eden Prairie.

We were also able to meet with Diego in Bogotá to finalize preparation for another scripture use workshop he was going to facilitate with the Tunebos. The third volume of the *Old Testament Summary* came off the press in June just in time to send it out with Diego. He left on the trip as scheduled. He was also looking forward to seeing his mother who lived in the area. He took his wife and children with him to meet her for the first time. However, when they arrived in Cubará they were confronted with a general strike. Nothing was open there or in the surrounding towns.

There was a curfew from 6:00 p.m. until dawn. He was unable to get to his mother's home because guerillas controlled the area. In addition, the Tunebos were too frightened to participate in the scripture use workshop. Diego cancelled it. He was also unable to get to the Tunebo home to deliver the *Old Testament Summary* books as planned. He left them in the church in town.

Diego relayed to us the frustrations of his trip. We were disappointed to hear of all his difficulties. I read again the story of Josiah[2] obeying the law when it was found in the walls of the temple and prayed again that the Tunebo Scriptures would someday be found and the message would get into their hands and hearts.

God's Protecting Angels

María was unable to accompany Nina to Bogotá because Tito had not been able to live at home for four months. He was in hiding from the guerillas who had him on a hit list. One night guerillas in search of Tito surrounded their home. They intended to go in and take Tito by force. María was unaware of the men approaching the house as she got up and went inside from the porch where she had been reading,

> Whoever dwells in the shelter of the Most High
> will rest in the shadow of the Almighty.
> I will say of the Lord, "He is my refuge and my fortress,
> my God, in whom I trust."

> Surely he will save you
> from the fowler's snare
> and from the deadly pestilence.
> He will cover you with his feathers,

---

2   See chapter 21.

and under his wings you will find refuge;
his faithfulness will be your shield and rampart.
You will not fear the terror of night,
nor the arrow that flies by day,
nor the pestilence that stalks in the darkness,
nor the plague that destroys at midday.
A thousand may fall at your side,
ten thousand at your right hand,
but it will not come near you.
You will only observe with your eyes
and see the punishment of the wicked.

If you say, "The Lord is my refuge,"
and you make the Most High your dwelling,
no harm will overtake you,
no disaster will come near your tent.
For he will command his angels concerning you
to guard you in all your ways;
they will lift you up in their hands,
so that you will not strike your foot against a stone.
You will tread on the lion and the cobra;
you will trample the great lion and the serpent.

"Because he loves me," says the Lord, "I will rescue him;
I will protect him, for he acknowledges my name.
He will call on me, and I will answer him;
I will be with him in trouble,
I will deliver him and honor him.
With long life I will satisfy him
and show him my salvation." (Ps, 91:1–15, NIV)

One of the men, who had been with the guerillas, later told María of their evening visit. He said, "We were all ready to attack when we saw all those people in white surrounding the house. We decided we better leave. We crept quietly away." The Lord had indeed sent His angels to protect María and the family.

When Diego arrived back in Bogotá, he brought only Nina, not María. He relayed the sad news that her parents were planning to leave their home, not knowing where they would go. Tito and María planned to place each of their children in a different home. It broke our hearts to think that the family was being separated because they had helped us in the work of Bible translation. Once again, we cast ourselves upon the Lord. We were filled with questions. *How do we go about helping this precious family? Will they listen to any ideas we might give them? If María leaves the area, who will be there to stimulate interest in the Scriptures when they are finally published? What will happen to Juan? Is it wise to send him back to his home area?* We had to leave these questions with the Lord. We had to walk by faith, not by sight.

We took Nina to the clinic where she had another surgery and was able to stay while we waited to see what her parents planned to do. Tito and María planned to move out of their home area little by little so as not to raise suspicion. In mid-July Tito boarded a night bus for Bogotá with two of their daughters in the first step of their move. They arrived safely at the home where we were staying. Two days later, we drove them to a poor section of Bogotá where he had arranged to place the children in different homes with friends. We hoped this would be only a temporary situation.

We approached Marion Price, the director of the WEC clinic, who had been so gracious in her care of Nina, about the plight of the family. At the time, she was also the acting director of the orphanage in Villavicencio. We were aware that they had a lot of facilities that were not being used to the fullest as well as a small farm that needed upkeep. We asked her about the possibility of María's family staying on the orphanage property. Paul, Tito, and Marion took the three-and-a-half-hour road trip down the mountain in a public taxi. They worked out a plan to have the whole family live there and for Tito to work on the grounds.

First Tito made the dangerous trip back home to get María and the two youngest children. In order not to raise suspicion, they went to a town in the opposite direction. From there, they caught the night bus to Bogotá. When María arrived in Bogotá, she was relieved to be out of danger but nervous, filled with fear, and suffering from bad dreams. After a week with us in the city, the arrangements were finalized for them to move to Villavicencio. They settled in quickly.

This brought another big challenge for us. How do we balance work and family? Juan was still living with us in Lomalinda, and María was in Villavicencio, a half-an-hour flight from Lomalinda. Ron was starting his senior year in high school. We made a plan we followed for the next nine months; Paul went to Villavicencio for two weeks, we spent a week together at Lomalinda, then I went to Villavicencio for a week, and then we had another week together. Then we started the cycle again.

During that year, Paul and I each worked on different books. For example, at one time, Paul was incorporating consultant suggestions on Hebrews with María and 2 Corinthians with Juan while I was revising Luke with María and the Gospel of Mark with Juan. Working on two gospels at the same time made it easier to harmonize them. We needed to make sure we used the same expressions in passages that were the same in several books. Each book had to be back-translated literally into English or Spanish for a consultant to check for faithfulness or accuracy to the original text. The consultant then made suggestions for changes. Some were required for approval; others were optional.

The constant daily news of guerrilla warfare became so distracting we quit reading the paper in order to concentrate on translation. However, by November 1985, the upheaval in

Colombia was so great we couldn't avoid it. The Palace of Justice in Bogotá was taken over by M-19 insurgents. In the aftermath of the takeover thirty-five M-19 members were dead, along with eleven supreme court justices and forty-eight Colombian soldiers. The Palace of Justice building and the records in it were destroyed. Again, security came to the forefront of all we did. The M-19 was the same group that had kidnapped and killed Chet Bitterman.

In addition to the insecurity, a volcano erupted in Tolima, Colombia, killing twenty thousand people. JAAR's planes helped transport supplies to survivors.

Juan successfully completed his school year (February to November), and on December 16, we had a farewell party for him. He went to Villavicencio to spend the Christmas holidays with María and her family.

After Christmas, we met María and Juan in Bogotá and traveled on to the city of Bucaramanga for a committee check of key portions of the New Testament. Five Tunebos helped us carefully go through the chosen passages. First Juan or María would read the portion aloud as the others followed along. Then Paul or I would ask questions to check for comprehension. If the passage was not clear, we made revisions as necessary. We also discussed choices of words, such as whether to use the borrowed Spanish word for *Holy Spirit* or the Tunebo-constructed phrase. The committee chose the Tunebo term. One of the committee members exclaimed when he heard the term, "So that is what the Holy Spirit is!"

The next months we continued with editing, proofreading, and revising with many more trips to Villavicencio to work with María. We were coming near the finish line and our deadline to be done working with María by the time Ron graduated from high school. On one trip to Villavicencio, I stayed for two weeks rather than the usual one week. Each evening, I had to work to be ready for the next day. I told María on Friday we needed to work on Saturday. Her response was that she couldn't do it. I lost it and blurted out, "We give and give and give, and you can't even give your Saturday." I don't think she got the point of giving time because after that she started giving us gifts. O dear! I had to apologize for my ugly outburst.

The school year was coming to a close. May 1 was field day—Ron's day to shine. He got first place in eight out of nine of the high school events. He threw the shot put about twice as far as the others.

Just three days later, on Sunday afternoon, one of the school teachers, Joanie, a very special friend of Joy, was sunbathing with a group of teenagers on a floating dock some distance from shore. Joanie swam to shore alone. A deranged man who had been indoctrinated against SIL sat waiting for her when she arrived. He grabbed her and stabbed her in the heart, killing her instantly. The teenagers on the floating dock watched helplessly from the distance. Ron helped in the search for the assailant who was soon apprehended and jailed.

It was a devastated group of high schoolers that gathered for their youth meeting in our living room that evening. We led them in prayer and discussion of their feelings about the tragedy they had witnessed that day. School closed and work came to a halt the next day for the funeral.

On May 15, Ron graduated from high school along with six others, four of whom he had gone to school with since kindergarten. He was chomping at the bit to leave Colombia to begin life in the States. He went through his room and gave most of his things to his friends. He left for California the day after graduation. We finished more details of the New Testament with María and followed two weeks later to join Ron in California.

After a brief stay in California, we traveled to Longview, Texas, where Ron would be studying aviation at LeTourneau College. We helped settle him into a summer orientation program for missionary kids. It was hard to say good-bye, and I choked up and shed tears as we left him and headed for Minnesota. This good-bye, however, was a little easier than leaving Joy two years earlier. We would only be a phone call away and would see him again in a month. Joy stayed with us and got a job in a daycare for the summer.

Grace Church of Edina graciously prepared their mission home for us to live as well as space in the church for us to work. Much more proofreading and editing still needed to be done to ready the New Testament for printing. Dick Lundborg from the missions committee even provided a printer to make the necessary copies for proofreading. Mrs. Osborne came to help with typing, and Helen Gibbs, a nurse and our substitute grandma in Lomalinda, came to help with proofreading.

By August 28, we had finished all the proofreading and editing we could do on our own. We traveled to Texas again where we attended the fall parent orientation at Letourneau College and helped get Ron settled. From there, we went to work with the Printing Arts Department at the International Linguistic Center in Dallas. We had the latest printout of the New Testament in hand and a copy on the computer.

One of the things the director of the Printing Arts Department wanted was assurance that we had used consistency in spelling. Did we spell the same word the same way in Revelation as we did in Matthew? When one creates an alphabet and decides how words should be spelled, it is easy to be inconsistent. Word-processing programs were relatively new at that point. There was no spelling program to point out our inconsistencies. The computer specialists made word lists of all the words in the New Testament and where those words were used. We laboriously went over these lists, figured out what words were spelled inconsistently, decided on the spelling, and corrected them one by one.

Even with all the editing we had done before we went to Dallas, the New Testament was not in as good a shape as we thought. We had to extend our time working with the computer specialists several times for yet another proofreading. Verse numbers and page breaks needed to be checked; maps and pictures chosen and placed; book, chapter, and section headings decided on.[1]

Finally November 24, 1986, just three days before Thanksgiving, we turned in the completed photo-ready manuscript of the *Tunebo New Testament* for printing. We signed off saying we wouldn't make any more changes! It was the culmination of the main focus of our work for twenty-two years. We were numb from working so hard. Even at that time, we were acutely aware that years of work remained before the Scriptures would be in use by the Tunebo people. In spite of that, it felt good to know that we had done what God wanted us to do. We could join our family that Thanksgiving, rejoicing in God's faithfulness and the faithfulness of His people who backed us with prayer and finances. We were also grateful to have a change of pace and to be able to relate to those who partnered with us in the work.

In May 1987, we made a necessary trip to Colombia to renew our visas. While there, we learned that the New Testament manuscript, which had been sent to a printshop in Bogotá was on hold. Due to complications in printing a New Testament in another language, the SIL administration had decided to send the *Tunebo New Testament* to Korea for printing. We were disappointed to say the least. Our supervisor asked if we would like to remain in the States another year while the New Testament was being printed. We decided it would be good to

---

[1] We chose to use Spanish section headings to help Spanish-speaking missionaries more easily find a portion of scripture they wanted to share with the Tunebos.

have more time closer to Joy and Ron as well as do some further study ourselves.

We planned to help other translators in the future. We began our upgrading by taking a concentrated summer course in translation consulting at the University of Oklahoma. In the fall, we moved to Dallas again where Paul taught forty-four students translation principles at Texas SIL. I attended Dallas Baptist University. Ron transferred to the aviation program at Mountain View Community College in Dallas and lived with us.

33

ARRIVAL OF PRINTED NEW TESTAMENT

A Dream Come True

IN APRIL 1988, a package arrived from Korea. I opened the package and held in my hands the beautifully bound and printed *Tunebo New Testament*.[2] I couldn't do anything but cry. What a thrill after so many years! The fruit of the labor of our whole adult lives and the dream of our youth was there in my hands.

Some were tears of sheer joy at seeing the wonderful job that had been done on the printing and of reading the clear gospel message in Tunebo. Other tears were for the many hard things that we, María, and others had endured to see the completion of the New Testament—all the plans and dreams thwarted. Still other tears were for the present situation with the Tunebos, but God is able to bring His work to completion.

In May, I received my BA from Dallas Baptist University. We helped get Ron set up in an apartment in Dallas. He had a good job as a cargo handler for Delta Airlines. We traveled to Bemidji, Minnesota, to attend Joy's graduation from Oak Hills Bible Institute with an AA in Bible. After graduation, we helped her settle in a home with other girls in Minneapolis.

---

2   The International Bible Society paid the final printing costs.

Grace Church held a lovely dedication of the *Tunebo New Testament.* A few days later, we were on our way back to Colombia.

A New Assignment

What a change! We were headed to a new assignment, coordinating the translation work on the northern coast of Colombia. Both kids were now on their own, and we were finished with the translation of the New Testament. It was the same as when we had gone to Colombia twenty-five years earlier—just Paul and me. We held hands in the plane headed back to Colombia, lost in our own thoughts. I wondered, *When will the New Testaments get to Colombia? Will the office staff be able to get them out of customs? Will Joy and Ron be all right? What will our new assignment be like?*

God seemed to confirm our assignment on the coast by leading us to two apartments in a new building. We were looking for an apartment for the Mansens, translators for the Wayuu, as well as ourselves. Telephones were a scarce commodity in the city of Santa Marta on the northern coast where we were planning to settle. The rental agency required an advance payment of six months on each of the apartments. We needed desperately to contact the Mansens. Early one day we tried to phone the Mansens from the public telephone office but hadn't succeeded. That evening we went to meet friends to go out to dinner with them. They were temporarily staying in a home. It "happened" that the home had a phone, and that was the only phone number the Mansens knew in the city. They called during the fifteen minutes we were there. They agreed to the arrangements, and we rented the two apartments. God's timing is perfect.

I went ahead of Paul to Bogotá on an early-morning flight. When I arrived in a taxi at the SIL group house, there was a truck unloading boxes. In bold black letters on the side of a box, it read, "Tunebo New Testament." Praise God. It was like He was saying to me, "I don't want you to worry a single day about getting the New Testaments through customs." Once again I saw God's perfect timing. Isn't that just like God's great love?

The next day we personally delivered the first copy of God's Word in their language to Tito and María. They were moved to see the fruit of our combined labor all beautifully bound in a book they could hold in their hands. It thrilled our hearts to hear María read God's Word fluently in the Tunebo language. The four of us laid hands on the New Testament and had a prayer of dedication.

Prior to working with us, María had prayed one evening and asked the Lord to use her. That night, she had a dream in which she saw herself reading Scripture to her people. Now years later, María went to Lomalinda and spent two weeks reading Scripture before we moved to our new assignment. She read the Gospel of John and other portions from the *Tunebo New Testament* while Paul audio-recorded. God was fulfilling the dream He had given her years earlier.

While Paul and María recorded, I began preparing for our move. With the help of Colombian Christians interested in working with indigenous groups, I sealed each New Testament in plastic to protect it and packed them for shipping. We mailed complimentary copies to people who might have contact or interest in reaching the Tunebos. There were some Spanish-speaking churches in the towns at the foot of the mountains surrounding them. We prepared packages of New Testaments for each of these churches as well as the Roman Catholic bishop and the priest at the local mission station. We also placed larger quantities for storage with the Cuadrangular church in Bucaramanga, in Diego's church, and with María. I hadn't forgotten the story of Josiah in the Old Testament. When the scroll was found hidden in the wall of the temple, Josiah had it read, and led his people in following the Lord. My hope was that in placing Tunebo Scriptures in a number of places, one day they would be discovered, read, and obeyed.

When all the things from our house in Lomalinda were packed, we hired a man with a truck. Our friends on the center came and loaded the truck. The driver took off for Santa Marta on what turned out to be a week's trip for him. We went ahead on a commercial flight. Paul hired two men in Santa Marta who hand-carried everything, including the refrigerator, the five flights of stairs to our apartment. We settled into our apartment and new assignment.

In late September, we traveled to the city of Bucaramanga to attend the Cuadrangular Church we had been in communication with since 1981. On September 25, 1988, the pastor, Juan Encinales, dedicated the *Tunebo New Testament*. In the service, he made Colombian Christians aware of the need of the Tunebos as well as other groups to be evangelized. He especially wanted them to know the Scripture in the language of the people was available to teach and evangelize this group who didn't understand Spanish. A number of people came forward at the pastor's invitation willing to serve in missions if the Lord called them.

Although there were a half dozen or so Tunebos in town, not one of them showed up at the dedication. Tears streamed down my face as I stood in front of the church. It was hard not to be discouraged and start questioning again. Didn't the New Testament in their language matter to any of the Tunebos? Was it really worth it all? Had the Tunebos not responded to the message of God's Word because we weren't good witnesses? Was this really God's plan or just our idea? Again I had to give my anxious thoughts to God and trust His timing.

By November, Tito was eager for all his friends and family to have copies of the New Testament. We were concerned for his safety but deeply touched and grateful that he was willing to venture back into his home area and distribute copies. He packed eleven Tunebo New Testaments, nineteen cassette tapes with recordings of the Gospel of John, and other portions in his small pack and boarded the bus for Cubará. There was no dedication in the area, no parade in the street and no fanfare—just one man secretly going quietly to his friends and giving them a copy of the precious Word of God. Tito was satisfied that he had delivered the books safely to their destination on the fringes of the traditional Tunebo area.

We settled into our work of helping other translators in Santa Marta. However, our thoughts and efforts to see the New Testament in use never waned. A young man from a nearby city learned of our presence and the need for Scripture distribution. He came to visit us, and we mentored him and developed a ministry method for him to use Tunebo Scripture tapes. He came for instruction a number of times. However, he could not follow through because he didn't have the necessary identification papers, and his father would not allow him to go.

Another great opportunity was teaching a cross-cultural communication course at a TEAM Mission Bible Institute. We were able to raise awareness of the need of the indigenous groups of Colombia, particularly the Tunebos. One of the women in the course made a trip and distributed fourteen more *Tunebo New Testament*. Juan accompanied her. She even gathered seven Tunebos and brought them to Bogotá. Paul met them there for a Christian Indian Congress in the soccer stadium. Singing praises to the Lord with hundreds of indigenous Christians and hearing God's Word were real encouragement to the believers from many different indigenous groups, especially those who stood alone in their community.

We invested more time preparing another Scripture Use Conference for the Tunebos, and training Diego and María to teach the material. When they arrived in Cubará, they found the area quieter. A few Tunebos came to the conference; others were still too afraid to attend. At the conference, María introduced the *Tunebo New Testament*. Diego did most of the teaching while María read the Scripture and translated for him. They joyfully reported that one young man accepted the Lord.

The highlights of our time in Santa Marta were visits from Juan and Naomi. Juan came to spend Holy Week with us during his school break. Daily we had the joy of seeing him make personal application of the New Testament. It was a joy and a relief to read and study God's Word in Tunebo without having to analyze how it needed to be translated. We taught Juan a method that could be used to study any passage.[1] As always, he wanted to sing the Tunebo hymns and choruses over and over. Together we put the final touches on the latest chorus he had translated, "Dios Donde Quieras Está" (God Is Everywhere).

He was finding it a challenge to remain faithful to God as he faced the pressures of animistic leaders on one hand and atheistic ideologies on the other. One problem we were able to help him with was arranging for him to live with other Christians while attending school in the city.

After the Christian Indian Congress in Bogotá in July, Naomi came to Santa Marta with Paul. For two weeks, we sat together daily to read and study God's Word from the book of Acts. She took seriously the Bible study question, "Is there either a command or an example in this passage relating something good I should do?" In Acts 2, she saw the command Peter gave to repent and be baptized. Then she saw the response of the people who repented and were baptized. Naomi answered, "I need to be baptized." When she got back to the local town near her home, she followed through and was baptized.

Another time we were reading Ephesians. When I asked her what she thought was the meaning of the verse, "And be ye kind one to another, tenderhearted, forgiving one another, even as

---

[1] Adapted from Richard Hohulin, SIL Philippine Branch. Four questions: (1) What does this passage teach about God? (2) What does this passage teach about Jesus? (3) Is there something good in this passage I should do? (command or example), (4) Is there something bad in this passage I should avoid? (command or example).

God for Christ's sake hath forgiven you"(Eph. 4:32, KJV), Naomi replied, "It means I need to forgive the person who stole all the manioc I planted near my daughter's house." She got the message. It was clear, accurate, and natural.

A Painful Decision

August 30, 1989, the director of the consul of the US embassy in Bogotá called the SIL director with a security advisory issued by the US Department of State, warning of the potential danger to our personnel in the country. After receiving the advisory, our leaders asked each family to prayerfully consider their situation. We were to consult with SIL's administration, embassy officials, and local authorities, and then to decide before the Lord whether we should stay or leave. At the time, I was in Dallas with Ron helping him in a number of areas.

When I returned, Paul and I talked and prayed for almost three days straight, considering what we should do. In addition to the potential danger to all SIL personnel, we had received a call from one of our dear friends warning us that the guerillas were asking a lot of questions about us. Apparently, the recent activities of the *Tunebo New Testament* distribution, the Scripture Use Conference, the Tunebos going to the Christian congress in Bogotá, and recent visitors had provoked those opposed to our work. They didn't like the fact that we still had influence even though we were not in the area.

Our supervisor came to Santa Marta to consult with us. Once again we weighed the issues as we had with our colleagues and director in 1981. This time it was different. The commitment I had made when studying the life of David seventeen years earlier had been fulfilled. Like David who prepared the materials for his son to build the temple, Paul and I had prepared the materials for the next generation of God's servants to build the Tunebo church. The materials for the Tunebo church were ready and available in several locations. The foundation was started with a few lone believers. The building blocks for the church included the following: the *Tunebo New Testament*,[2] a three-volume *Old Testament Summary*, selected Psalms and Proverbs, a hymn book and CDs, a simplified grammar with dialogues to learn the language, a basic Tunebo primer to teach reading, easy readers in Tunebo, a transition to Spanish primer, and a primer for Spanish speakers to transfer their reading skills to Tunebo. These materials were all stockpiled, ready, and waiting for the next generation of God's workers. We could go in peace, knowing God would call another one of His servants to use the materials to evangelize and disciple His church. In His perfect time, God would build His church among the Tunebos.

Although we had fulfilled our commitment, we still agonized over the decision. Finally, after taking both the security situation and our family situation into consideration, we came to the painful decision that we should leave. We decided to seek an assignment in Dallas, Texas, and made plans to leave one month later.

Even though the packing was a horrendous task, the most difficult job was writing to Diego and others who had been part of our team to reach the Tunebos to let them know we were leaving. Diego tried to negotiate with us, offering to leave his church in the city and take the pastorate in the small town at the foot of the mountains near the Tunebos if we would stay in Colombia. Although it was a sincere offer from his heart, we couldn't accept it.

We wrote letters to the Catholic priest and others reminding them they could get copies of the *Tunebo New Testament* through the SIL office in Bogotá. We carefully noted the locations of all the Tunebo books to keep for our own records and to leave with the SIL office. The Tunebo books we had in Santa Marta were sent back to Bogotá or other appropriate places. My last project,

---

[2] The Tunebo New Testament will soon also be in audio. The Gospel of Luke in video was completed in Tunebo in 2007. *Uwa/Tunebo Spanish Dictionary with a Grammar Introduction* was published in 1996.

the revision of the Tunebo primer to make it more natural and acceptable in the Tegría dialect, was in the Lomalinda printshop for printing. It was added to the inventory list.

Just a little over a month after we made the decision to leave, we somehow completed the huge task of packing, selling, and disposing of stuff, including the fifty-three boxes of books we had brought with us from Lomalinda and two filing cabinets of papers. Since Santa Marta is on the coast, we were able to ship a crate with books, one filing cabinet, and a few barrels to Houston on a banana boat. On October 19, 1989, we had everything in order, even the necessary papers for Ron's dog. We boarded the plane for the United States.

Reflection

Over the years since boarding the plane to begin a new phase of ministry in Dallas, I have continued to reflect on the questions I had in my mind as I stood at the dedication of the *Tunebo New Testament* in Bucaramanga. *Why hadn't the Tunebos responded to the gospel? Why wasn't there a people movement and many lives changed? Had it really been God's plan that we go to this group, or had it just been our own idea?*

Taking and teaching a number of different courses at Texas SIL and GIAL (Graduate Institute of Applied Linguistics) gave me a better understanding of our situation with the Tunebos. Sometimes, as I prepared lessons or listened to others teach, it was like the light dawned. There are many different aspects of the Uwa/Tunebo social, cultural, and religious situation that made them closed to the gospel.

Socially, the Tunebo/Uwa had been pushed into a rather small area of rugged mountains and were surrounded by Spanish-speaking Colombians who continue to encroach on their territory. They had maintained themselves as a people by their strict taboos, preventing any regular socialization with those from other cultures. They didn't even intermarry with Tunebos from other villages. As mentioned already, anyone or anything coming into a Tunebo home had to go through a purification ceremony preformed by the shaman. This prevented the entrance into the culture of any books or technology. They strongly resisted the road coming into the area, realizing it would bring more outsiders who would take their land and influence their people.

Their resistance to outsiders and their desire to maintain their traditional lands and culture reached international proportions in the 1990s when they became embroiled in a battle with Occidental Petroleum Company that was drilling on their traditional land. One evening while listening to the news in Dallas, I was jerked to attention when I heard the word *Uwa* (the current name for the Tunebo people). An earlier news article stated, "The US multinational spent about $12 million on seismic surveying before halting all operations in the face of U'wa threats to commit mass suicide if Occidental tried to drill for what the tribe view as 'the lifeblood of Mother Earth.'"[3] It became obvious to the oil industry that no amount of money could influence the Uwa's desire to maintain their traditional land and culture. Many ecology and anthropology activists joined the Uwa in their cause, including three American activists who went to the area and were killed by guerillas. The activists promoted the idea that the oil is the world's lifeblood and the Tunebo land is the heart of the world. This coincides with the Tunebo belief that their ceremonial dances sustain the world. If they didn't perform their dances, the world would come to an end. Their mass suicide would mean the end the dances and the world.[4]

---

[3] Reuters, August 25, 1999.

[4] There could be a book written on this whole topic. I only mention it here to illustrate the extent the Uwa will go to maintain their culture. For more information see https://en.wikipedia.org/wiki/U%27wa_people#Struggle_to_prevent_oil_drilling.

Similarly, if they were to become Christians and stop their ceremonies, the world would come to an end. This was a strong deterrent from accepting the Lord. José, our faithful language and translation assistant, was the main social chief and leader of these ceremonial dances. He seemed to believe the Scriptures that we translated, but his fear of the repercussions of stopping the ceremonies held him back from leading his people in a decision to follow Christ.

The Tunebo religion and culture were strongly unified. If a Tunebo did not submit to either a cultural or religious taboo, he was excluded from the village. Fear of exclusion from their closely knit community held them in bondage. They did not have freedom to commit to Christ even if they wanted to.[5]

The Tunebo animistic beliefs that each plant and animal has a spirit that must be appeased and their great fear of the spirits mentioned throughout the book were other factors that caused them to resist any change. From our cultural viewpoint, we can't begin to imagine how they could abandon two perfectly formed twin babies to die in the forest. But it is an example of the deep fear of spirits that controls them. They believe one of the babies is the child of an evil spirit who will bring harm to others if allowed to live. Not knowing which one it is, they leave both to die.

Between the Tunebo cultural taboos excluding outsiders, their fear of spirits, and their ceremonial dances maintaining the world, humanly speaking, we were obviously well over our heads in a spiritual battle. "For we wrestle not against flesh and blood, but against principalities, against powers, against the rulers of the

---

[5]   Dye, T. Wayne, June 7, 2008, "Social and Cultural Factors Necessary for the Acceptance of Vernacular Scripture Translations: The Eight Conditions of Scripture Use (revised)," *IJFM*. See seventh condition for the use of the Scriptures. "FREEDOM TO COMMIT: People are spiritually free to follow Christ wholeheartedly, including turning from ancestor worship, traditional magic, fetish worship and other practices when those conflict with the teaching of the Bible."

darkness of this world, against spiritual wickedness in high places" (Eph. 6:12, KJV). But God was on our side. We had the promise, "God hath chosen the foolish things of the world to confound the wise; and God hath chosen the weak things of the world to confound the things which are mighty (1 Cor. 1:27, NIV). God also promises, "So is my word that goes out from my mouth: It will not return to me empty, but will accomplish what I desire and achieve the purpose for which I sent it" (Isa. 55:11, NIV).

In response to his disciple's question about why they couldn't cast out an evil spirit, Jesus replied, "This kind can come out only by prayer" (Mark 9:29, NIV). Many of God's faithful servants have prayed for the Tunebos and are still praying. They are engaged in spiritual warfare against the forces that have controlled the Uwa/Tunebo for centuries. You, the reader, can join them in their prayers that there would be a significant number of Tunebos ready to make the decision for Christ at the same time so that they could remain in the area and be a witness to the others. You can believe with them that in God's perfect time, He will burden the hearts of people to use the translated Tunebo Scriptures to evangelize, disciple, and teach the Uwa. Finally, you can join them in asking God to raise up Uwa/Tunebo Christian leaders so that one day there will be a vibrant church among the Tunebo singing God's praises and learning from His Word in their own language.

God had called us as young people. We had responded to His call first to missions and then to Bible translation. He sent us to the Tunebos, the majority of whom were monolingual, speaking only their own language. If they were to understand God's message, it had to be in their language. When we arrived in Cobaría in 1964, the Tunebo had some awareness of a supreme being who was distant with no personal interest in them, but they had no effective knowledge of the gospel. We held on to His promise, "Therefore, my dear brothers and sisters, stand firm. Let nothing move you. Always give yourselves fully to the work of the Lord, because you know that your labor in the Lord is not in vain" (1 Cor. 15:58, NIV). When we left the area in 1982, they had an initial awareness of the gospel. It takes time for a group like the Tunebos to grasp the implications of the gospel, develop a positive attitude toward it, recognize their need for Christ, and make a decision to act. After that, they need discipleship and growth to become reproducing Christians.[6]

From the beginning, God had clearly shown us His direction over and over. He had worked a miracle by causing the Tunebos to give us a house in the village and putting it in José's heart to teach us the language, even though it had been previously prohibited. God had consistently provided Tunebo speakers to assist us with language learning and translation. Even with the

---

[6] See James F. Engel and H. Wilber Norton. *What's Gone Wrong with the Harvest: A Communication Strategy for the Church and World Evangelism* (Grand Rapids: Zondervan, 1975) 45.

The Engel Scale was developed by James F. Engel as a way of representing the journey from no knowledge of God through to spiritual maturity as a Christian believer. The model is used by some Christians to emphasize the process of conversion, and the various decision-making steps that a person goes through before they become a Christian. (Wikipedia)

+5 Stewardship
+4 Communion with God
+3 Conceptual and behavioral growth
+2 Incorporation into Body
+1 Post-decision evaluation
New birth
-1 Repentance and faith in Christ
-2 Decision to act
-3 Personal problem recognition
-4 Positive attitude towards Gospel
-5 Grasp implications of Gospel
-6 Awareness of fundamentals of Gospel
-7 Initial awareness of Gospel
-8 Awareness of supreme being, no knowledge of Gospel

taboo against having written materials in their homes, God had enabled us to finish and test a primer series with young men who came to Lomalinda. God had given Andrés a desire to minister to Juan and Aarón by teaching them to read and helping them accept Christ. God had sent María when we were looking for direction as to whether to continue with the translation. He had worked through our colleagues and leaders to encourage us to finish the translation. God had sent Diego to partner with us by going to the Tunebo area when we couldn't. God had raised a great crowd of supporters and coworkers to help us complete the translation task. He had cared for us and protected us from harm. He had repeatedly showed us His grace was sufficient even in our weakest moments.

The Apostle Paul said, "I planted the seed, Apollos watered it, but God has been making it grow" (1 Cor. 3:6, NIV). "Let us not become weary in doing good, for at the proper time we will reap a harvest if we do not give up" (Gal. 6:9, NIV). Paul and I prepared the seed, God's Word in the Tunebo language, and did some planting of that seed. We didn't give up and are waiting to see the harvest that will be reaped in God's time as He raises up others to continue to plant and water the seed of His word.

The story of the Tunebo church isn't finished yet!

EPILOGUE

AFTER LEAVING COLOMBIA in late 1989, we settled in Dallas, Texas, near the International Linguistics Center. In the spring semester of 1990, we both began teaching in Texas SIL (later it became GIAL, Graduate Institute of Applied Linguistics). Paul taught translation principles, and I taught several different courses but mainly Intercultural Communication and Training, and Second Language and Culture Acquisition. At the same time, Paul studied and earned a master's degree in biblical studies at Dallas Baptist University. I studied and received a master's degree from the University of Texas in Arlington in interdisciplinary studies: Spanish and linguistics.

Ron married Angélica Arcipreste and has our only grandchild, Carlos. Ron has used his aviation education mostly representing companies in sales. His knowledge of Spanish has been a real asset. Joy married John Tymony and lives out of state. She continues to keep up with her Lomalinda friends.

We returned to Colombia for the 1993–1994 school year and worked with Tunebo assistants on the Uwa/Tunebo-Spanish bilingual dictionary with its grammar introduction, which was also my master's thesis. The time there provided opportunities to encourage our friends. We were at Lomalinda on March 31, 1994, when our coworker Ray Rising was kidnapped by the leftist guerillas. We were in Bogotá two years and eighty days later, in August 1996, when he was released.

By 1996, the security situation in and around Lomalinda had deteriorated to the point that it was no longer safe for SIL personnel. Sadly, the center was closed after many years of being the hub of translation activity. The remaining personnel moved to Bogotá or other cities to complete the unfinished translations. Linguists were unable to live in most of the indigenous areas due to insecurity. The JAARS program operated out of Bogotá for a short time but found it wasn't feasible. Provision was made in Bogotá for offices for the linguists and housing for their indigenous translation assistants. Several Colombian mission organizations were started, including Misincol, Avancemos, and AGA, to continue the work with the indigenous groups.

During the time we taught in Texas SIL, we made yearly trips to Colombia to encourage the use of the Scriptures and to train others interested in working with the Uwa/Tunebo. The security situation in the Tunebo area and the surrounding vicinity remained very tenuous. For our own safety and that of our friends, we did not go there. We did, however, have a number of workshops in the church of a friend in a city some distance from Cubará. He made trips and brought in people. In the scripture use workshops, we studied both the New and Old Testaments using a variety of methods including drama. As a result of a class on translating songs, more Christian songs have been translated and recorded.

In 2000, I began teaching classes in cultural anthropology with an Emphasis in Cross-Cultural Communication in Spanish for a Mexican mission, *Bienestar para las Naciones*. This opened opportunities to teach in other countries of Latin America.

By mutual agreement with the government, SIL dissolved their official contract in 2000. Even though very few SIL personnel were left in Colombia, we were reassigned there from 2002 to 2005. (We had maintained our resident visas.) We taught in the FACET training program for Colombians, did translation consulting, and facilitated three translation projects. During that time, we also had opportunity to further encourage use of the Uwa/Tunebo Scriptures and make the needs of the Tunebos known to young Colombians interested in missions.

New Testament translations have been completed in more than thirty-five languages in Colombia. In many languages, there are also Old Testament stories or summaries.[7] The Gospel of Luke in video has been dubbed in a number of languages and some of the New Testaments have been audio-recorded by a Colombian partner organization, AGA (Audio Grabaciones Autóctonas), which works with Faith Comes by Hearing.[8]

Tunebo was dubbed into the Gospel of Luke DVD in late 2006 or early 2007. It has been viewed with interest by many Uwa when visiting Cubará. Faith Comes by Hearing is currently sponsoring the audio recording of the entire New Testament in Uwa. It will be put on preloaded Proclaimers, a device that can run on solar panels, batteries, or electricity. It has enough volume to be heard by a whole church. Pray that these tools would be used to further the spread of the gospel and the conversion of the people.

I had the privilege of serving the Americas area as the Scripture Use Coordinator from 2006 to 2011. During that time, Paul and I traveled to countries as far distant as Northern Canada and Argentina. Our experiences with the Tunebos prepared us for consulting and training others in translation and cross-cultural living.

Currently we are serving SIL as retired volunteers. Paul is an editor for Spanish Translator's Notes (commentaries for translators) and I am a Scripture Engagement Consultant, working mostly in trauma healing.

Our dear friend and faithful language assistant José died in the late 1980s. Current security concerns make it impossible to bring you up to date as we would like on most of the people who played important roles in the story of the translation of the Scriptures into the Uwa/Tunebo language. Some are still involved.

---

[7] Some of these areas need workers to go and teach the use of the available materials to build God's church.

[8] Much of this material is available on http://www.scriptureearth.org.

Acknowledgments

I WANT TO acknowledge God, who daily gave me the grace and strength to live and write this story. His strength is made perfect in weakness. To Him be the glory!

I want to thank Paul, my husband of more than fifty years, for his partnership, support, and encouragement in writing this book. He has been with me in every experience reiterated in this book. This is our story.

I want to thank our children Joy and Ron (Blake), who shared us with the Tunebos all their growing-up years. They are precious to us.

I want to acknowledge José, the Tunebo chief. Without his help, we could never have learned the Tunebo language or translated Scripture. We are deeply grateful for him.

I also want to thank María, Juan, and all the Tunebos mentioned in this book who helped us with the translation and testing of Scripture and literacy materials. It was a team effort. We could not have done the work without them.

I want to recognize Diego, who came alongside, making trips when we could no longer go to the area. He was a real partner enabling us to continue when at an impasse.

I would like to mention our parents who were committed to letting us serve, prayed for us, and sacrificed for us to be on the field.

I would like to recognize the part Edina Baptist Church had in my formation—Glenn Anderson, Sunday school teachers, youth leaders, guest missionaries, and others, many of whom have gone to be with the Lord. Discipleship from Navigators also prepared me for missionary service.

Both Paul and I would like to express deep gratitude to a whole host of prayer and financial supporters who have been part of the Tunebo team, making a translation of the Scripture in Tunebo a reality.

I would like to acknowledge the multitude of colleagues who served with us in Colombia. Without the work of administrators, pilots, school teachers, maintenance personnel, consultants, doctors, radio technicians, and others, we would not have been able to translate for the Uwa/Tunebo.

I want to acknowledge my brother, Dick (Dr. Richard Blake) who spent countless hours, researching, editing, and gently prodding me to make my writing more interesting, "Show, don't tell." He and his wife, Thelma, have been our cheerleaders and partners in ministry since the beginning.

I am deeply grateful to Luis Palau for taking time from his busy important ministry to write the foreword of this book. It is an honor to know him and his wife, Pat.

I am indebted to Dr. Steve Walter's insightful suggestions that made the book more cohesive.

I also want to thank Vurnell Cobbey, Karen McIntosh, Victor Glenn, and Jenny Hoffman for their editorial input on the rough draft.

Made in the USA
Lexington, KY
14 February 2018